OXFORD READINGS IN PHILOSOPHY

PERCEPTUAL KNOWLEDGE

Also published in this series

The Concept of Evidence, edited by Peter Achinstein
The Philosophy of Law, edited by Ronald M. Dworkin
Moral Concepts, edited by Joel Feinberg
Theories of Ethics, edited by Philippa Foot
The Philosophy of History, edited by Patrick Gardiner
The Philosophy of Mind, edited by Jonathan Glover
Knowledge and Belief, edited by A. Phillips Griffiths
Scientific Revolutions, edited by Ian Hacking
Philosophy and Economic Theory, edited by Frank Hahn and
Martin Hollis
Divine Commands and Morality, edited by Paul Helm
Hegel, edited by Michael Inwood
The Philosophy of Linguistics, edited by Jerrold J. Katz
Reference and Modality, edited by Leonard Linsky
The Philosophy of Religion, edited by Basil Mitchell
The Concept of God, edited by Thomas V. Morris
A Priori Knowledge, edited by Paul K. Moser
Aesthetics, edited by Harold Osborne
The Theory of Meaning, edited by G. H. R. Parkinson
The Philosophy of Education, edited by R. S. Peters
Political Philosophy, edited by Anthony Quinton
Practical Reasoning, edited by Joseph Raz
The Philosophy of Social Explanation, edited by Alan Ryan
Consequentialism and its Critics, edited by Samuel Scheffler
The Philosophy of Language, edited by J. R. Searle
Semantic Syntax, edited by Pieter A. M. Seuren
Applied Ethics, edited by Peter Singer
Philosophical Logic, edited by P. F. Strawson
Locke on Human Understanding, edited by I. C. Tipton
Theories of Rights, edited by Jeremy Waldron
Kant on Pure Reason, edited by Ralph C. S. Walker
Free Will, edited by Gary Watson
The Philosophy of Action, edited by Alan R. White
Leibniz: Metaphysics and Philosophy of Science, edited by
R. S. Woolhouse

Other volumes are in preparation

PERCEPTUAL KNOWLEDGE

EDITED BY

JONATHAN DANCY

OXFORD UNIVERSITY PRESS
1988

Oxford University Press, Walton Street, Oxford OX2 6DP

Oxford New York Toronto
Delhi Bombay Calcutta Madras Karachi
Kuala Lumpur Singapore Hong Kong Tokyo
Nairobi Dar es Salaam Cape Town
Melbourne Auckland
and associated companies in
Berlin Ibadan

Oxford is a trade mark of Oxford University Press

Published in the United States
by Oxford University Press, New York

Introduction and selection © Oxford University Press 1988

British Library Cataloguing in Publication Data
Perceptual Knowledge.—(Oxford Readings in Philosophy)
1. Perception (Philosophy)
I. Dancy, Jonathan
121'.3   B828.45
ISBN 0–19–875075–7
ISBN 0–19–875074–9 (Pbk)

Library of Congress Cataloging in Publication Data
Perceptual knowledge/edited by Jonathan Dancy.
—(Oxford readings in philosophy)
Bibliography: p.   Includes index.
1. Perception (Philosophy) 2. Knowledge, Theory of.
I. Dancy, Jonathan.   II. Series.
B828.45.P48   1988   121'.3—dc19   87-35216
ISBN 0-19-875075-7
ISBN 0-19-875074-9 (pbk.)

CONTENTS

INTRODUCTION

Perceptual knowledge is the sort of knowledge that we get about the things around us by looking at them, feeling them, tasting them, and so on. It is said that seeing is believing, but seeing is often knowing too. Normally, to see that something is happening is to know that it is happening. And it is largely by using our senses that we come to know anything about the world we live in. So the senses normally give us knowledge, and that knowledge occupies a privileged position since it is by means of it that we are able to come to know other things. The task of philosophy here is to help us to understand how this can be so: to write an account of ourselves, of our senses, and of the world which shows the nature and role of perceptual knowledge.

This enterprise stands at the intersection of two large areas of philosophical contention. The first is epistemology, that is, the theory of knowledge and of justification. The epistemologist attempts to give an account of what knowledge is and of what it is for a belief to be justified, and to use that account to show not only the extent and nature of our cognitive grasp on the world but also our right to that grasp: to show how far we are rational in taking the world to be the way it seems to us.

The second broad area is that of the philosophy of perception. The philosopher of perception tries to give an account of what it is to perceive something, but this broad aim can be broken up into several parts, most of which are represented in this collection. Perhaps the most important of these is the attempt to give an account of the nature of perceptual experience. And this shows that the philosophy of perception is only a chapter in the general philosophy of mind. We have to work our views about perception into a more general theory of awareness, desire, and choice.

To decide whether and under what conditions the senses yield knowledge, we need first to decide what knowledge is. The sharp edge of this enquiry is to distinguish between knowledge and mere true belief. What is the difference between these? Almost every conceivable answer has been offered to this question. The traditional 'tripartite' analysis held that knowledge is belief which is both justified and true. This was probably the mainstream view thirty or forty years ago. Its opponents held that knowledge was not a form of belief at all—that a state of mind could not be changed from being belief to being knowledge by the addition of seemingly extraneous elements such as further and better justification, or by becoming true when it had previously been false. Now there are well-known counterexamples to the mainstream view, which seem to show that a belief may be both true and justified without being knowledge.[1] In response to these, some philosophers who wish to remain within the mainstream tradition have attempted to replace the justification condition by something else; others try to give an account of justification which undermines the counterexamples. Robert Nozick offers an account of the former type. He argues that A knows that p if and only if

(1) p is true
(2) A believes that p
(3) If p were not true, A would not believe that p
(4) If, in changed circumstances, p were still true, A would still believe that p.

When a true belief satisfies conditions (3) and (4), Nozick says that it *tracks* the truth, since it seems to vary with the truth in just the way a superior cognitive state should. He defends this analysis against objections, and then goes on to show how to use it in order to undermine a classic sceptical argument. This argument, in modern dress, urges that we have no reason whatever to believe that we are not brains in vats, wired to a super-computer controlled by an ingenious scientist which is generating in us the experiences we are currently having. It seems to follow from this that we have no reason to believe, and so do not know to be true, anything which would not be true if we were brains in vats. For to know that these things are true we would surely have to know that we are not brains in vats, which we have admitted that we don't. Nozick argues, however, that we should pay careful attention to the differences between statements like (3) and (4) in his analysis, which are about what *would* be true in certain circumstances, and those which the sceptic uses, which typically concern what *might* be true. Using this, he shows that on his account of knowledge it is possible to know that one is sitting reading, even though one knows that if one were a brain in a vat one would not be sitting reading and does not know that one is not a brain in a vat.

---

[1] The *locus classicus* for these examples is E. L. Gettier, 'Is Justified True Belief Knowledge?' *Analysis*, 23 (1963), 121–3.

This is an important if contentious result, which contributes to the account of perceptual knowledge in two ways. First, it is plausible to suppose that we can only reasonably rely on our senses if we have some general reason to believe that our senses are not serving to distort the world for us. Nozick's position, if sound, removes this worry from us. Second, it gives a focus to the desire to show that perception yields knowledge. For all we now have to show is that our perceptual states *do* generally track the truth, and how we might come to enjoy such splendid states.

While thoughts about perception are consequences of Nozick's account of knowledge, in the essay by Alvin Goldman they are at the centre of attention. He starts by offering an adaptation of his earlier causal theory of knowledge, rather on the lines of Nozick's tracking requirement (but with some important differences too). The initial thought is that those true beliefs are knowledge which are produced by a 'reliable' mechanism. A reliable mechanism is understood as one which not only produces true beliefs in actual situations, but which would continue to produce true beliefs or at least to inhibit false ones in other relevantly different circumstances. Goldman then goes on to use this approach to give an account of what he calls non-inferential perceptual knowledge. He sums this up on p. 59. 'What our analysis says is that S has perceptual knowledge if and only if not only does his perceptual mechanism produce true belief, but there are no relevant counterfactual situations in which the same belief would be produced via an equivalent percept and in which the belief would be false.'

Goldman would not claim to have provided here a complete theory of perceptual knowledge. As he says, he takes for granted certain notions which a complete theory would explain. He assumes that to perceive an object is to have a percept caused by that object; but of course there are many causes of our percepts which are not themselves perceived, such as the electrical activity in our own brains, and Goldman makes no attempt to say which of the causally relevant objects are perceived and which are not. He assumes that the way to do this is to pick out a particular causal relation in which we or our percepts stand only to the things that we see. The second notion that Goldman takes for granted is that of a perceptual belief. He says that such beliefs are non-inferentially caused by percepts. But so are others, and he makes no attempt to say which are which.

Perhaps the most important matter on which Goldman is silent, however, is the question what a percept is. What we learn is that percepts are a special class of internal states, sometimes spoken of as 'perceptual experiences'. We perceive when and only when such experiences are caused in us by our surroundings, and perceptual beliefs are those caused in us by those experiences. So we know that the experiences are not identical with the beliefs they cause. But beyond that we are left in the dark as to how to conceive of perceptual experience.

I think that it would have been impossible for Goldman to make his first assumption so blithely had Paul Grice's classic essay, of which only relevant excerpts are reprinted here, not succeeded in rehabilitating causal theories of perception. The 'assumption' that to perceive an object is to have a percept suitably caused by that object is the core of what Grice calls the causal theory of perception, though Grice expresses it in terms of 'sense-datum statements' instead of percepts. Although the notion of a sense-datum has a distinct history and is strongly associated with a particular account of perceptual experience, Grice is very careful not to subscribe to all of that. He tells us only that sense-datum statements are among those which describe how an object looks, and goes no further. This is because his main concern is to defend causal theories of perception against two influential objections. The first of these is that they have the unfortunate consequence that material objects are invisible. The objection was that on causal theories material objects are not themselves objects of awareness; we are aware only of our percepts, and we *infer* the probable presence of material things causing those percepts. The material objects themselves are invisible because they are hidden behind the 'veil of perception'. The second objection is the familiar sceptical charge that perception never yields knowledge, because there is always the possibility that things are not the way they look. Grice succeeds in showing that causal theories as such are not vulnerable to these reproaches, without himself subscribing to any particular account of what we have previously been calling perceptual experience. This shows us that adherence to a causal theory does not itself determine how we should conceive of the state caused.

I said that Goldman takes it for granted that we will be able to give an account of the special causal relation in which we stand to those objects which we perceive. Grice tackles this difficulty by suggesting that we can specify that causal relation by using examples. He offers the following version of a causal theory: 'It is true that X perceives M if, and only if, some present-tense sense-datum statement is true of X which reports a state of affairs for which M, in a way to be indicated by example, is causally responsible.' Grice's approach to this problem has been generally thought to be unsatisfactory, and the essay by David Lewis is one of many attempts to improve on it. Lewis's *analysandum* is, however, slightly different from Grice's (and from Goldman's). First, in common with so many theorists of perception, he concentrates entirely on seeing, assuming that sight is relevantly similar to the other senses. Second, he is concerned with what it is to see the whole scene before one, rather than what it is to see some particular object which is part of that scene. Lewis starts with the claim that someone sees if and only if the scene before his eyes causes matching visual experience. The question then is what is the difference between seeing and having a hallucination which happens to be true. (This might remind us of the question what the difference is between knowing that p and merely believing truly that p.) His answer is that a veridical hallucination does not stand in a suitable relation of counterfactual dependence on the scene before the eyes. In the case of seeing, changes in the scene would be accompanied by corresponding changes in one's visual experience; with hallucination, this is not so.

Lewis has only partial success in dealing with a counter-example at the end of his paper. But it will be clear that his approach to perception fits very well with Goldman's, and both fit well Nozick's account of knowledge. A strong general theory or family of theories is developing here, which will give answers to three questions: what is it to see, what is it to see some particular object O, and what is it to see *that* something is happening or to see *that* some proposition is true? And it will give an account along Nozickian lines of why seeing is so often knowing.

Such an account will still not be a complete theory of perceptual knowledge, for the reason that it has nothing to say about the nature of perceptual states themselves, the perceptual experiences caused in us by the things we see. So causal theories need supplementation. And there are of course other complaints about causal theories. Not everyone agrees that the right way to distinguish the object we see from other causally relevant objects is to tighten up on the causal relation. Fred Dretske argues that the solution to this puzzle should be given in informational rather than causal terms,[2]

[2] See his *Knowledge and the Flow of Information* (Cambridge, Mass., 1981), 153–68.

and Paul Snowdon's essay argues that there may be something wrong with the puzzle itself.

We now turn to the notion of a perceptual experience, which is the crucial element in any theory of perception. The essay by Sir Peter Strawson addresses itself to one of the main topics which must be resolved by anyone hoping to understand that notion, the question what are the proper objects of perception. Answers to this question, at least among those philosophers who do not deny the existence of an independent material world, are of broadly two sorts. Representationalism (sometimes called indirect realism) is the view that the immediate objects of perception are mental objects, which represent a physical reality to the perceiver. These mental objects have been variously called sense-data, ideas, or percepts (to mention just a few names). The opposing view, called direct realism, holds that we are capable of being directly aware of a physical object; our awareness of physical things does not need to be mediated by or exist in virtue of awareness of a mental object. There are, however, many different variants on these two general accounts of the objects of perception. Strawson's essay provides a very helpful map to the possibilities here.[3] His own view, in keeping with positions he has adopted on other topics, is that we can somehow adopt theories of both types. But not everyone will find this suggestion easy to accept.

Representationalism has been traditionally associated with causal theories of perception. A classic view, held for instance by John Locke, is that to perceive an object is to have an idea in the mind which is caused by and resembles that object. We have already seen that this sort of simple reference to causation is insufficient. Locke also runs into problems with his suggestion that mental objects, which for him are ideas immediately present to the mind, represent to us those physical things which resemble them. It is hard to accept that our mental objects can only represent physical things by resembling them. A visual appearance of a tree, thought of as an internal mental object which may be present to the mind whether there is a tree there or not, seems not to have any of the primary qualities of shape, size, and mobility. Visual appearances are themselves neither small nor large, neither square nor round, neither fast-moving nor slow. It seems, then, that a mental object or idea can represent a physical one as having a certain property

[3] I give a slightly more detailed map in my *Introduction to Contemporary Epistemology* (Oxford, 1985), ch. 10.

without itself having that property. The idea has what we might call a representational property, the property of being an idea *of* a square thing, without having the intrinsic property of being square.[4] But surely anything that has representational properties must have intrinsic properties as well, and the representational properties must exist in virtue of the intrinsic ones. For instance, a drawing of a house has representational properties, but they could only exist in virtue of some intrinsic properties—the distribution of charcoal on the paper, for instance. So we ask what are the intrinsic properties of mental objects such as sense-data or Locke's ideas. There is the danger that either such mental objects have no intrinsic properties at all, or such intrinsic properties as they do enjoy are quite unsuited to act as properties in virtue of which they have their representational properties. For instance, mental objects no doubt last for a certain length of time; they may be distinct or indistinct; they may be familiar or unusual, and so on. But these admittedly intrinsic properties are not of the right sort to ground the rich array of representational properties which the mental objects must have if they are to play the role assigned to them in representationalist theories of perception.

Locke's account of a perceptual experience as the occurrence of an idea immediately present to the mind is one version of what is called an act–object analysis of experience. Act–object accounts distinguish two elements in a perceptual experience, an act of awareness and an internal object of awareness. Each perceptual experience has its own distinctive nature, which it has whether or not the surrounding world really is the way that experience represents it as being. Act–object accounts analyse the differences between experiences as differences between their internal objects. Frank Jackson argues strongly in favour of an act–object analysis. Anyone who accepts that analysis is likely to be a representationalist, and Jackson is no exception. His arguments are only part of a sustained attempt to resurrect representationalism, which has currently fallen out of general favour.

Opposition to the act–object analysis is likely to stem from the sort of consideration raised two paragraphs ago, which casts doubt on the status of the internal object as an *object*. Opponents claim that the distinctive nature of an experience is not to be understood in terms of differences between non-physical objects of awareness.

---

[4] For these distinctions see C. Peacocke, *Sense and Content* (Oxford, 1983), ch. 1.

For them, an experience is the way one is aware of the world around one. The experience itself is not something of which one is aware—or at least not normally—nor does it contain something of which one is aware as a part. The experience is one's awareness of an external world, and should not be broken up into an act of awareness and a new object of awareness. Indeed there are obvious dangers of an infinite regress in so doing.

Those who take this line have to provide their own account of how one such act of awareness differs from the next. The most popular account is one which expands the idea that the nature of my experience is just the *way* the world looks to me into what is called the adverbial theory of experience. Adverbial theorists hold that the way in which we speak of having an experience or a sensation, or of the appearances which things present to us, misleadingly suggests that experiences, sensations, and appearances are private mental objects caused in us by the things they are experiences *of*. In their view, it would be less misleading to talk about *how* things look and feel. For instance, we should concentrate less on the expression 'I have a pain in my knee', which leads us to suppose that pains are special sorts of objects which exist if not in the knee then in the head, and more on the expression 'my knee hurts', which suggests instead that the pain is not so much an object of awareness as a *way* we feel. Similarly, the expression 'this thing looks red' is preferable to 'this thing has a red look'. The redness of the look is to be analysed as a way in which the material thing appears to us, and not as a property of a mental object such as a sense-datum. So the different contents of our experiences are to be conceived, not as different internal objects of awareness, but as different ways of experiencing the world.

Direct realists, who deny the existence of internal mental objects of awareness, have often been tempted by an adverbial account as an alternative which manifestly avoids any danger of creating some new object of awareness, intermediate between us and the physical world. But the adverbial theory is not the only way in which a direct realist might try to avoid the act–object analysis of perceptual experience. To see this we need to introduce a further distinction, which gives us a new puzzle to solve. How are we to conceive of perceptual awareness? There are two familiar sorts of awareness, which seem to exhaust the field.[5] The first is belief. Our beliefs about the world around us constitute a sort of awareness of it. The

---

[5] See C. McGinn, *The Character of Mind* (Oxford, 1982), ch. 1.

second is sensation. Pain is often taken as a good example of a sensation. Unlike beliefs, sensations such as pain have an intrinsic nature to them; they have a certain phenomenal feel. Beliefs do not *feel* like anything; they have no phenomenal nature. How then should we conceive of perceptual awareness? It seems to be in a way like belief and in a way like sensation. It is like belief because, generally at least, to see a house is to believe that there is a house before one. Seeing more or less *is* believing, sometimes. But it is unlike belief in having a certain phenomenal feel; there are distinctive styles to the different forms of perceptual awareness—seeing, feeling, hearing, tasting, and smelling—which are rather like the distinctive styles of different sorts of sensations. A complete philosophy of perception has to take account of both these aspects of perceptual experience, and do justice to both. Different thinkers try to take different aspects as central and then somehow include the other afterwards. Both adverbial theorists and act–object theorists take perceptual awareness as being some form of sensation; they differ only on how to analyse it. But a more extreme form of direct realism will take the other view. David Armstrong argues in favour of an account of perception as basically a form of belief—as a cognitive state rather than as what we might call a sensational one. He attempts to deal with the obvious objection, mentioned above, that perceptual awareness seems to have a characteristic style, or rather several characteristic styles, one for each of the senses. But there is no doubt that this trenchant view faces an uphill struggle. It offers pleasing simplification in one's philosophy of mind, but we should be careful not to insist on a simple theory if the facts refuse to be simplified.

In Essay VIII Fred Dretske argues that the facts are against Armstrong and any attempt to see perception as a purely cognitive activity. He provides impressive reasons, some from the province of cognitive psychology, for supposing that no purely cognitive account of perception will do justice to the facts. According to Dretske, we need to keep to a general distinction between sensory perception or perceptual experience, on the one hand, and cognitive activities such as belief, judgement, classification, and recognition on the other. 'Our sensory experience is information-ally rich and profuse in a way that our cognitive utilization of it is not. . . . It is this fact that makes the sensory representation more like a *picture* of, and the consequent belief a *statement about*, the source' (p. 160). Perceptual experience provides us with far more information than we can actually use, and cognition is the extraction of some few elements from this rich source. Dretske concludes that 'if perception is understood as a creature's *experience* of his surroundings, then, perception itself is cognitively neutral' (p. 162).

This is in direct opposition to any attempt such as Armstrong's to see perception as a cognitive state or process. A probable response would see the sensory perception of a scene as a set of tendencies to believe, in Armstrong's sense, only some of which can actually be implemented. But Dretske would have a reply to this. For, in his example of the girl learning to identify daffodils, we would not want to say that in her awareness of the flowers before her she already had a tendency to believe that the ones in this patch are daffodils, a tendency which will remain unactualized until she acquires the concept of a daffodil. Tendencies to believe only exist in those who already have the cognitive apparatus ready to select some items from the rich information present in the perceptual experience.

Dretske's position here can be challenged. Is there not a sense in which our knowledge and expectations can affect the nature of the information which the senses offer us? It is very tempting to say that the engine of a car looks one way to a mechanic and quite different to those unversed in such things, or that a piece of jazz sounds different to a novice from the way it sounds to people who understand what they are hearing. Dretske argues against this possibility at the end of his essay. I suspect, however, that there is room for allowing that the information present in a perceptual experience can be affected by our cognitive states without abandoning his crucial distinction between the sorts of ways in which perceptual and cognitive states carry information.

We now turn our attention away from the theory of perception proper, and begin to return to epistemology. We have seen that a full theory of perception will offer answers to these questions:

(1) What are the objects of perception?
(2) Should we accept the act–object or the adverbial account of perceptual experience (or some other)?
(3) Are we to understand perceptual experience as a form of cognition, of sensation, or as some combination of the two?

Let us suppose that we are armed with answers to these questions, and with a suitable view about what knowledge is. Are we now in a position to give an account of perceptual knowledge? We started by saying that such an account would tell us two things:

(4) Why is perception (or the beliefs which perception generates) normally knowledge?

(5) Do perceptual beliefs have a special status, and if so why?

What makes the area with which this collection is concerned so
interesting and challenging is the attempt to make one's answers to
these questions fit each other. There is a classic theory that achieves
this sort of fit, and which has therefore been so influential that
most contemporary discussion starts from it. I call this package
classical foundationalism.

Classical foundationalism is the view that all our knowledge rests
on foundations, which are beliefs about our own sensory experiences. Such beliefs are different from the sensory experiences
themselves, but are always true; they are infallible. This means that
they are all justified, and therefore (on the tripartite theory of
knowledge) they are all knowledge. All other justified beliefs are
justified 'by appeal to' these basic beliefs, which stand as foundations for the rest. So there are two sorts of justified beliefs, the
inferentially justified ones which are the superstructure and the
non-inferentially justified ones which are the base.

Classical foundationalism accepts the act–object analysis of
experience and the representationalism which is closely associated
with it, and sees experience as a form of sensation rather than of
cognition. It provides a very neat package of answers to our
questions (1)–(3), which generate answers to questions (4)–(5).

Let us take, as an example of a perceptual belief, the belief of a
subject S that he is sitting in a car. This belief, like other perceptual
beliefs about the things around us, is one for which S has 'the
evidence of his senses'. According to classical foundationalism,
such a belief is always justified, so that where it is true it is knowledge. Of course it is only inferentially justified, since it is part of
the superstructure rather than of the base. So there must be some
principle of inference which takes S from basic beliefs about his
sensations and experience to his belief that he is sitting in a car.
This might be:

PJ: If it sensibly seems to me that p, then it is probably true
that p.

Our foundationalist understands the first half of PJ as concerning
the nature of one's experience. The principle has the form: if my
experience is in such and such a way, the world probably is in such

and such a way. (Compare this with Armstrong, who would understand it as saying roughly: if I am tempted to believe that *p*, it is probably true that *p*.)

The question then is what justifies us in accepting PJ. Classical foundationalism held that we know a priori that PJ is true. Knowing this, and knowing the nature of our own experience, the beliefs we form by the use of PJ have a special status, in virtue of which when true they count as knowledge, and which enables them to stand as our *firmest* knowledge about anything other than our own sensations and experiences.

Essentially the same account will be given of our knowledge of our past actions (to take another example for a moment). The foundationalist will appeal to a principle:

MJ: If I remember having done *A*, then I probably did *A*,

interpreting the first half of this as concerning the nature of my memory experiences. Both memory knowledge and perceptual knowledge will count as empirical knowledge, on this approach; for both rest in the same sort of way on present experience. And if we want to say that perceptual knowledge is more secure than memory knowledge, this can be achieved by giving different weighting to the two principles PJ and MJ.

Among the attractions of classical foundationalism is that it promises an answer to scepticism, because of the directness of its account of perceptual knowledge, and that it makes good sense of the empiricist belief that all our knowledge rests somehow on our experience. But every element of it can be and has been questioned. Even if we retain the distinctive foundationalist contrast between inferentially and non-inferentially justified beliefs, there still remains a number of different options we might take. First, it is hard to accept that our beliefs about our own sensations and experiences are infallible, which means that we need a different account of why such beliefs are always justified. Second, it is difficult to show how we know the truth of PJ a priori, if PJ is given a foundationalist interpretation; we should hope to do better here. Turning more to the theory of perception, we may abandon the act–object analysis of experience, and try to think in terms of the adverbial theory instead. And there is a more dramatic variant which holds that some beliefs about the material world are basic. But all these changes remain within the spirit of classical foundationalism.

There are two more radical moves we could make. The first is to abandon entirely any talk of foundations and superstructure in favour of a coherentist theory of justification. Coherentism is the view that there are no basic beliefs which justify others in a way different from that in which they are themselves justified. Instead, all justified beliefs are justified in the same way, by the contribution they make to the coherence of the belief set of which they are members. A belief is justified, that is, if the set of which it is a member is more coherent with it than without it.

An immediate objection to such a theory is that it will be unable to give any sense to the idea that perceptual beliefs have a special status, or are more firmly anchored in a belief set than are many others. For the notion that in experience we acquire a basis by appeal to which other beliefs are assessed for justification looks very like a form of foundationalism. The coherentist cannot simply say that perceptual beliefs have no special status. He needs to give some special weight to the perceptual in order to ward off the classic objection to coherentism, which is that it sees no epistemic difference between a set of empirically justified beliefs about the world we live in and a set restricted to the contents of a novel such as *Crime and Punishment*. Both are equally coherent, and so unless we can prefer one for being empirically grounded we will have to say that both are equally justified. The question is therefore whether there is a way in which coherentism can speak of empirical grounding without collapsing into foundationalism. Roderick Firth considers various less extreme versions of both approaches and argues that a coherentist can give a good sense to the notion of empirical knowledge.

If he is right, we still need to say exactly how coherentism does offer an account of the special status of perceptual beliefs. Just as the foundationalist gets from basic to non-basic beliefs by use of some principle of inference, so the coherentist is likely to use principles of inference to tie together the different members of his belief set in the relation he calls coherence. As far as this goes, he can make use of PJ and MJ. And a coherentist is not condemned to holding that we know the truth of these principles a priori. Instead he can say, consistent with his general approach, that our acceptance of PJ is justified by the increase in coherence in our belief set if we add to it the beliefs warranted by PJ. In particular, if we had two competing principles, we should accept the one whose use will generate more coherence in our growing belief set.

The essay by Wilfred Sellars is an attempt to carry this programme through. Sellars wants to maintain that principles like PJ and MJ *both* provide criteria for adjudicating certain empirical knowledge claims *and* are empirical knowledge claims in their own right. But how can we be justified in accepting particular beliefs because they are generated by the principles and in accepting the principles because of the particular beliefs which they generate? Sellars argues at paragraphs 84–6 that there is no circularity here. It is our acceptance of the principles that makes our acceptance of the particular beliefs reasonable, and our *explanation* of why such beliefs are likely to be true rests on particular beliefs of that sort.

I said that there were two radical ways in which we could move away from classical foundationalism. The second of these is to abandon the stress on inference, and on the principles in accordance with which the inferences are made, with all the trouble this generates about what sort of justification we can provide for the principles, a priori or empirical. Instead we concentrate on causation. We say that perceptual beliefs are not inferred from experience, but caused in us by our experience. This approach, like the other, relies on a general principle, such as:

CJ: If *S*'s experience causes in him a perceptual belief that *p*, *S* is justified in believing that *p*.

One could then work from this, using an account of knowledge in terms of justification, or go directly for:

CK: If *S*'s experience causes in him a true perceptual belief that *p*, *S* knows that *p*.

These principles need sharpening up. In particular, we need to restrict the admissible sorts of causation, rather as we saw in discussion of the causal theory of perception (to which this new causal approach is very congenial). But my aim at the moment is to distinguish between classical approaches which exploit the notion of inference and those which use instead something like CJ and CK. The former have been called internalist and the latter externalist.

The contrast between internalism and externalism is not yet very clear in the literature. What lies behind it is a clash of intuitions. The externalist feels that all we want from our beliefs is that they have a good strong grip on the world. If that grip is strong, it just doesn't matter whether we know about its strength. The internalist feels that the enterprise of epistemology is the attempt to make good sense of ourselves to ourselves, so that from the material available to each of us we can show not only the extent and nature of our cognitive grasp on the world but also our *right* to that grasp, so as to substantiate our sense that it is *rational* for us to have the beliefs we do. I can hardly be proud of forming beliefs that are reliable if I have no notion of their reliability. We may express the internalist's point thus:

I: Only propositions believed by S can be relevant to the epistemic status of a belief of S's.[6]

Externalism proper might be expressed as the claim:

E: The relevance of a true proposition to the epistemic status of a belief of S's is not affected by the question whether S believes that proposition.

It is possible to be generally sympathetic to E but find it too strong. Suppose that there is a crystal ball which gives the names of winning horses 99 per cent of the time. I use this ball for the first time, and it tells me that Sundowner will win the 2.30 at Ascot. If I believe this proposition, is my belief justified? An externalist could say that it is, urging that though I may not know that the belief is justified, it is still justified because it is highly reliable. But however much my belief that p may be justified by the reliability of its source, it would be *more* justified if I knew about this reliability. This requires a change in E, perhaps to yield:

E*: A true proposition may be already relevant to the epistemic status of a belief of S's, even if that relevance is increased by S's believing that proposition.

The same point can be made about internalism. The strong form represented in I maintains that a proposition's relevance to the epistemic status of a belief of S's is entirely unaffected by the question whether that proposition is true. An internalist might argue for this position by saying that all that we can require of someone is that he do as well as possible epistemically (i.e. in the formation and rejection of beliefs) by his own lights. An analogy is commonly drawn here with the thought in ethics that all we can require of people is that they follow their own conscience. But the relevance of one belief of S's to the justification of another is surely increased if the first belief is true. If, for instance, S holds our

---

[6] I ignore a variant which starts 'Only propositions justifiably believed by S . . .', for reasons which I give on pp. 134-5 of my *Contemporary Epistemology*.

principle PJ, and this fact serves to justify the beliefs which S accepts in accordance with that principle, the justification so created is much greater if PJ is true. This yields a weaker form of internalism:

> I*: A proposition believed by S may be already relevant to the justification of a belief of S's, even if that relevance is increased by the truth of that proposition.

On this showing both internalism and externalism are agreed on a distinction between internal and external justification (sometimes called the distinction between subjective and objective justification), and on the view that the best thing is to have both at once. But the internalist says that a belief may be well justified even if all its justification is internal, while the externalist says that a belief may be well justified even if all its justification is external. We can ask two questions here. First, are both of these positions internally consistent? Second, if they are, how might we decide the issue?

On the first question, it seems to me that there are doubts about the weak form of internalism represented by I*. This is because it may not be compatible with the original motive for internalism, the sense that all that we can require of someone is that he do as well as possible by his own lights. There is a tension in this position, which appears also in any view that our moral obligations are primarily subjective, but that there are also objective obligations, which are in some ill-defined way more of the same sort of thing. The weak form of externalism may be subject to similar doubts, on the grounds that the only reasons for weakening E are internalist reasons. But perhaps the contribution of the fact that S believes the relevant true propositions may be conceived as further objective justification, rather than new justification of a rather different sort.

What considerations should affect our eventual choice? We have already seen some of the intuitions underlying the debate—and it should be said that much of the discussion in the literature has been conducted at an intuitive level. These appeals to intuition seem to me insufficient to settle the issue. There are two further points made. The first is that strong internalism makes life more difficult than does externalism. For the externalist we may know or be justified, whether we can show that we are or not. For the internalist, our justification depends (roughly) upon our ability to show it. This leads to the sort of trouble for the foundationalist which we have already seen; adopting an internalist approach, he needed to show that whatever principles of inference do in fact justify S's perceptual beliefs are ones which S himself accepts. This is a tough job, if only because of the antecedent improbability that all cognitive agents do believe anything like the principles of inference that we, as epistemologists, would like them to. So there is a permanent danger that internalism will lead to scepticism.

The second sort of argument involves an appeal to moral philosophy, some of which we have already seen. When we ask whether some action of S's was a good one, we are surely concerned with the light in which S saw the action, for it is his beliefs, desires, and intentions that determine the moral quality of the action. Maybe, for instance, Bill's enquiry after the health of his friend James's wife did cause great offence, but it was kindly meant. Bill had forgotten that she had just left James and taken with her all the money in their joint bank account. The action was unfortunate, perhaps, but still well intended; and as such it was a good action, the sort we want people to do more of. This is, as it were, a strong internalist position. There are two sorts of attack on it. The first argues that we should distinguish between the action and the agent. An agent can be blameless even when his action is wrong, if he did it under some misapprehension. So S's action was wrong itself, though S cannot be condemned for it. The analogue of this position in epistemology is the claim that internal questions about S's other beliefs are irrelevant to questions about the justification of this perceptual belief. S may be cognitively blameless in adopting this belief, even though as a matter of fact there is no justification for it. The second sort of attack argues that the moral value of an action is partly dependent on the way the agent saw things, but also partly dependent on whether things were the way the agent thought they were. The moral value of action and of agent coincide, on this approach, and they are only partly dependent on the agent's beliefs, desires, and intentions. It is no real excuse, when one treads on someone's baby, to say that one did not notice the baby on the floor. This is the point that led us originally to weak internalism. If the point is good, and weak internalism is incoherent, there must be something wrong with the strong internalism from which we started.

The drift of the discussion has perhaps favoured some form of externalism. But I have been trying more to introduce the relevant considerations than to argue for one side or the other, and anyway two warning notes need to be sounded. First, the analogy with ethics may itself be questioned. Second, it is not clear that the distinction between subjective and objective is much better understood on the moral side, in which case the analogy, even if sound, would not decide the issue for us. My own view is that the analogy is sound but that the contrast between subjective and objective is misconceived; and so I expect the eventual emergence of a third position, which will vindicate neither internalism nor externalism.

We now return to the attempt to give an account of perceptual knowledge. This will require, not only an account of perception and of knowledge, but also a choice between foundationalist and coherentist theories of justification and between internalist and externalist conceptions of justification. Classical foundationalism, as we saw, was representationalist and internalist, and accepted the tripartite account of knowledge. Nozick and Goldman offer externalist theories of knowledge, which would fit well with a causal theory of perception (though internalist versions of causal theories are possible); but it is not clear what account of perceptual experience they would adopt. Sellars runs a traditional internalist form of coherentism. There is a wide variety of options, and our problem is to try to tell a complete story in which all the parts fit.

What sort of theory of perception is likely to attract a coherentist? I say 'likely' because just as a foundationalist can accept the adverbial theory of sensation, so a coherentist *can* opt for representationalism. But the most probable choice is some form of direct realism, either via the adverbial theory or via Armstrong's account of perception as belief. This is because of the coherentist's distrust of any notion of a datum which all our beliefs must fit. However this may be, the first half of Sellars's essay attacks representationalism in favour of what he calls 'direct apprehension' theories of perceptual awareness. In his view, representationalists admit the possibility of direct awareness of *something* (namely our own sensations/experiences) and they have no real reason for refusing to accept that we can be directly aware of physical things. In fact that refusal is likely to generate an infinite regress, as we saw, once we admit that our knowledge of our own sensations is fallible.

The sort of direct realism at issue here is one which holds that we can stand in just the same relation to a physical object as the representationalist says we stand to his internal objects. Whether we think that this is possible will depend on, or will be, our answer to the notorious argument from illusion.[7] This argument starts from the undeniable fact of perceptual error. We sometimes make mistakes about the nature of the objects around us, and sometimes suppose that there is something there when in fact there is nothing (the drunkard's pink rats are a favourite example). In such cases we take it that there are two stories to be told. The first is about how it is with us, and the second is about how it is with the world; and the two stories fail to coincide. What this tells us is that, even when we do not make mistakes, there are still two distinct stories to be told, but this time the stories coincide or match in some way. Our perceptual states, then (the subject of the first story), are distinct from any state of the world (the subject of the second). And our question is what is the relation between the two stories when we are said to *see* the things around us. Some sort of a causal answer to this question seems inevitable, and this is how we find ourselves engaged in the enterprise of working out exactly how a causal theory of perception should go. Paul Snowdon argues that this is not inevitable, and that there may be room for a different, two-pronged or disjunctive account of perceptual experiences. On this account there are two sorts of experiences. The first of these is as before, a perceptual state whose nature is logically independent of the nature of the surrounding world, and which represents that world to us, with varying degrees of success, in very much the sort of way that interests the causal theorists. The second is quite different. There are some perceptual states which are not logically distinct from but logically tied to the states of affairs which they represent to us, so that one could not be in such a state if the world was not as it seems to us to be. Such a state is error free. One may of course be mistaken about whether one is in such a state or not, but this is as much as we should admit to the argument from illusion.

The position here may remind us of the distinction mentioned earlier between accounts of knowledge as a rather grand form of belief and accounts which suppose that knowledge is a state distinct from belief, a state tied in a distinct way to the factuality (as Sellars puts it) of that which it represents. The argument about the merits of the disjunctive account of perceptual experience has important consequences for our account of perceptual knowledge, and indeed generally for our epistemology. In his essay, partly reworked from

[7] A classic statement of this argument is in A. J. Ayer, *The Foundations of Empirical Knowledge* (London, 1969), chs. 1–2.

the final part of a much longer one, John McDowell pursues these implications in an attempt to see how best we should avoid the ever-present danger of scepticism. On the sort of approach favoured by the causal theory, there will always be the possibility, however strong our evidence for some perceptual belief, that the world is different from the way it appears to us. We cannot know that it is not, and so how can we hope to know that we are sitting in a car when for all we know we are not? McDowell's attempt to find a way through this question amounts, in his view, to a position intermediate between internalism and externalism. But he is pessimistic about the thought that such a position is one with which we are going to find it easy to come to terms.[8]

February 1987   J.D.

[8] I am grateful to Paul Snowdon and Mark Sainsbury for advice about this collection, and particularly to David Bakhurst for help with the introduction.

I

KNOWLEDGE AND SCEPTICISM

R. NOZICK

You think you are seeing these words, but could you not be hallucinating or dreaming or having your brain stimulated to give you the
experience of seeing these marks on paper although no such thing is
before you? More extremely, could you not be floating in a tank
while super-psychologists stimulate your brain electrochemically to
produce exactly the same experiences as you are now having, or
even to produce the whole sequence of experiences you have had in
your lifetime thus far? If one of these other things was happening,
your experience would be exactly the same as it now is. So how can
you know none of them is happening? Yet if you do not know these
possibilities don't hold, how can you know you are reading this
book now? If you do not know you haven't always been floating in
the tank at the mercy of the psychologists, how can you know
anything—what your name is, who your parents were, where you
come from?

The sceptic argues that we do not know what we think we do.
Even when he leaves us unconverted, he leaves us confused. Granting that we do know, how *can* we? Given these other possibilities he
poses, how is knowledge possible? In answering this question, we
do not seek to convince the sceptic, but rather to formulate hypotheses about knowledge and our connection to facts that show how
knowledge can exist even given the sceptic's possibilities. These
hypotheses must reconcile our belief that we know things with our
belief that the sceptical possibilities are logical possibilities.

The sceptical possibilities, and the threats they pose to our
knowledge, depend upon our knowing things (if we do) mediately,
through or by way of something else. Our thinking or believing that
some fact *p* holds is connected somehow to the fact that *p*, but is
not itself identical with that fact. Intermediate links establish the

Abridged by permission of the publishers and the author from *Philosophical
Explanations*, Cambridge, Mass.: Harvard University Press/Oxford University
Press. Copyright © 1981 by Robert Nozick.

connection. This leaves room for the possibility of these intermediate stages holding and producing our belief that *p*, without the fact that *p* being at the other end. The intermediate stages arise in a completely different manner, one not involving the fact that *p* although giving rise to the appearance that *p* holds true.

Are the sceptic's possibilities indeed logically possible? Imagine reading a science fiction story in which someone is raised from birth floating in a tank with psychologists stimulating his brain. The story could go on to tell of the person's reactions when he is brought out of the tank, of how the psychologists convince him of what had been happening to him, or how they fail to do so. This story is coherent, there is nothing self-contradictory or otherwise impossible about it. Nor is there anything incoherent in imagining that you are now in this situation, at a time before being taken out of the tank. To ease the transition out, to prepare the way, perhaps the psychologists will give the person in the tank thoughts of whether floating in the tank is possible, or the experience of reading a book that discusses this possibility, even one that discusses their easing his transition. (Free will presents no insuperable problem for this possibility. Perhaps the psychologists caused all your experiences of choice, including the feeling of freely choosing; or perhaps you do freely choose to act while they, cutting the effector circuit, continue the scenario from there.)

Some philosophers have attempted to demonstrate there is no such coherent possibility of this sort.[1] However, for any reasoning that purports to show this sceptical possibility cannot occur, we can imagine the psychologists of our science fiction story feeding *it* to their tank-subject, along with the (inaccurate) feeling that the reasoning is cogent. So how much trust can be placed in the apparent cogency of an argument to show the sceptical possibility isn't coherent?

The sceptic's possibility is a logically coherent one, in tension with the existence of (almost all) knowledge; so we seek a hypothesis to explain how, even given the sceptic's possibilities, knowledge is possible. We may worry that such explanatory hypotheses are *ad hoc*, but this worry will lessen if they yield other facts as well, fit in with other things we believe, and so forth. Indeed, the theory of knowledge that follows was not developed in order to explain how knowledge is possible. Rather, the motivation was external to epistemology; only after the account of knowledge was

---

[1] See Hilary Putnam, *Reason, Truth and History* (Cambridge, 1981), ch. 1.

developed for another purpose did I notice its consequences for scepticism, for understanding how knowledge is possible. So whatever other defects the explanation might have, it can hardly be called *ad hoc*.

I. KNOWLEDGE

Our task is to formulate further conditions to go alongside

(1) p is true
(2) S believes that p.

We would like each condition to be necessary for knowledge, so any case that fails to satisfy it will not be an instance of knowledge. Furthermore, we would like the conditions to be jointly sufficient for knowledge, so any case that satisfies all of them will be an instance of knowledge. We first shall formulate conditions that seem to handle ordinary cases correctly, classifying as knowledge cases which are knowledge, and as non-knowledge cases which are not; then we shall check to see how these conditions handle some difficult cases discussed in the literature.

One plausible suggestion is causal, something like: the fact that p (partially) causes S to believe that p, that is, (2) because (1). But this provides an inhospitable environment for mathematical and ethical knowledge; also there are well-known difficulties in specifying the type of causal connection. If someone floating in a tank oblivious to everything around him is given (by direct electrical and chemical stimulation of the brain) the belief that he is floating in a tank with his brain being stimulated, then even though that fact is part of the cause of his belief, still he does not know that it is true.

Let us consider a different third condition:

(3) If p were not true, S would not believe that p.

Throughout this work, let us write the subjunctive 'if-then' by an arrow, and the negation of a sentence by prefacing 'not-' to it. The above condition thus is rewritten as:

(3) not-p $\rightarrow$ not-(S believes that p).

This subjunctive condition is not unrelated to the causal condition. Often when the fact that p (partially) causes someone to believe that p, the fact also will be causally necessary for his having the belief—without the cause, the effect would not occur. In that case, the subjunctive condition (3) also will be satisfied. Yet this condition is not equivalent to the causal condition. For the causal condition will be satisfied in cases of causal overdetermination, where either two sufficient causes of the effect actually operate, or a back-up cause (of the same effect) would operate if the first one didn't; whereas the subjunctive condition need not hold for these cases.[2] When the two conditions do agree, causality indicates knowledge because it acts in a manner that makes the subjunctive (3) true.

The subjunctive condition (3) serves to exclude cases of the sort first described by Edward Gettier, such as the following. Two other people are in my office and I am justified on the basis of much evidence in believing the first owns a Ford car; though he (now) does not, the second person (a stranger to me) owns one. I believe truly and justifiably that someone (or other) in my office owns a Ford car, but I do not know someone does. Concluded Gettier, knowledge is not simply justified true belief.

The following subjunctive, which specifies condition (3) for this Gettier case, is not satisfied: if no one in my office owned a Ford car, I wouldn't believe that someone did. The situation that would obtain if no one in my office owned a Ford is one where the stranger does not (or where he is not in the office); and in that situation I still would believe, as before, that someone in my office does own a Ford, namely, the first person. So the subjunctive condition (3) excludes this Gettier case as a case of knowledge.

The subjunctive condition is powerful and intuitive, not so easy to satisfy, yet not so powerful as to rule out everything as an instance of knowledge. A subjunctive conditional 'if p were true, q would be true', $p \rightarrow q$, does not say that p entails q or that it is logically impossible that p yet not-q. It says that in the situation that would obtain if p were true, q also would be true. This point is brought out especially clearly in recent 'possible-worlds' accounts of subjunctives: the subjunctive is true when (roughly) in all those worlds in which p holds true that are closest to the actual world, q also is true. (Examine those worlds in which p holds true closest to the actual world, and see if q holds true in all these.) Whether or not q is true in p worlds that are still farther away from the actual world is irrelevant to the truth of the subjunctive. I do not mean to endorse any particular possible-worlds account of subjunctives, nor am I committed to this type of account.[3] I sometimes shall use it, though, when it illustrates points in an especially clear way.

[2] I should note here that I assume bivalence throughout this chapter, and consider only statements that are true if and only if their negations are false.

[3] See Robert Stalnaker, 'A Theory of Conditionals', in N. Rescher, ed., *Studies*

The subjunctive condition (3) also handles nicely cases that cause difficulties for the view that you know that p when you can rule out the relevant alternatives to p in the context. For, as Gail Stine writes, 'what makes an alternative relevant in one context and not another? . . . if on the basis of visual appearances obtained under optimum conditions while driving through the countryside Henry identifies an object as a barn, normally we say that Henry knows that it is a barn. Let us suppose, however, that unknown to Henry, the region is full of expertly made papier-mâché facsimiles of barns. In that case, we would not say that Henry knows that the object is a barn, unless he has evidence against it being a papier-mâché facsimile, which is now a relevant alternative. So much is clear, but what if no such facsimiles exist in Henry's surroundings, although they once did? Are either of these circumstances sufficient to make the hypothesis (that it's a papier-mâché object) relevant? Probably not, but the situation is not so clear.'[4] Let p be the statement that the object in the field is a (real) barn, and q the one that the object in the field is a papier-mâché barn. When papier-mâché barns are scattered through the area, if p were false, q would be true or might be. Since in this case (we are supposing) the person still would believe p, the subjunctive

(3) not-$p \rightarrow$ not-(S believes that p)

is not satisfied, and so he doesn't know that p. However, when papier-mâché barns are or were scattered around another country, even if p were false q wouldn't be true, and so (for all we have been told) the person may well know that p. A hypothesis q contrary to p clearly is relevant when if p weren't true, q would be true; when not-$p \rightarrow q$. It clearly is irrelevant when if p weren't true, q also would not be true; when not-$p \rightarrow$ not-q. The remaining possibility is that neither of these opposed subjunctives holds; q might (or might not) be true if p weren't true. In this case, q also will be relevant, according to an account of knowledge incorporating condition (3) and treating subjunctives along the lines sketched above. Thus, condition (3) handles cases that befuddle the 'relevant alternatives' account; though that account can adopt the above subjunctive

in Logical Theory (Oxford 1968); David Lewis, *Counterfactuals* (Cambridge 1973); and Jonathan Bennett's critical review of Lewis, 'Counterfactuals and Possible Worlds', *Canadian Journal of Philosophy*, 4/2 (Dec. 1974), 381–402. Our purposes require, for the most part, no more than an intuitive understanding of subjunctives.

[4] G. C. Stine, 'Skepticism, Relevant Alternatives and Deductive Closure', *Philosophical Studies*, 29 (1976), 252, who attributes the example to Carl Ginet.

criterion for when an alternative is relevant, it then becomes merely an alternate and longer way of stating condition (3).

Despite the power and intuitive force of the condition that if *p* weren't true the person would not believe it, this condition does not (in conjunction with the first two conditions) rule out every problem case. There remains, for example, the case of the person in the tank who is brought to believe, by direct electrical and chemical stimulation of his brain, that he is in the tank and is being brought to believe things in this way; he does not know this is true. However, the subjunctive condition is satisfied: if he weren't floating in the tank, he wouldn't believe he was.

The person in the tank does not know he is there, because his belief is not sensitive to the truth. Although it is caused by the fact that is its content, it is not sensitive to that fact. The operators of the tank could have produced any belief, including the false belief that he wasn't in the tank; if they had, he would have believed that. Perfect sensitivity would involve beliefs and facts varying together. We already have one portion of that variation, subjunctively at least: if *p* were false he wouldn't believe it. This sensitivity as specified by a subjunctive does not have the belief vary with the truth or falsity of *p* in all possible situations, merely in the ones that would or might obtain if *p* were false.

The subjunctive condition

(3) not-*p* → not-(*S* believes that *p*)

tells us only half the story about how his belief is sensitive to the truth-value of *p*. It tells us how his belief state is sensitive to *p*'s falsity, but not how it is sensitive to *p*'s truth; it tells us what his belief state would be if *p* were false, but not what it would be if *p* were true.

To be sure, conditions (1) and (2) tell us that *p* is true and he does believe it, but it does not follow that his believing *p* is sensitive to *p*'s being true. This additional sensitivity is given to us by a further subjunctive: if *p* were true, he would believe it.

(4) *p* → *S* believes that *p*.

Not only is *p* true and *S* believes it, but if it were true he would believe it. Compare: not only was the photon emitted and did it go to the left, but (it was then true that): if it were emitted it would go to the left. The truth of antecedent and consequent is not alone sufficient for the truth of a subjunctive; (4) says more than (1) and (2). Thus, we presuppose some (or another) suitable account of subjunctives. According to the suggestion tentatively made above, (4) holds true if not only does he actually truly believe *p*, but in the 'close' worlds where *p* is true, he also believes it. He believes that *p* for some distance out in the *p* neighbourhood of the actual world; similarly, condition (3) speaks not of the whole not-*p* neighbourhood of the actual world, but only of the first portion of it. (If, as is likely, these explanations do not help, please use your own intuitive understanding of the subjunctives (3) and (4).)

The person in the tank does not satisfy the subjunctive condition (4). Imagine as actual a world in which he is in the tank and is stimulated to believe he is, and consider what subjunctives are true in that world. It is not true of him there that if he were in the tank he would believe it; for in the close world (or situation) to his own where he is in the tank but they don't give him the belief that he is (much less instil the belief that he isn't) he doesn't believe he is in the tank. Of the person actually in the tank and believing it, it is not true to make the further statement that if he were in the tank he would believe it—so he does not know he is in the tank.

The subjunctive condition (4) also handles a case presented by Gilbert Harman.[5] The dictator of a country is killed; in their first edition, newspapers print the story, but later all the country's newspapers and other media deny the story, falsely. Everyone who encounters the denial believes it (or does not know what to believe and so suspends judgement). Only one person in the country fails to hear any denial and he continues to believe the truth. He satisfies conditions (1)–(3) (and the causal condition about belief) yet we are reluctant to say he knows the truth. The reason is that if he had heard the denials, he too would have believed them, just like everyone else. His belief is not sensitively tuned to the truth, he doesn't satisfy the condition that if it were true he would believe it. Condition (4) is not satisfied.

There is a pleasing symmetry about how this account of knowledge relates conditions (3) and (4), and connects them to the first two conditions. The account has the following form.

(1)
(2)
(3) not-1 → not-2
(4) 1 → 2

[5] Gilbert Harman, *Thought* (Princeton; 1973), ch. 9, 142–54.

I am not inclined, however, to make too much of this symmetry, for I found also that with other conditions experimented with as a possible fourth condition there was some way to construe the resulting third and fourth conditions as symmetrical answers to some symmetrical looking questions, so that they appeared to arise in parallel fashion from similar questions about the components of true belief.

Symmetry, it seems, is a feature of a mode of presentation, not of the contents presented. A uniform transformation of symmetrical statements can leave the results non-symmetrical. But if symmetry attaches to mode of presentation, how can it possibly be a deep feature of, for instance, laws of nature that they exhibit symmetry? (One of my favourite examples of symmetry is due to Groucho Marx. On his radio programme he spoofed a commercial, and ended, 'And if you are not completely satisfied, return the unused portion of our product and we will return the unused portion of your money.') Still, to present our subject symmetrically makes the connection of knowledge to true belief especially perspicuous. It seems to me that a symmetrical formulation is a sign of our understanding, rather than a mark of truth. If we cannot understand an asymmetry as arising from an underlying symmetry through the operation of a particular factor, we will not understand why that asymmetry exists in that direction. (But do we also need to understand why the underlying asymmetrical factor holds instead of its opposite?)

A person knows that p when he not only does truly believe it, but also would truly believe it and wouldn't falsely believe it. He not only actually has a true belief, he subjunctively has one. It is true that p and he believes it; if it weren't true he wouldn't believe it, and if it were true he would believe it. To know that p is to be someone who would believe it if it were true, and who wouldn't believe it if it were false.

It will be useful to have a term for this situation when a person's belief is thus subjunctively connected to the fact. Let us say of a person who believes that p, which is true, that when (3) and (4) hold, his belief *tracks* the truth that p. To know is to have a belief that tracks the truth. Knowledge is a particular way of being connected to the world, having a specific real factual connection to the world: tracking it.

[*A section which introduces some refinements is omitted here.*]

II. SCEPTICISM

The sceptic about knowledge argues that we know very little or nothing of what we think we know, or at any rate that this position is no less reasonable than the belief in knowledge. The history of philosophy exhibits a number of different attempts to refute the sceptic: to prove him wrong or show that in arguing against knowledge he presupposes there is some and so refutes himself. Others attempt to show that accepting scepticism is unreasonable, since it is more likely that the sceptic's extreme conclusion is false than that all of his premises are true, or simply because reasonableness of belief just means proceeding in an anti-sceptical way. Even when these counter-arguments satisfy their inventors, they fail to satisfy others, as is shown by the persistent attempts against scepticism. The continuing felt need to refute scepticism, and the difficulty in doing so, attests to the power of the sceptic's position, the depth of his worries.

An account of knowledge should illuminate sceptical arguments and show wherein lies their force. If the account leads us to reject these arguments, this had better not happen too easily or too glibly. To think the sceptic overlooks something obvious, to attribute to him a simple mistake or confusion or fallacy, is to refuse to acknowledge the power of his position and the grip it can have upon us. We thereby cheat ourselves of the opportunity to reap his insights and to gain self-knowledge in understanding why his arguments lure us so. Moreover, in fact, we cannot lay the spectre of scepticism to rest without first hearing what it shall unfold.

Our goal is not, however, to refute scepticism, to prove it is wrong or even to argue that it is wrong. We have elsewhere distinguished between philosophy that attempts to prove, and philosophy that attempts to explain how something is possible. Our task here is to explain how knowledge is possible, given what the sceptic says that we do accept (for example, that it is logically possible that we are dreaming or are floating in the tank). In doing this, we need not convince the sceptic, and we may introduce explanatory hypotheses that he would reject. What is important for our task of explanation and understanding is that *we* find those hypotheses acceptable or plausible, and that they show us how the existence of knowledge fits together with the logical possibilities the sceptic points to, so that these are reconciled within our own belief system. These hypotheses are to explain to ourselves how knowledge is possible, not to prove to someone else that knowledge *is* possible.[6]

Sceptical Possibilities

The sceptic often refers to possibilities in which a person would believe something even though it was false: really, the person is cleverly deceived by others, perhaps by an evil demon, or the person is dreaming, or he is floating in a tank near Alpha Centauri with his brain being stimulated. In each case, the p he believes is false, and he believes it even though it is false.

How do these possibilities adduced by the sceptic show that someone does not know that p? Suppose that someone is you; how do these possibilities count against your knowing that p? One way might be the following. (I shall consider other ways later.) If there is a possible situation where p is false yet you believe that p, then in that situation you believe that p even though it is false. So it appears you do not satisfy condition (3) for knowledge.

(3) If p were false, S wouldn't believe that p.

For a situation has been described in which you do believe that p even though p is false. How then can it also be true that if p were false, you wouldn't believe it? If the sceptic's possible situation shows that (3) is false, and if (3) is a necessary condition for knowledge, then the sceptic's possible situation shows that there isn't knowledge.

So construed, the sceptic's argument plays on condition (3); it aims to show that condition (3) is not satisfied. The sceptic may seem to be putting forth

R: Even if p were false, S still would believe p.

This conditional, with the same antecedent as (3) and the contradictory consequent, is incompatible with the truth of (3). If (3) is true, then R is not. However, R is stronger than the sceptic needs in order to show (3) is false. For (3) is false when if p were false, S might believe that p. This last conditional is weaker than R, and is

---

[6] From the perspective of explanation rather than proof, the extensive philosophical discussion, deriving from Charles S. Peirce, of whether the sceptic's doubts are real is beside the point. The problem of explaining how knowledge is possible would remain the same, even if no one ever claimed to doubt that there was knowledge.

merely (3)'s denial:

T: not-[not-$p \rightarrow$ not-(S believes that p)].

Whereas R does not simply deny (3), it asserts an opposing subjunctive of its own. Perhaps the possibility the sceptic adduces is not enough to show that R is true, but it appears at least to establish the weaker T; since this T denies (3), the sceptic's possibility appears to show that (3) is false.

However, the truth of (3) is not incompatible with the existence of a possible situation where the person believes p though it is false. The subjunctive

(3)   not-$p \rightarrow$ not-(S believes p)

does not talk of all possible situations in which p is false (in which not-p is true). It does not say that in all possible situations where not-p holds, S doesn't believe p. To say there is no possible situation in which not-p yet S believes p, would be to say that not-p entails not-(S believes p), or logically implies it. But subjunctive conditionals differ from entailments; the subjunctive (3) is not a statement of entailment. So the existence of a possible situation in which p is false yet S believes p does not show that (3) is false; (3) can be true even though there is a possible situation where not-p and S believes that p.

What the subjunctive (3) speaks of is the situation that would hold if p were false. Not every possible situation in which p is false is the situation that would hold if p were false. To fall into possible worlds talk, the subjunctive (3) speaks of the not-p world that is closest to the actual world, or of those not-p worlds that are closest to the actual world. And it is of this or these not-p worlds that it says (in them) S does not believe that p. What happens in yet other more distant not-p worlds is no concern of the subjunctive (3).

The sceptic's possibilities (let us refer to them as SK), of the person's being deceived by a demon or dreaming or floating in a tank, count against the subjunctive

(3)   if p were false then S wouldn't believe that p

only if (one of) these possibilities would or might obtain if p were false. Condition (3) says: if p were false, S still would not believe p. And this can hold even though there is some situation SK described by the sceptic in which p is false and S believes p. If p were false S still would not believe p, even though there is a situation SK in which p is false and S does believe p, provided that this situation SK wouldn't obtain if p were false. If the sceptic describes a situation

SK which would not hold even if *p* were false then this situation SK doesn't show that (3) is false and so does not (in this way at least) undercut knowledge. Condition C acts to rule out sceptical hypotheses.

C: not-*p* → SK does not obtain.

Any sceptical situation SK which satisfies condition C is ruled out. For a sceptical situation SK to show that we don't know that *p*, it must fail to satisfy C which excludes it; instead it must be a situation that might obtain if *p* did not, and so satisfy C's denial:

not-(not-*p* → SK doesn't obtain).

Although the sceptic's imagined situations appear to show that (3) is false, they do not; they satisfy condition C and so are excluded.

The sceptic might go on to ask whether we know that his imagined situations SK are excluded by condition C, whether we know that if *p* were false SK would not obtain. However, typically he asks something stronger: do we know that his imagined situation SK does not actually obtain? Do we know that we are not being deceived by a demon, dreaming, or floating in a tank? And if we do not know this, how can we know that *p*? Thus we are led to the second way his imagined situations might show that we do not know that *p*.

Sceptical Results

According to our account of knowledge, *S* knows that the sceptic's situation SK doesn't hold if and only if

(1) SK doesn't hold
(2) *S* believes that SK doesn't hold
(3) If SK were to hold, *S* would not believe that SK doesn't hold
(4) If SK were not to hold, *S* would believe it does not.

Let us focus on the third of these conditions. The sceptic has carefully chosen his situations SK so that if they held we (still) would believe they did not. We would believe we weren't dreaming, weren't being deceived, and so on, even if we were. He has chosen situations SK such that if SK were to hold, *S* would (still) believe that SK doesn't hold—and this is incompatible with the truth of (3).

Since condition (3) is a necessary condition for knowledge, it follows that we do not know that SK doesn't hold. If it were true that an evil demon was deceiving us, if we were having a particular dream, if we were floating in a tank with our brains stimulated in a specified way, we would still believe we were not. So, we do not know we're not being deceived by an evil demon, we do not know we're not in that tank, and we do not know we're not having that dream. So says the sceptic, and so says our account. And also so we say—don't we? For how could we know we are not being deceived that way, dreaming that dream? If those things *were* happening to us, everything would seem the same to us. There is no way we can know it is not happening for there is no way we could tell if it were happening; and if it were happening we would believe exactly what we do now—in particular, we still would believe that it was not. For this reason, we feel, and correctly, that we don't know—how could we?—that it is not happening to us. It is a virtue of our account that it yields, and explains, this result.

The sceptic asserts we do not know his possibilities don't obtain, and he is right. Attempts to avoid scepticism by claiming we do know these things are bound to fail. The sceptic's possibilities make us uneasy because, as we deeply realize, we do not know they don't obtain; it is not surprising that attempts to show we do know these things leave us suspicious, strike us even as bad faith. Nor has the sceptic merely pointed out something obvious and trivial. It comes as a surprise to realize that we do not know his possibilities don't obtain. It is startling, shocking. For we would have thought, before the sceptic got us to focus on it, that we did know those things, that we did know we were not being deceived by a demon, or dreaming that dream, or stimulated that way in that tank. The sceptic has pointed out that we do not know things we would have confidently said we knew. And if we don't know these things, what can we know? So much for the supposed obviousness of what the sceptic tells us.

Let us say that a situation (or world) is doxically identical for S to the actual situation when if S were in that situation, he would have exactly the beliefs (*doxa*) he actually does have. More generally, two situations are doxically identical for S if and only if he would have exactly the same beliefs in them. It might be merely a curiosity to be told there are non-actual situations doxically identical to the actual one. The sceptic, however, describes worlds doxically identical to the actual world in which almost everything believed is false.[7]

---

[7] I say almost everything, because there still could be some true beliefs such as 'I

Such worlds are possible because we know mediately, not directly. This leaves room for a divergence between our beliefs and the truth. It is as though we possessed only two-dimensional plane projections of three-dimensional objects. Different three-dimensional objects, oriented appropriately, have the same two-dimensional plane projection. Similarly, different situations or worlds will lead to our having the very same beliefs. What is surprising is how very different the doxically identical world can be—different enough for almost everything believed in it to be false. Whether or not the mere fact that knowledge is mediated always makes room for such a very different doxically identical world, it does so in our case, as the sceptic's possibilities show. To be shown this is non-trivial, especially when we recall that we do not know the sceptic's possibility doesn't obtain: we do not know that we are not living in a doxically identical world wherein almost everything we believe is false.

What more could the sceptic ask for or hope to show? Even readers who sympathized with my desire not to dismiss the sceptic too quickly may feel this has gone too far, that we have not merely acknowledged the force of the sceptic's position but have succumbed to it.

The sceptic maintains that we know almost none of what we think we know. He has shown, much to our initial surprise, that we do not know his (non-trivial) possibility SK doesn't obtain. Thus, he has shown of one thing we thought we knew, that we didn't and don't. To the conclusion that we know almost nothing, it appears but a short step. For if we do not know we are not dreaming or being deceived by a demon or floating in a tank, then how can I know, for example, that I am sitting before a page writing with a pen, and how can you know that you are reading a page of a book?

However, although our account of knowledge agrees with the sceptic in saying that we do not know that not-SK, it places no formidable barriers before my knowing that I am writing on a page with a pen. It is true that I am, I believe I am, if I weren't I wouldn't believe I was, and if I were, I would believe it. Also, it is true that you are reading a page (please, don't stop now!), you believe you are, if you weren't reading a page you wouldn't believe you were, and if you were reading a page you would believe you

exist.' More limited sceptical possibilities present worlds doxically identical to the actual world in which almost every belief of a certain sort is false, for example, about the past, or about other people's mental states.

were. So according to the account, I do know that I am writing on a page with a pen, and you do know that you are reading a page. The account does not lead to any general scepticism.

Yet we must grant that it appears that if the sceptic is right that we don't know we are not dreaming or being deceived or floating in the tank, then it cannot be that I know I am writing with a pen or that you know you are reading a page. So we must scrutinize with special care the sceptic's 'short step' to the conclusion that we don't know these things, for either this step cannot be taken or our account of knowledge is incoherent.

Non-closure

In taking the 'short step', the sceptic assumes that if S knows that p and he knows that 'p entails q' then he also knows that q. In the terminology of the logicians, the sceptic assumes that knowledge is closed under known logical implication; that the operation of moving from something known to something else known to be entailed by it does not take us outside of the (closed) area of knowledge. He intends, of course, to work things backwards, arguing that since the person does not know that q, assuming (at least for the purposes of argument) that he does know that p entails q, it follows that he does not know that p. For if he did know that p, he would also know that q, which he doesn't.

The details of different sceptical arguments vary in their structure, but each one will assume some variant of the principle that knowledge is closed under known logical implication. If we abbreviate 'knowledge that p' by 'Kp' and abbreviate 'entails' by the fishhook sign '-3', we can write this principle of closure as the subjunctive principle

P: $K(p-3q)$ & $Kp \rightarrow Kq$.

If a person were to know that p entails q and he were to know that p then he would know that q. The statement that q follows by *modus ponens* from the other two stated as known in the antecedent of the subjunctive principle P; this principle counts on the person to draw the inference to q.

You know that your being in a tank on Alpha Centauri entails your not being in place X where you are. (I assume here a limited readership.) And you know also the contrapositive, that your being at place X entails that you are not then in a tank on Alpha Centauri. If you knew you were at X you would know you're not in a tank (of a specified sort) at Alpha Centauri. But you do not know this last fact (the sceptic has argued and we have agreed) and so (he argues) you don't know the first. Another intuitive way of putting the sceptic's argument is as follows. If you know that two statements are incompatible and you know the first is true then you know the denial of the second. You know that your being at X and your being in a tank on Alpha Centauri are incompatible; so if you knew you were at X you would know you were not in the (specified) tank on Alpha Centauri. Since you do not know the second, you don't know the first.

No doubt, it is possible to argue over the details of principle P, to point out it is incorrect as it stands. Perhaps, though Kp, the person does not know that he knows that p (that is, not-KKp) and so does not draw the inference to q. Or perhaps he doesn't draw the inference because not-$KK(p \dashv 3 q)$. Other similar principles face their own difficulties: for example, the principle that $K(p \rightarrow q) \rightarrow (Kp \rightarrow Kq)$ fails if Kp stops $p \rightarrow q$ from being true, that is, if $Kp \rightarrow$ not-$(p \rightarrow q)$; the principle that $K(p \dashv 3 q) \rightarrow K(Kp \rightarrow Kq)$ faces difficulties if Kp makes the person forget that $(p \dashv 3 q)$ and so he fails to draw the inference to q. We seem forced to pile K upon K until we reach something like $KK(p \dashv 3 q)$ & $KKp \rightarrow Kq$; this involves strengthening considerably the antecedent of P and so is not useful for the sceptic's argument that p is not known. (From a principle altered thus, it would follow at best that it is not known that p is known.)

We would be ill-advised, however, to quibble over the details of P. Although these details are difficult to get straight, it will continue to appear that something like P is correct. If S knows that 'p entails q', and he knows that p and knows that '(p and p entails q) entails q' and he does draw the inference to q from all this and believes q via the process of drawing this inference, then will he not know that q? And what is wrong with simplifying this mass of detail by writing merely principle P, provided we apply it only to cases where the mass of detail holds, as it surely does in the sceptical cases under consideration? For example, I do realize that my being in the Van Leer Foundation Building in Jerusalem entails that I am not in a tank on Alpha Centauri; I am capable of drawing inferences now; I do believe I am not in a tank on Alpha Centauri (though not solely via this inference, surely); and so forth. Won't this satisfy the correctly detailed principle, and shouldn't it follow that I know I am not (in that tank) on Alpha Centauri? The sceptic agrees it should follow; so he concludes from the fact that I don't know I am not floating in the tank on Alpha Centauri that I don't know I am in Jerusalem. Uncovering difficulties in the details of particular formulations of P will not weaken the principle's intuitive appeal; such quibbling will seem at best like a wasp attacking a steamroller, at worst like an effort in bad faith to avoid being pulled along by the sceptic's argument.

Principle P is wrong, however, and not merely in detail. Knowledge is not closed under known logical implication. S knows that p when S has a true belief that p, and S wouldn't have a false belief that p (condition (3)) and S would have a true belief that p (condition (4)). Neither of these latter two conditions is closed under known logical implication.

Let us begin with condition

(3) if p were false, S wouldn't believe that p.

When S knows that p, his belief that p is contingent on the truth of p, contingent in the way the subjunctive condition (3) describes. Now it might be that p entails q (and S knows this), that S's belief that p is subjunctively contingent on the truth of p, that S believes q, yet his belief that q is not subjunctively dependent on the truth of q, in that it (or he) does not satisfy:

(3 ') if q were false, S wouldn't believe that q.

For (3 ') talks of what S would believe if q were false, and this may be a very different situation from the one that would hold if p were false, even though p entails q. That you were born in a certain city entails that you were born on earth.[8] Yet contemplating what (actually) would be the situation if you were not born in that city is very different from contemplating what situation would hold if you weren't born on earth. Just as those possibilities are very different, so what is believed in them may be very different. When p entails q (and not the other way around) p will be a stronger statement than q, and so not-q (which is the antecedent of (3 ')) will be a stronger statement than not-p (which is the antecedent of (3)). There is no reason to assume you will have the same beliefs in these two cases, under these suppositions of differing strengths.

There is no reason to assume the (closest) not-p world and the (closest) not-q world are doxically identical for you, and no reason to assume, even though p entails q, that your beliefs in one of these worlds would be a (proper) subset of your beliefs in the other.

---

[8] Here again I assume a limited readership, and ignore possibilities such as those described in James Blish, *Cities in Flight* (New York, 1982).

Consider now the two statements:

p = I am awake and sitting on a chair in Jerusalem;
q = I am not floating in a tank on Alpha Centauri being stimulated by electrochemical means to believe that p.

The first one entails the second: p entails q. Also, I know that p entails q; and I know that p. If p were false, I would be standing or lying down in the same city, or perhaps sleeping there, or perhaps in a neighbouring city or town. If q were false, I would be floating in a tank on Alpha Centauri. Clearly these are very different situations, leading to great differences in what I then would believe. If p were false, if I weren't awake and sitting on a chair in Jerusalem, I would not believe that p. Yet if q were false, if I was floating in a tank on Alpha Centauri, I would believe that q, that I was not in the tank, and indeed, in that case, I would still believe that p. According to our account of knowledge, I know that p yet I do not know that q, even though (I know) p entails q.

This failure of knowledge to be closed under known logical implication stems from the fact that condition (3) is not closed under known logical implication; condition (3) can hold of one statement believed while not of another known to be entailed by the first. It is clear that any account that includes as a necessary condition for knowledge the subjunctive condition (3), not-$p \rightarrow$ not-(S believes that p), will have the consequence that knowledge is not closed under known logical implication.

When p entails q and you believe each of them, if you do not have a false belief that p (since p is true) then you do not have a false belief that q. However, if you are to know something not only don't you have a false belief about it, but also you wouldn't have a false belief about it. Yet, we have seen how it may be that p entails q and you believe each and you wouldn't have a false belief that p yet you might have a false belief that q (that is, it is not the case that you wouldn't have one). Knowledge is not closed under the known logical implication because 'wouldn't have a false belief that' is not closed under known logical implication.

If knowledge were the same as (simply) true belief then it would be closed under known logical implication (provided the implied statements were believed). Knowledge is not simply true belief, however; additional conditions are needed. These further conditions will make knowledge open under known logical implication, even when the entailed statement is believed, when at least one of the further conditions itself is open. Knowledge stays closed (only) if all of the additional conditions are closed. I lack a general non-trivial characterization of those conditions that are closed under known logical implication; possessing such an illuminating characterization, one might attempt to prove that no additional conditions of that sort could provide an adequate analysis of knowledge.

Still, we can say the following. A belief that p is knowledge that p only if it somehow varies with the truth of p. The causal condition for knowledge specified that the belief was 'produced by' the fact, but that condition did not provide the right sort of varying with the fact. The subjunctive conditions (3) and (4) are our attempt to specify that varying. But however an account spells this out, it will hold that whether a belief that p is knowledge partly depends on what goes on with the belief in some situations when p is false. An account that says nothing about what is believed in any situation when p is false cannot give us any mode of varying with the fact.

Because what is preserved under logical implication is truth, any condition that is preserved under known logical implication is most likely to speak only of what happens when p, and q, are true, without speaking at all of what happens when either one is false. Such a condition is incapable of providing 'varies with'; so adding only such conditions to true belief cannot yield an adequate account of knowledge.

A belief's somehow varying with the truth of what is believed is not closed under known logical implication. Since knowledge that p involves such variation, knowledge also is not closed under known logical implication. The sceptic cannot easily deny that knowledge involves such variation, for his argument that we don't know that we're not floating in that tank, for example, uses the fact that knowledge does involve variation. ('If you were floating in the tank you would still think you weren't, so you don't know that you're not.') Yet, though one part of his argument uses that fact that knowledge involves such variation, another part of his argument presupposes that knowledge does not involve any such variation. This latter is the part that depends upon knowledge being closed under known logical implication, as when the sceptic argues that since you don't know that not-SK, you don't know you are not floating in the tank, then you also don't know, for example, that you are now reading a book. That closure can hold only if the variation does not. The sceptic cannot be right both times. According to our view he is right when he holds that knowledge involves such variation and so concludes that we don't know, for example, that we are not floating in that tank; but he is wrong when he assumes knowledge is closed under known logical implication and concludes that we know hardly anything.[9]

Knowledge is a real factual relation, subjunctively specifiable, whose structure admits our standing in this relation, tracking, to *p* without standing in it to some *q* which we know *p* to entail. Any relation embodying some variation of belief with the fact, with the truth (value), will exhibit this structural feature. The sceptic is right that we don't track some particular truths—the ones stating that his sceptical possibilities SK don't hold—but wrong that we don't stand in the real knowledge-relation of tracking to many other truths, including ones that entail these first mentioned truths we believe but don't know.

The literature on scepticism contains writers who endorse these sceptical arguments (or similar narrower ones), but confess their inability to maintain their sceptical beliefs at times when they are not focusing explicitly on the reasoning that led them to sceptical conclusions. The most notable example of this is Hume:

> I am ready to reject all belief and reasoning, and can look upon no opinion even as more probable or likely than another . . . Most fortunately it

[9] Reading an earlier draft of this chapter, friends pointed out to me that Fred Dretske already had defended the view that knowledge (as one among many epistemic concepts) is not closed under known logical implication. (See his 'Epistemic Operators', *Journal of Philosophy*,67, (1970), 1007–23.) Furthermore, Dretske presented a subjunctive condition for knowledge (in his 'Conclusive Reasons', *Australasian Journal of Philosophy*, 49, (1971), 1–22), holding that *S* knows that *p* on the basis of reasons *R* only if: *R* would not be the case unless *p* were the case. Here Dretske ties the evidence subjunctively to the fact, and the belief based on the evidence subjunctively to the fact through the evidence. The independent statement and delineation of the position here I hope will make clear its many merits.

After Goldman's paper on a causal theory of knowledge, in *Journal of Philosophy*, 64, (1967), an idea then already 'in the air', it required no great leap to consider subjunctive conditions. Some 2 months after the first version of this chapter was written, Goldman himself published a paper on knowledge utilizing counterfactuals ('Discrimination and Perceptual Knowledge', Essay II in this collection), also talking of relevant possibilities (without using the counterfactuals to identify which possibilities are relevant); and R. Shope has called my attention to a paper of L. S. Carrier ('An Analysis of Empirical Knowledge', *Southern Journal of Philosophy*, 9, (1971), 3–11) that also used subjunctive conditions including our condition (3). Armstrong's reliability view of knowledge (*Belief, Truth and Knowledge*, Cambridge, 1973, pp. 166, 169) involved a lawlike connection between the belief that *p* and the state of affairs that makes it true. Clearly, the idea is one whose time has come.

happens that since reason is incapable of dispelling these clouds, nature herself suffices to that purpose, and cures me of this philosophical melancholy and delirium, either by relaxing this bent of mind, or by some avocation, and lively impression of my senses, which obliterate all these chimeras. I dine, I play a game of backgammon, I converse, and am merry with my friends; and when after three or four hours' amusement, I would return to these speculations, they appear so cold, and strained, and ridiculous, that I cannot find in my heart to enter into them any farther. (*A Treatise of Human Nature*, Book I, Part IV, section VII.)

The great subverter of Pyrrhonism or the excessive principles of skepticism is action, and employment, and the occupations of common life. These principles may flourish and triumph in the schools; where it is, indeed, difficult, if not impossible, to refute them. But as soon as they leave the shade, and by the presence of the real objects, which actuate our passions and sentiments, are put in opposition to the more powerful principles of our nature, they vanish like smoke, and leave the most determined skeptic in the same condition as other mortals . . . And though a Pyrrhonian may throw himself or others into a momentary amazement and confusion by his profound reasonings; the first and most trivial event in life will put to flight all his doubts and scruples, and leave him the same, in every point of action and speculation, with the philosophers of every other sect, or with those who never concerned themselves in any philosophical researches. When he awakes from his dream, he will be the first to join in the laugh against himself, and to confess that all his objections are mere amusement. (*An Enquiry Concerning Human Understanding*, Section XII, Part II.)

The theory of knowledge we have presented explains why sceptics of various sorts have had such difficulties in sticking to their far-reaching sceptical conclusions 'outside the study', or even inside it when they are not thinking specifically about sceptical arguments and possibilities SK.

The sceptic's arguments do show (but show only) that we don't know the sceptic's possibilities SK do not hold; and he is right that we don't track the fact that SK does not hold. (If it were to hold, we would still think it didn't.) However, the sceptic's arguments don't show we do not know other facts (including facts that entail not-SK) for we do track these other facts (and knowledge is not closed under known logical entailment). Since we do track these other facts—you, for example, the fact that you are reading a book; I, the fact that I am writing on a page—and the sceptic tracks such facts too, it is not surprising that when he focuses on them, on his relationship to such facts, the sceptic finds it hard to remember or maintain his view that he does not know those facts. Only by shifting his attention back to his relationship to the (different) fact that not-SK, which relationship is not tracking, can he revive his sceptical belief and make it salient. However, this sceptical triumph is evanescent, it vanishes when his attention turns to other facts. Only by fixating on the sceptical possibilities SK can he maintain his sceptical virtue; otherwise, unsurprisingly, he is forced to confess to sins of credulity.

II

DISCRIMINATION AND PERCEPTUAL KNOWLEDGE

A. I. GOLDMAN

This paper presents a partial analysis of perceptual knowledge, an analysis that will, I hope, lay a foundation for a general theory of knowing. Like an earlier theory I proposed,[1] the envisaged theory would seek to explicate the concept of knowledge by reference to the causal processes that produce (or sustain) belief. Unlike the earlier theory, however, it would abandon the requirement that a knower's belief that *p* be causally connected with the fact, or state of affairs, that *p*.

What kinds of causal processes or mechanisms must be responsible for a belief if that belief is to count as knowledge? They must be mechanisms that are, in an appropriate sense, 'reliable'. Roughly, a cognitive mechanism or process is reliable if it not only produces true beliefs in actual situations, but would produce true beliefs, or at least inhibit false beliefs, in relevant counterfactual situations. The theory of knowledge I envisage, then, would contain an important counterfactual component.

To be reliable, a cognitive mechanism must enable a person to *discriminate* or *differentiate* between incompatible states of affairs. It must operate in such a way that incompatible states of the world would generate different cognitive responses. Perceptual mechanisms illustrate this clearly. A perceptual mechanism is reliable to the extent that contrary features of the environment (for example, an object's being red, versus its being yellow) would produce contrary perceptual states of the organism, which would, in turn, produce suitably different beliefs about the environment. Another belief-governing mechanism is a reasoning mechanism,

Reprinted from the *Journal of Philosophy*, 73/20 (18 Nov. 1976), 771–91, by permission of the author and Managing Editor.

[1] 'A Causal Theory of Knowing', *Journal of Philosophy*, 64/12 (22 June 1967), 357–72; reprinted in M. Roth and L. Galis, eds., *Knowing* (New York, 1970).

which, given a set of antecedent beliefs, generates or inhibits various new beliefs. A reasoning mechanism is reliable to the extent that its functional procedures would generate new true beliefs from antecedent true beliefs.

My emphasis on discrimination accords with a sense of the verb 'know' that has been neglected by philosophers. The OED lists one (early) sense of 'know' as '*to distinguish* (one thing) *from* (another)', as in 'I know a hawk from a handsaw' (*Hamlet*) and 'We'll teach him to know Turtles from Jayes' (*Merry Wives of Windsor*). Although it no longer has great currency, this sense still survives in such expressions as 'I don't know him from Adam', 'He doesn't know right from left', and other phrases that readily come to mind. I suspect that this construction is historically important and can be used to shed light on constructions in which 'know' takes propositional objects. I suggest that a person is said to know that *p* just in case he *distinguishes* or *discriminates* the truth of *p* from relevant alternatives.

A knowledge attribution imputes to someone the discrimination of a given state of affairs from possible alternatives, but not necessarily all logically possible alternatives. In forming beliefs about the world, we do not normally consider all logical possibilities. And in deciding whether someone knows that *p* (its truth being assumed), we do not ordinarily require him to discriminate *p* from all logically possible alternatives. Which alternatives are, or ought to be considered, is a question I shall not fully resolve in this paper, but some new perspectives will be examined. I take up this topic in Section I.

I

Consider the following example. Henry is driving in the country-side with his son. For the boy's edification Henry identifies various objects on the landscape as they come into view. 'That's a cow', says Henry, 'That's a tractor', 'That's a silo', 'That's a barn', etc. Henry has no doubt about the identity of these objects; in particular, he has no doubt that the last-mentioned object is a barn, which indeed it is. Each of the identified objects has features characteristic of its type. Moreover, each object is fully in view, Henry has excellent eyesight, and he has enough time to look at them reasonably carefully, since there is little traffic to distract him.

Given this information, would we say that Henry *knows* that the object is a barn? Most of us would have little hesitation in saying this, so long as we were not in a certain philosophical frame of mind. Contrast our inclination here with the inclination we would have if we were given some additional information. Suppose we are told that, unknown to Henry, the district he has just entered is full of papier-mâché facsimiles of barns. These facsimiles look from the road exactly like barns, but are really just façades, without back walls or interiors, quite incapable of being used as barns. They are so cleverly constructed that travellers invariably mistake them for barns. Having just entered the district, Henry has not encountered any facsimiles; the object he sees is a genuine barn. But if the object on that site were a facsimile, Henry would mistake it for a barn. Given this new information, we would be strongly inclined to withdraw the claim that Henry *knows* the object is a barn. How is this change in our assessment to be explained?

Note first that the traditional justified-true-belief account of knowledge is of no help in explaining this change. In both cases Henry truly believes (indeed, is certain) that the object is a barn. Moreover, Henry's 'justification' or 'evidence' for the proposition that the object is a barn is the same in both cases. Thus, Henry should either know in both cases or not know in both cases. The presence of facsimiles in the district should make no difference to whether or not he knows.

My old causal analysis cannot handle the problem either. Henry's belief that the object is a barn is caused by the presence of the barn; indeed, the causal process is a perceptual one. None the less, we are not prepared to say, in the second version, that Henry knows.

One analysis of propositional knowledge that might handle the problem is Peter Unger's non-accidentality analysis.[2] According to this theory, S knows that p if and only if it is not at all accidental that S is right about its being the case that p. In the initial description of the example, this requirement appears to be satisfied; so we say that Henry knows. When informed about the facsimiles, however, we see that it is accidental that Henry is right about its being a barn. So we withdraw our knowledge attribution. The 'non-accidentality' analysis is not very satisfying, however, for the notion of 'non-accidentality' itself needs explication. Pending explication, it isn't clear whether it correctly handles all cases.

---

[2] 'An Analysis of Factual Knowledge', *Journal of Philosophy*, 45/6 (21 Mar. 1968), 157–70; reprinted in Roth and Galis, *Knowing*.

Another approach to knowledge that might handle our problem is the 'indefeasibility' approach.[3] On this view, S knows that p only if S's true belief is justified *and* this justification is not defeated. In an unrestricted form, an indefeasibility theory would say that S's justification j for believing that p is defeated if and only if there is some true proposition q such that the conjunction of q and j does not justify S in believing that p. In slightly different terms, S's justification j is defeated just in case p would no longer be evident for S if q were evident for S. This would handle the barn example, presumably, because the true proposition that there are barn facsimiles in the district is such that, if it were evident for Henry, then it would no longer be evident for him that the object he sees is a barn.

The trouble with the indefeasibility approach is that it is too strong, at least in its unrestricted form. On the foregoing account of 'defeat', as Gilbert Harman shows,[4] it will (almost) always be possible to find a true proposition that defeats S's justification. Hence, S will never (or seldom) know. What is needed is an appropriate restriction on the notion of 'defeat', but I am not aware of an appropriate restriction that has been formulated thus far.

The approach to the problem I shall recommend is slightly different. Admittedly, this approach will raise problems analogous to those of the indefeasibility theory, problems which will not be fully resolved here. Nevertheless, I believe this approach is fundamentally on the right track.

What, then, is my proposed treatment of the barn example? A person knows that p, I suggest, only if the actual state of affairs in which p is true is *distinguishable* or *discriminable* by him from a relevant possible state of affairs in which p is false. If there is a relevant possible state of affairs in which p is false and which is indistinguishable by him from the actual state of affairs, then he fails to know that p. In the original description of the barn case there is no hint of any relevant possible state of affairs in which the object in question is not a barn but is indistinguishable (by Henry) from the actual state of affairs. Hence, we are initially inclined to say that Henry knows. The information about the facsimiles, how-

---

[3] See e.g. Keith Lehrer and Thomas Paxson, Jr., 'Knowledge: Undefeated Justified True Belief', *Journal of Philosophy*, 46/8 (24 Apr. 1969), 225–37, and Peter D. Klein, 'A Proposed Definition of Propositional Knowledge', *Journal of Philosophy*, 48/16 (19 Aug. 1971), 471–482.

[4] *Thought* (Princeton, 1973), 152.

ever, introduces such a relevant state of affairs. Given that the district Henry has entered is full of barn facsimiles, there is a relevant alternative hypothesis about the object, namely, that it is a facsimile. Since, by assumption, a state of affairs in which such a hypothesis holds is indistinguishable by Henry from the actual state of affairs (from his vantage point on the road), this hypothesis is not 'ruled out' or 'precluded' by the factors that prompt Henry's belief. So, once apprised of the facsimiles in the district, we are inclined to deny that Henry knows.

Let us be clear about the bearing of the facsimiles on the case. The presence of the facsimiles does not 'create' the possibility that the object Henry sees is a facsimile. Even if there were no facsimiles in the district, it would be possible that the object on that site is a facsimile. What the presence of the facsimiles does is make this possibility *relevant*; or it makes us *consider* it relevant.

The qualifier 'relevant' plays an important role in my view. If knowledge required the elimination of all logically possible alternatives, there would be no knowledge (at least of contingent truths). If only *relevant* alternatives need to be precluded, however, the scope of knowledge could be substantial. This depends, of course, on which alternatives are relevant.

The issue at hand is directly pertinent to the dispute—at least one dispute—between sceptics and their opponents. In challenging a claim to knowledge (or certainty), a typical move of the sceptic is to adduce an unusual alternative hypothesis that the putative knower is unable to preclude: an alternative compatible with his 'data'. In the sceptical stage of his argument, Descartes says that he is unable to preclude the hypothesis that, instead of being seated by the fire, he is asleep in his bed and dreaming, or the hypothesis that an evil and powerful demon is making it appear to him as if he is seated by the fire. Similarly, Bertrand Russell points out that, given any claim about the past, we can adduce the 'sceptical hypothesis' that the world sprang into being five minutes ago, exactly as it then was, with a population that 'remembered' a wholly unreal past.[5]

One reply open to the sceptic's opponent is that these sceptical hypotheses are just 'idle' hypotheses, and that a person can know a proposition even if there are 'idle' alternatives he cannot preclude. The problem, of course, is to specify when an alternative is 'idle' and when it is 'serious' ('relevant'). Consider Henry once again. Should we say that the possibility of a facsimile before him is a

[5] *The Analysis of Mind* (London, 1921), 159–60.

serious or relevant possibility if there are no facsimiles in Henry's district, but only in Sweden? Or if a single such facsimile once existed in Sweden, but that none exists now?

There are two views one might take on this general problem. The first view is that there is a 'correct' answer, in any given situation, as to which alternatives are relevant. Given a complete specification of Henry's situation, a unique set of relevant alternatives is determined: either a set to which the facsimile alternative belongs or one to which it doesn't belong. According to this view, the semantic content of 'know' contains (implicit) rules that map any putative knower's circumstances into a set of relevant alternatives. An analysis of 'know' is incomplete unless it specifies these rules. The correct specification will favour either the sceptic or the sceptic's opponent.

The second view denies that a putative knower's circumstances uniquely determine a set of relevant alternatives. At any rate, it denies that the semantic content of 'know' contains rules that map a set of circumstances into a single set of relevant alternatives. According to this second view, the verb 'know' is simply not so semantically determinate.

The second view need not deny that there are *regularities* governing the alternative hypotheses a speaker (that is, an attributer or denier of knowledge) thinks of, and deems relevant. But these regularities are not part of the semantic content of 'know'. The putative knower's circumstances do not *mandate* a unique selection of alternatives; but psychological regularities govern which set of alternatives are in fact selected. In terms of these regularities (together with the semantic content of 'know'), we can explain the observed use of the term.

It is clear that some of these regularities pertain to the (description of the) putative knower's circumstances. One regularity might be that the more *likely* it is, given the circumstances, that a particular alternative would obtain (rather than the actual state of affairs), the more probable it is that a speaker will regard this alternative as relevant. Or, the more *similar* the situation in which the alternative obtains to the actual situation, the more probable it is that a speaker will regard this alternative as relevant. It is not only the circumstances of the putative knower's situation, however, that influence the choice of alternatives. The speaker's own linguistic and psychological context are also important. If the speaker is in a class where Descartes's evil demon has just been discussed, or

Russell's five-minute-old-world hypothesis, he may think of alternatives he would not otherwise think of and will perhaps treat them seriously. This sort of regularity is entirely ignored by the first view.

What I am calling the 'second' view might have two variants. The first variant can be imbedded in Robert Stalnaker's framework for pragmatics.[6] In this framework, a proposition is a function from possible words into truth values; the determinants of a proposition are a sentence and a (linguistic) context. An important contextual element is what the utterer of a sentence presupposes, or takes for granted. According to the first variant of the second view, a sentence of the form '*S* knows that *p*' does not determine a unique proposition. Rather, a proposition is determined by such a sentence together with the speaker's presuppositions concerning the relevant alternatives.[7] Sceptics and non-sceptics might make different presuppositions (both presuppositions being 'legitimate'), and, if so, they are simply asserting or denying different propositions.

One trouble with this variant is its apparent implication that, if a speaker utters a knowledge sentence without presupposing a fully determinate set of alternatives, he does not assert or deny any proposition. That seems too strong. A second variant of the second view, then, is that sentences of the form '*S* knows that *p*' express vague or indeterminate propositions (if they express 'propositions' at all), which can, but need not, be made more determinate by full specification of the alternatives. A person who *assents* to a knowledge sentence says that *S* discriminates the truth of *p* from relevant alternatives; but he may not have a distinct set of alternatives in mind. (Similarly, according to Paul Ziff, a person who says something is 'good' says that it answers to *certain* interests;[8] but he may not have a distinct set of interests in mind.) Someone who *denies* a knowledge sentence more commonly has one or more alternatives in mind as relevant, because his denial may stem from a particular alternative *S* cannot rule out. But even the denier of a knowledge sentence need not have a full set of relevant alternatives in mind.

I am attracted by the second view under discussion, especially its second variant. In the remainder of this paper, however, I shall be

[6] 'Pragmatics', in Donald Davidson and Gilbert Harman, eds., *Semantics of Natural Language* (Boston, 1972).

[7] Something like this is suggested by Fred Dretske, in 'Epistemic Operators', *Journal of Philosophy*, 47/24 (24 Dec. 1970), 1007–23, p. 1022.

[8] That 'good' means *answers to certain interests* is claimed by Ziff in *Semantic Analysis* (Ithaca, NY, 1960), ch. 6.

officially neutral. In other words, I shall not try to settle the question of whether the semantic content of 'know' contains rules that map the putative knower's situation into a unique set of relevant alternatives. I leave open the question of whether there is a 'correct' set of relevant alternatives, and if so, what it is. To this extent, I also leave open the question of whether sceptics or their opponents are 'right'. In defending my analysis of 'perceptually knows', however, I shall have to discuss particular examples. In treating these examples I shall assume some (psychological) regularities concerning the selection of alternatives. Among these regularities is the fact that speakers do not *ordinarily* think of 'radical' alternatives, but are caused to think of such alternatives, and take them seriously, if the putative knower's circumstances call attention to them. Since I assume that radical or unusual alternatives are not *ordinarily* entertained or taken seriously, I may appear to side with the opponents of scepticism. My official analysis, however, is neutral on the issue of scepticism.

II

I turn now to the analysis of 'perceptually knows'. Suppose that Sam spots Judy on the street and correctly identifies her as Judy, that is, believes she is Judy. Suppose further that Judy has an identical twin, Trudy, and the possibility of the person's being Trudy (rather than Judy) is a relevant alternative. Under what circumstances would we say that Sam *knows* it is Judy?

If Sam regularly identifies Judy as Judy and Trudy as Trudy, he apparently has some (visual) way of discriminating between them (though he may not know how he does it, that is, what cues he uses). If he does have a way of discriminating between them, which he uses on the occasion in question, we would say that he *knows* it is Judy. But if Sam frequently mistakes Judy for Trudy, and Trudy for Judy, he presumably does not have a way of discriminating between them. For example, he may not have sufficiently distinct (visual) memory 'schemata' of Judy and Trudy. So that, on a particular occasion, sensory stimulation from either Judy *or* Trudy would elicit a Judy-identification from him. If he happens to be right that it is Judy, this is just accidental. He doesn't *know* it is Judy.

The crucial question in assessing a knowledge attribution, then, appears to be the truth value of a counterfactual (or set of counterfactuals). Where Sam correctly identifies Judy as Judy, the crucial counterfactual is: 'If the person before Sam were Trudy (rather than Judy), Sam would believe her to be Judy.' If this counterfactual is true, Sam doesn't know it is Judy. If this counterfactual is false (and all other counterfactuals involving relevant alternatives are also false), then Sam may know it is Judy.

This suggests the following analysis of (non-inferential) perceptual knowledge.

> S (non-inferentially) *perceptually knows that p* if and only if
>
> (1) S (non-inferentially) perceptually believes that p,
> (2) p is true, and
> (3) there is no relevant contrary q of p such that, if q were true (rather than p), then S would (still) believe that p.

Restricting attention to relevant possibilities, these conditions assert in effect that the only situation in which S would believe that p is a situation in which p is true. In other words, S's believing that p is sufficient for the truth of p. This is essentially the analysis of non-inferential knowledge proposed by D. M. Armstrong in *A Materialist Theory of the Mind* (though without any restriction to 'relevant' alternatives), and refined and expanded in *Belief, Truth and Knowledge*.[9]

This analysis is too restrictive. Suppose Oscar is standing in an open field containing Dack the dachshund. Oscar sees Dack and (non-inferentially) forms a belief in P:

> P The object over there is a dog.

Now suppose that Q:

> Q The object over there is a wolf.

is a relevant alternative to P (because wolves are frequenters of this field). Further suppose that Oscar has a tendency to mistake wolves for dogs (he confuses them with malamutes, or German shepherds). Then if the object Oscar saw were Wiley the wolf, rather than Dack the dachshund, Oscar would (still) believe P. This means that Oscar fails to satisfy the proposed analysis with respect to P, since (3) is violated. But surely it is wrong to deny—for the indicated reasons —that Oscar *knows* P to be true. The mere fact that he would erroneously take a wolf to be a dog hardly shows that he doesn't know a *dachshund* to be a dog! Similarly, if someone looks at a

---

[9] *A Materialist Theory of the Mind* (New York, 1968), 189 ff., and *Belief, Truth and Knowledge* (New York, 1973), chs. 12 and 13.

huge redwood and correctly believes it to be a tree, he is not disqualified from knowing it to be a tree merely because there is a very
small plant he would wrongly believe to be a tree, that is, a bonsai
tree.

The moral can be formulated as follows. If Oscar believes that a
dog is present because of a certain way he is 'appeared to', then this
true belief fails to be knowledge if there is an alternative situation
in which a non-dog produces the same belief by means of the same,
or a very similar, appearance. But the wolf situation is not such an
alternative: although it would produce in him the same belief, it
would not be by means of the same (or a similar) appearance. An
alternative that disqualifies a true perceptual belief from being
perceptual knowledge must be a 'perceptual equivalent' of the
actual state of affairs.[10] A *perceptual equivalent* of an actual state
of affairs is a possible state of affairs that would produce the same,
or a sufficiently similar, perceptual experience.

The relation of perceptual equivalence must obviously be relativized to *persons* (or organisms). The presence of Judy and the
presence of Trudy might be perceptual equivalents for Sam, but not
for the twins' own mother (to whom the twins look quite different).
Similarly, perceptual equivalence must be relativized to *times*, since
perceptual discriminative capacities can be refined or enhanced
with training or experience, and can deteriorate with age or disease.

How shall we specify alternative states of affairs that are candidates for being perceptual equivalents? First, we should specify the
object involved. (I assume for simplicity that only one object is in
question.) As the Judy–Trudy case shows, the object in the alternative state of affairs need not be identical with the actual object.
Sometimes, indeed, we may wish to allow non-actual possible
objects. Otherwise our framework will be unable in principle to
accommodate some of the sceptic's favourite alternatives, for
example, those involving demons. If the reader's ontological
sensibility is offended by talk of possible objects, I invite him to
replace such talk with any preferred substitute.

Some alternative states of affairs involve the same object but
different properties. Where the actual state of affairs involves a
certain ball painted blue, an alternative might be chosen involving
the same ball painted green. Thus, specification of an alternative

---

[10] My notion of a perceptual equivalent corresponds to Jaakko Hintikka's notion
of a 'perceptual alternative'. See 'On the Logic of Perception', in N. S. Care and
R. H. Grimm, eds., *Perception and Personal Identity* (Cleveland, Ohio, 1969).

requires not only an object, but properties of the object (at the time in question). These should include not only the property in the belief under scrutiny, or one of its contraries, but other properties as well, since the property in the belief (or one of its contraries) might not be sufficiently determinate to indicate what the resultant percept would be like. For full generality, let us choose a *maximal set of* (non-relational) *properties*. This is a set that would exhaustively characterize an object (at a single time) in some possible world.[11]

An object plus a maximal set of (non-relational) properties still does not fully specify a perceptual alternative. Also needed are relations between the object and the perceiver, plus conditions of the environment. One relation that can affect the resultant percept is *distance*. Another relational factor is *relative orientation*, both of object *vis-à-vis* perceiver and perceiver *vis-à-vis* object. The nature of the percept depends, for example, on which side of the object faces the perceiver, and on how the perceiver's bodily organs are oriented, or situated, *vis-à-vis* the object. Thirdly, the percept is affected by the current state of the *environment*, for example, the illumination, the presence or absence of intervening objects, and the direction and velocity of the wind.

To cover all such elements, I introduce the notion of a *distance–orientation–environment* relation, for short, a *DOE relation*. Each such relation is a conjunction of relations or properties concerning distance, orientation, and environmental conditions. One DOE relation is expressed by the predicate 'x is 20 feet from y, the front side of y is facing x, the eyes of x are open and focused in y's direction, no opaque object is interposed between x and y, and y is in moonlight'.

Since the health of sensory organs can affect percepts, it might be argued that this should be included in these relations, thereby opening the condition of these organs to counterfactualization. For simplicity I neglect this complication. This does not mean that I don't regard the condition of sensory organs as open to

---

[11] I have in mind here purely qualitative properties. Properties like *being identical with Judy* would be given by the selected object. If the set of qualitative properties (at a given time) implied which object it was that had these properties, then specification of the object would be redundant, and we could represent states of affairs by ordered pairs of maximal sets of (qualitative) properties and DOE relations. Since this is problematic, however, I include specification of the object as well as the set of (qualitative) properties.

counter-factualization. I merely omit explicit incorporation of this factor into our exposition.

We can now give more precision to our treatment of perceptual equivalents. Perceptual states of affairs will be specified by ordered triples, each consisting of (1) an object, (2) a maximal set of non-relational properties, and (3) a DOE relation. If S perceives object b at t and if b has all the properties in a maximal set J and bears DOE relation R to S at t, then the actual state of affairs pertaining to this perceptual episode is represented by the ordered triple $\langle b,J,R \rangle$. An alternative state of affairs is represented by an ordered triple $\langle c,K,R^* \rangle$, which may (but need not) differ from $\langle b,J,R \rangle$ with respect to one or more of its elements.

Under what conditions is an alternative $\langle c,K,R^* \rangle$ a perceptual equivalent of $\langle b,J,R \rangle$ for person S at time t? I said that a perceptual equivalent is a state of affairs that would produce 'the same, or a very similar' perceptual experience. That is not very committal. Must a perceptual equivalent produce exactly the same percept? Given our intended use of perceptual equivalence in the analysis of perceptual knowledge, the answer is clearly no. Suppose that a Trudy-produced percept would be qualitatively distinct from Sam's Judy-produced percept, but similar enough for Sam to mistake Trudy for Judy. This is sufficient grounds for saying that Sam fails to have knowledge. Qualitative identity of percepts, then, is too strong a requirement for perceptual equivalence.

How should the requirement be weakened? We must not weaken it too much, for the wolf alternative might then be a perceptual equivalent of the dachshund state of affairs. This would have the unwanted consequence that Oscar doesn't know Dack to be a dog.

The solution I propose is this. If the percept produced by the alternative state of affairs would not differ from the actual percept in any respect this is causally relevant to S's belief, this alternative situation is a perceptual equivalent for S of the actual situation. Suppose that a Trudy-produced percept would differ from Sam's Judy-produced percept to the extent of having a different eyebrow configuration. (A difference in shape between Judy's and Trudy's eyebrows does not ensure that Sam's percepts would 'register' this difference. I assume, however, that the eyebrow difference would be registered in Sam's percepts.) But suppose that Sam's visual 'concept' of Judy does not include a feature that reflects this contrast. His Judy-concept includes an 'eyebrow feature' only in the sense that the absence of eyebrows would inhibit a Judy-classification. It does not include a more determinate eyebrow feature, though: Sam hasn't learned to associate Judy with distinctively shaped eyebrows. Hence, the distinctive 'eyebrow shape' of his actual (Judy-produced) percept is not one of the percept-features that is causally responsible for his believing Judy to be present. Assuming that a Trudy-produced percept would not differ from his actual percept in any *other* causally relevant way, the hypothetical Trudy-situation is a perceptual equivalent of the actual Judy-situation.

Consider now the dachshund–wolf case. The hypothetical percept produced by a wolf would differ from Oscar's actual percept of the dachshund in respects that *are* causally relevant to Oscar's judgement that a dog is present. Let me elaborate. There are various kinds of objects, rather different in shape, size, colour, and texture, that would be classified by Oscar as a dog. He has a number of visual 'schemata', we might say, each with a distinctive set of features, such that any percept that 'matches' or 'fits' one of these schemata would elicit a 'dog' classification. (I think of a schema not as a template, but as a set of more or less abstract—though iconic—features.)[12] Now, although a dachshund and a wolf would each produce a dog-belief in Oscar, the percepts produced by these respective stimuli would differ in respects that are causally relevant to Oscar's forming a dog-belief. Since Oscar's dachshund-schema includes such features as having an elongated, sausage-like shape, a smallish size, and droopy ears, these features of the percept are all causally relevant, when a dachshund is present, to Oscar's believing that a dog is present. Since a hypothetical wolf-produced percept would differ in these respects from Oscar's dachshund-produced percept, the hypothetical wolf state of affairs is not a perceptual equivalent of the dachshund state of affairs for Oscar.

The foregoing approach requires us to relativize perceptual equivalence once again, this time to the belief in question, or the property believed to be exemplified. The Trudy-situation is a perceptual equivalent for Sam of the Judy-situation *relative to the property of being* (identical with) *Judy*. The wolf-situation is not a perceptual equivalent for Oscar of the dachshund-situation *relative to the property of being a dog*.

---

[12] For a discussion of iconic schemata, see Michael I. Posner, *Cognition: An Introduction* (Glenview, Ill., 1973), ch. 3.

I now propose the following definition of perceptual equivalence:

> If object *b* has the maximal set of properties *J* and is in DOE relation *R* to *S* at *t*, if *S* has some percept *P* at *t* that is perceptually caused by *b*'s having *J* and being in *R* to *S* at *t*, and if *P* non-inferentially causes *S* to believe (or sustains *S* in believing) of object *b* that it has property *F*, then
>
> ⟨*c,K,R**⟩ is a *perceptual equivalent of* ⟨*b,J,R*⟩ *for S at t relative to property F* if and only if
>
> (1) if at *t* object *c* had *K* and were in *R** to *S*, then this would perceptually cause *S* to have some percept *P** at *t*,
> (2) *P** would cause *S* non-inferentially to believe (or sustain *S* in believing) of object *c* that it has *F*, and
> (3) *P** would not differ from *P* in any respect that is causally relevant to *S*'s *F*-belief.

Since I shall analyse the *de re, relational*, or *transparent* sense of 'perceptually knows', I shall want to employ, in my analysis, the *de re* sense of 'believe'. This is why such phrases as 'believe . . . *of* object *b*' occur in the definition of perceptual equivalence. For present purposes, I take for granted the notion of (perceptual) *de re* belief. I assume, however, that the object *of which* a person perceptually believes a property to hold is the object he perceives, that is, the object that 'perceptually causes' the percept that elicits the belief. The notion of *perceptual causation* is another notion I take for granted. A person's percept is obviously caused by many objects (or events), not all of which the person is said to perceive. One problem for the theory of perception is to explicate the notion of perceptual causation, that is, to explain which of the causes of a percept a person is said to perceive. I set this problem aside here.[13] A third notion I take for granted is the notion of a (non-inferential) *perceptual belief*, or perceptual 'taking'. Not all beliefs that are non-inferentially caused by a percept can be considered perceptual 'takings'; 'indirectly' caused beliefs would not be so considered. But I make no attempt to delineate the requisite causal relation.

Several other comments on the definition of perceptual equivalence are in order. Notice that the definition is silent on whether *J* or *K* contains property *F*, that is, whether *F* is exemplified in either the actual or the alternative states of affairs. The relativization to *F* (in the definiendum) implies that an *F-belief* is produced in both

13 I take this problem up in 'Perceptual Objects', *Synthese*, 35/3 (July, 1977).

situations, not that F is exemplified (in either or both situations). In applying the definition to cases of putative knowledge, we shall focus on cases where F belongs to J (so S's belief is true in the actual situation) but does not belong to K (so S's belief is false in the counterfactual situation). But the definition of perceptual equivalence is silent on these matters.

Though the definition does not say so, I assume it is possible for object c to have all properties in K, and possible for c to be in R^* to S while having all properties in K. I do not want condition (1) to be vacuously true, simply by having an impossible antecedent.

It might seem as if the antecedent of (1) should include a further conjunct, expressing the supposition that object b is absent. This might seem necessary to handle cases in which, if c were in R^* to S, but b remained in its actual relation R to S, then b would 'block' S's access to c. (For example, b might be an orange balloon floating over the horizon, and c might be the moon.) This can be handled by the definition as it stands, by construing R^*, where necessary, as including the absence of object b from the perceptual scene. (One cannot *in general* hypothesize that b is absent, for we want to allow object c to be identical with b.)

The definition implies that there is no temporal gap between each object's having its indicated properties and DOE relation and the occurrence of the corresponding percept. This simplification is introduced because no general requirement can be laid down about how long it takes for the stimulus energy to reach the perceiver. The intervals in the actual and alternative states may differ because the stimuli might be at different distances from the perceiver.

III

It is time to turn to the analysis of perceptual knowledge, for which the definition of perceptual equivalence paves the way. I restrict my attention to perceptual knowledge of the possession, by physical objects, of non-relational properties. I also restrict the analysis to *non-inferential* perceptual knowledge. This frees me from the complex issues introduced by inference, which require separate treatment.

It may be contended that all perceptual judgement is based on inference and, hence, that the proposed restriction reduces the scope of the analysis to nil. Two replies are in order. First, although cognitive psychology establishes that percepts are affected by cognitive factors, such as 'expectancies', it is by no means evident that these causal processes should be construed as inferences. Second, even if we were to grant that there is in fact no non-inferential perceptual belief, it would still be of epistemological importance to determine whether non-inferential perceptual knowledge of the physical world is conceptually possible. This could be explored by considering merely possible cases of non-inferential perceptual belief, and seeing whether, under suitable conditions, such belief would count as knowledge.

With these points in mind, we may propose the following (tentative) analysis:

At t S non-inferentially perceptually knows of object b that it has property F if and only if

(1)   for some maximal set of non-relational properties J and some DOE relation R, object b has (all the members of) J at t and is in R to S at t,

(2) F belongs to J,

(3A) b's having J and being in R to S at t perceptually causes S at t to have some percept P,[14]

---

[14] Should (3A) be construed as implying that *every* property in J is a (perceptual) cause of P? No. Many of b's properties are exemplified in its interior or at its backside. These are not causally relevant, at least in visual perception. (3A) must therefore be construed as saying that P is (perceptually) caused by b's having (jointly) *all* the members of J, and leaving open which, among these members, are individually causally relevant. It follows, however, that (3A) does not require that *b's-having-F*, in particular, is a (perceptual) cause of P, and this omission might be regarded as objectionable. 'Surely,' it will be argued, 'S perceptually knows b to have F only if *b's-having-F* (perceptually) causes the percept.' The reason I omit this requirement is the following. Suppose F is the property of being a dog. Can we say that *b's-being-a-dog* is a cause of certain light waves' being reflected? This is very dubious. It is the molecular properties of the surface of the animal that are causally responsible for this transmission of light, and hence for the percept.

One might say that, even if the percept needn't be (perceptually) caused by *b's-having-F*, it must at least be caused by microstructural properties of b that *ensure b's-having-F*. As the dog example again illustrates, however, this is too strong. The surface properties of the dog that reflect the light waves do not *ensure* that the object is a dog, either logically or nomologically. Something could have that surface (on one side) and still have a non-dog interior and backside. The problem should be solved, I think, by reliance on whether there are relevant perceptual equivalents. If there are no relevant perceptual equivalents in which K excludes being a dog, then the properties of the actual object that are causally responsible for the percept suffice to yield knowledge. We need not require either that the percept be (perceptually) caused by *b's-having-F*, nor by any subset of J that 'ensures' *b's-having-F*, nor by any subset of J that 'ensures' *b's-having-F*.

(3B) P non-inferentially causes S at t to believe (or sustains S in believing) of object b that it has property F, and

(3C) there is no alternative state of affairs $\langle c, K, R^* \rangle$ such that

(i) $\langle c, K, R^* \rangle$ is a relevant perceptual equivalent of $\langle b, J, R \rangle$ for S at t relative to property F, and

(ii) F does not belong to K

Conditions (1) and (2) jointly entail the truth condition for knowledge: S knows b to have F (at t) only if b does have F (at t). Condition (3B) contains the belief condition for knowledge, restricted, of course, to (non-inferential) perceptual belief. The main work of the conditions is done by (3C). It requires that there be no relevant alternative that is (i) a perceptual equivalent to the actual state of affairs relative to property F, and (ii) a state of affairs in which the appropriate object lacks F (and hence S's F-belief is false).

How does this analysis relate to my theme of a 'reliable discriminative mechanism'? A perceptual cognizer may be thought of as a two-part mechanism. The first part constructs percepts (a special class of internal states) from receptor stimulation. The second part operates on percepts to produce beliefs. Now, in order for the conditions of the analysans to be satisfied, each part of the mechanism must be sufficiently discriminating, or 'finely tuned'. If the first part is not sufficiently discriminating, patterns of receptor stimulation from quite different sources would result in the same (or very similar) percepts, percepts that would generate the same beliefs. If the second part is not sufficiently discriminating, then even if different percepts are constructed by the first part, the same beliefs will be generated by the second part. To be sure, even an undiscriminating bipartite mechanism may produce a belief that, luckily, is true; but there will be other, counterfactual, situations in which such a belief would be false. In this sense, such a mechanism is unreliable. What our analysis says is that S has perceptual knowledge if and only if not only does his perceptual mechanism produce true belief, but there are no relevant counterfactual situations in which the same belief would be produced via an equivalent percept and in which the belief would be false.

Let me now illustrate how the analysis is to be applied to the barn example, where there are facsimiles in Henry's district. Let S = Henry, b = the barn Henry actually sees, and F = the property of being a barn. Conditions (1)–(3B) are met by letting J

take as its value the set of all non-relational properties actually possessed by the barn at t, R take as its value the actual DOE relation the barn bears to Henry at t, and P take as its value the actual (visual) percept caused by the barn. Condition (3C) is violated, however. There *is* a relevant triple that meets subclauses (i) and (ii), that is, the triple where $c = $ a suitable barn facsimile, $K = $ a suitable set of properties (excluding, of course, the property of being a barn), and $R^* = $ approximately the same DOE relation as the actual one. Thus, Henry does not (non-inferentially) perceptually *know* of the barn that it has the property of being a barn.

In the dachshund–wolf case, $S = $ Oscar, $b = $ Dack the dachshund, and $F = $ being a dog. The first several conditions are again met. Is (3C) met as well? There is a relevant alternative state of affairs in which Wiley the wolf is believed by Oscar to be a dog, but lacks that property. This state of affairs doesn't violate (3C), however, since it isn't a *perceptual equivalent* of the actual situation relative to being a dog. So this alternative doesn't disqualify Oscar from knowing Dack to be a dog.

Is there another alternative that *is* a perceptual equivalent of the actual situation (relative to being a dog)? We can imagine a DOE relation in which fancy devices between Wiley and Oscar distort the light coming from Wiley and produce in Oscar a Dack-like visual percept. The question here, however, is whether this perceptual equivalent is *relevant*. Relevance is determined not only by the hypothetical object and its properties, but also by the DOE relation. Since the indicated DOE relation is highly unusual, this will count (at least for a non-sceptic) against the alternative's being relevant and against its disqualifying Oscar from knowing.[15]

[15] It is the 'unusualness' of the DOE relation that inclines us not to count the alternative as relevant; it is not the mere fact that the DOE relation differs from the actual one. In general, our analysis allows knowledge to be defeated or disqualified by alternative situations in which the DOE relation differs from the DOE relation in the actual state of affairs. Our analysis differs in this respect from Fred Dretske's analysis in 'Conclusive Reasons', *Australasian Journal of Philosophy*, 49/1 (May 1971), 1–22. Dretske's analysis, which ours resembles on a number of points, considers only those counterfactual situations in which everything that is 'logically and causally independent of the state of affairs expressed by P' (pp. 7–8) is the same as in the actual situation. (P is the content of S's belief.) This implies that the actual DOE relation cannot be counterfactualized, but must be held fixed. (It may also imply—depending what P is—that one cannot counterfactualize the perceived object nor the full set of properties J.) This unduly narrows the class of admissible alternatives. Many *relevant* alternatives, that do disqualify knowledge, involve DOE relations that differ from the actual DOE relation.

The following 'Gettierized' example, suggested by Marshall Swain, might appear to present difficulties. In a dark room there is a candle several yards ahead of *S* which *S* sees and believes to be ahead of him. But he sees the candle only indirectly, via a system of mirrors (of which he is unaware) that make it appear as if he were seeing it directly.[16] We would surely deny that *S* knows the candle to be ahead of him. (This case does not really fit our intended analysandum, since the believed property *F* is relational. This detail can be ignored, however.) Why? If we say, with Harman, that all perceptual belief is based on inference, we can maintain that *S* infers that the candle is ahead of him from the premiss that he sees whatever he sees *directly*. This premiss being false, *S*'s knowing is disqualified on familiar grounds.

My theory suggests another explanation, which makes no unnecessary appeal to inference. We deny that *S* knows, I suggest, because the system of mirrors draws our attention to a perceptual equivalent in which the candle is *not* ahead of *S*, that is, a state of affairs where the candle is behind *S* but reflected in a system of mirrors so that it appears to be ahead of him. Since the actual state of affairs involves a system of reflecting mirrors, we are impelled to count this alternative as relevant, and hence to deny that *S* knows.

Even in ordinary cases, of course, where *S* sees a candle directly, the possibility of reflecting mirrors constitutes a perceptual equivalent. In the ordinary case, however, we would not count this as relevant; we would not regard it as a 'serious' possibility. The Gettierized case impels us to take it seriously because there the actual state of affairs involves a devious system of reflecting mirrors. So we have an explanation of why people are credited with knowing in ordinary perceptual cases but not in the Gettierized case.

The following is a more serious difficulty for our analysis. *S* truly believes something to be a tree, but there is a relevant alternative in which an electrode stimulating *S*'s optic nerve would produce an equivalent percept, which would elicit the same belief. Since this is assumed to be a relevant alternative, it ought to disqualify *S* from knowing. But it doesn't satisfy our definition of a perceptual equivalent, first because the electrode would not be a perceptual cause of the percept (we would not say that *S perceives* the

---

[16] Harman has a similar case, in *Thought*, pp. 22–3. In that case, however, *S* does not see the candle; it is not a cause of his percept. Given our causal requirement for perceptual knowledge, that case is easily handled.

electrode), and second because S would not believe *of the electrode* (nor *of* anything else) that it is a tree. A similar problem arises where the alternative state of affairs would involve S's having a hallucination.

To deal with these cases, we could revise our analysis of perceptual knowledge as follows. (A similar revision in the definition of perceptual equivalence would do the job equally well.) We could reformulate (3C) to say that there must neither be a relevant perceptual equivalent of the indicated sort (using our present definition of perceptual equivalence) *nor* a relevant alternative situation in which an equivalent percept occurs and prompts a *de dicto* belief that something has F, but where there is nothing that *perceptually* causes this percept and nothing *of which* F is believed to hold. In other words, knowledge can be disqualified by relevant alternative situations where S doesn't perceive anything and doesn't have any *de re* (F-) belief at all. I am inclined to adopt this solution, but will not actually make this addition to the analysis.

Another difficulty for the analysis is this. Suppose Sam's 'schemata' of Judy and Trudy have hitherto been indistinct, so Judy-caused percepts sometimes elicit Judy-beliefs and sometimes Trudy-beliefs, and similarly for Trudy-caused percepts. Today Sam falls down and hits his head. As a consequence a new feature is 'added' to his Judy-schema, a mole-associated feature. From now on he will believe someone to be Judy only if he has the sort of percept that would be caused by a Judy-like person with a mole over the left eye. Sam is unaware that this change has taken place and will remain unaware of it, since he isn't conscious of the cues he uses. Until today, neither Judy nor Trudy has had a left-eyebrow mole; but today Judy happens to develop such a mole. Thus, from now on Sam can discriminate Judy from Trudy. Does this mean that he will *know* Judy to be Judy when he correctly identifies her? I am doubtful.

A possible explanation of Sam's not knowing (on future occasions) is that Trudy-with-a-mole is a relevant perceptual equivalent of Judy. This is not Trudy's actual condition, of course, but it might be deemed a relevant possibility. I believe, however, that the mole case calls for a further restriction, one concerning the *genesis* of a person's propensity to form a certain belief as a result of a certain percept. A merely fortuitous or accidental genesis is not enough to support knowledge. I do not know exactly what requirement to impose on the genesis of such a propensity. The mole case intimates that the genesis should involve certain 'experience' with objects, but this may be too narrow. I content myself with a very vague addition to our previous conditions, which completes the analysis:

(4) *S*'s propensity to form an *F*-belief as a result of percept *P* has an appropriate genesis.

Of course this leaves the problem unresolved. But the best I can do here is identify the problem.

IV

A few words are in order about the intended significance of my analysis. One of its purposes is to provide an alternative to the traditional 'Cartesian' perspective in epistemology. The Cartesian view combines a theory of knowledge with a theory of justification. Its theory of knowledge asserts that *S* knows that *p* at *t* only if *S* is (fully, adequately, etc.) justified at *t* in believing that *p*. Its theory of justification says that *S* is justified at *t* in believing that *p* only if either (i) *p* is self-warranting for *S* at *t*, or (ii) *p* is (strongly, adequately, etc.) supported or confirmed by propositions each of which is self-warranting for *S* at *t*. Now propositions about the state of the external world at *t* are not self-warranting. Hence, if *S* knows any such proposition *p* at *t*, there must be some other propositions which strongly support *p* and which are self-warranting for *S* at *t*. These must be propositions about *S*'s mental state at *t* and perhaps some obvious necessary truths. A major task of Cartesian epistemology is to show that there is some such set of self-warranting propositions, propositions that support external-world propositions with sufficient strength.

It is impossible to canvass all attempts to fulfill this project; but none has succeeded, and I do not think that any will. One can conclude either that we have no knowledge of the external world or that Cartesian requirements are too demanding. I presuppose the latter conclusion in offering my theory of perceptual knowledge. My theory requires no justification for external-world propositions that derives entirely from self-warranting propositions. It requires only, in effect, that beliefs in the external world be suitably caused, where 'suitably' comprehends a process or mechanism that not only produces true belief in the actual situation, but would not produce false belief in relevant counterfactual situations. If one wishes, one can so employ the term 'justification' that belief causation of *this* kind counts as justification. In this sense, of course, my theory does require justification. But this is entirely different from the sort of justification demanded by Cartesianism.

My theory protects the possibility of knowledge by making Cartesian-style justification unnecessary. But it leaves a door open to scepticism by its stance on relevant alternatives. This is not a failure of the theory, in my opinion. An adequate account of the term 'know' should make the temptations of scepticism comprehensible, which my theory does. But it should also put scepticism in a proper perspective, which Cartesianism fails to do.

In any event, I put forward my account of perceptual knowledge not primarily as an antidote to scepticism, but as a more accurate rendering of what the term 'know' actually means. In this respect it is instructive to test my theory and its rivals against certain metaphorical or analogical uses of 'know'. A correct definition should be able to explain extended and figurative uses as well as literal uses, for it should explain how speakers arrive at the extended uses from the central ones. With this in mind, consider how tempting it is to say of an electric-eye door that it 'knows' you are coming (at least that *something* is coming), or 'sees' you coming. The attractiveness of the metaphor is easily explained on my theory: the door has a reliable mechanism for discriminating between something being before it and nothing being there. It has a 'way of telling' whether or not something is there: this 'way of telling' consists in a mechanism by which objects in certain DOE relations to it have differential effects on its internal state. By contrast, note how artificial it would be to apply more traditional analyses of 'know' to the electric-eye door, or to other mechanical detecting devices. How odd it would be to say that the door has 'good reasons', 'adequate evidence', or 'complete justification' for thinking something is there; or that it has 'the right to be sure' something is there. The oddity of these locutions indicates how far from the mark are the analyses of 'know' from which they derive.

The trouble with many philosophical treatments of knowledge is that they are inspired by Cartesian-like conceptions of justification or vindication. There is a consequent tendency to overintellectualize or overrationalize the notion of knowledge. In the spirit of naturalistic epistemology,[17] I am trying to fashion an account of

[17] Cf. W. V. Quine, 'Epistemology Naturalized', in *Ontological Relativity, and Other Essays* (New York, 1969).

knowing that focuses on more primitive and pervasive aspects of cognitive life, in connection with which, I believe, the term 'know' gets its application. A fundamental facet of animate life, both human and infra-human, is telling things apart, distinguishing predator from prey, for example, or a protective habitat from a threatening one. The concept of knowledge has its roots in this kind of cognitive activity.

III

THE CAUSAL THEORY OF PERCEPTION

H. P GRICE

I

The Causal Theory of Perception (CTP) has for some time received comparatively little attention, mainly, I suspect, because it has been generally assumed that the theory either asserts or involves as a consequence the proposition that material objects are unobservable, and that the unacceptability of this proposition is sufficient to dispose of the theory. I am inclined to regard this attitude to the CTP as unfair or at least unduly unsympathetic and I shall attempt to outline a thesis which might not improperly be considered to be a version of the CTP, and which is, if not true, at least not too obviously false.

What is to count as holding a causal theory of perception? (1) I shall take it as being insufficient merely to believe that the perception of a material object is always to be causally explained by reference to conditions the specification of at least one of which involves a mention of the object perceived; that, for example, the perception is the terminus of a causal sequence involving at an earlier stage some event or process in the history of the perceived object. Such a belief does not seem to be philosophical in character; its object has the appearance of being a very general contingent proposition; though it is worth remarking that if the version of the CTP with which I shall be primarily concerned is correct, it (or something like it) will turn out to be a necessary rather than a contingent truth. (2) It may be held that the elucidation of the notion of perceiving a material object will include some reference to the role of the material object perceived in the causal ancestry of the perception or of the sense-impression or sense-datum involved in the perception. This contention is central to what I regard as a

Abridged from *Proc. of the Aristotelian Society*, suppl. vol. 35 (1961), 121–52, © 1961. Reprinted by courtesy of the author and the Editor of the Aristotelian Society.

standard version of the CTP. (3) It might be held that it is the task of the philosopher of perception not to elucidate or characterize the ordinary notion of perceiving a material object, but to provide a rational reconstruction of it, to replace it by some concept more appropriate to an ideal or scientific language: it might further be suggested that such a redefinition might be formulated in terms of the effect of the presence of an object upon the observer's sense-organ and nervous system or upon his behaviour or 'behaviour-tendencies' or in terms of both of these effects. A view of this kind may perhaps deserve to be called a causal theory of perception; but I shall not be concerned with theories on these lines. (4) I shall distinguish from the adoption of a CTP the attempt to provide for a wider or narrower range of propositions ascribing properties to material objects a certain sort of causal analysis: the kind of analysis which I have in mind is that which, on *one* possible interpretation, Locke could be taken as suggesting for ascriptions of, for example, colour and temperature; he might be understood to be holding that such propositions assert that an object would, in certain standard conditions, cause an observer to have certain sorts of ideas or sense-impressions.

In Professor Price's *Perception*,[1] there appears a preliminary formulation of the CTP which would bring it under the second of the headings distinguished in the previous paragraph. The CTP is specified as maintaining (1) that in the case of all sense-data (not merely visual and tactual) 'belonging to' simply means *being caused by*, so that '*M* is present to my senses' will be equivalent to '*M* causes a sense-datum with which I am acquainted'; (2) that perceptual consciousness is fundamentally an inference from effect to cause. Since it is, I think, fair to say that the expression 'present to my senses' was introduced by Price as a special term to distinguish one of the possible senses of the verb 'perceive',[2] the first clause of the quotation above may be taken as propounding the thesis that 'I am perceiving *M*' (in one sense of that expression) is to be regarded as equivalent to 'I am having (or sensing) a sense-datum which is caused by *M*.' (The second clause I shall for the time being ignore.) I shall proceed to consider the feature which this version of the CTP shares with other non-causal theories of perception, namely, the claim that perceiving a material object

---

[1] London, 1932, 66.
[2] Cf. ibid. 21–5.

involves having or sensing a sense-datum; for unless this claim can be made out, the special features of the CTP become otiose.

II

The primary difficulty facing the contention that perceiving involves having or sensing a sense-datum is that of giving a satisfactory explanation of the meaning of the technical term 'sense-datum'. One familiar method of attempting this task is that of trying to prove, by means of some form of the Argument from Illusion, the existence of objects of a special sort for which the term 'sense-datum' is offered as a class-name. Another method (that adopted in a famous passage by Moore) is that of giving directions which are designed to enable one to pick out items of the kind to which the term 'sense-datum' is to be applied. The general character of the objections to each of these procedures is also familiar, and I shall, for present purposes, assume that neither procedure is satisfactory.

Various philosophers have suggested that though attempts to indicate, or demonstrate the existence of, special objects to be called sense-data have all failed, nevertheless the expression 'sense-datum' can (and should) be introduced as a technical term; its use would be explicitly defined by reference to such supposedly standard locutions as 'So-and-so looks Φ (e.g. blue) to me', 'It looks (feels) to me as if there were a Φ so-and-so', 'I seem to see something Φ', and so on. Now it is not to my present purpose to consider how in detail such an explicit definition of the notion of a sense-datum might be formulated. I should, however, remark that this programme may be by no means so easy to carry through as the casual way in which it is sometimes proposed might suggest; various expressions are candidates for the key role in this enterprise, for example, 'looks' ('feels' etc.), 'seems', 'appears', and the more or less subtle differences between them would have to be investigated; and furthermore even if one has decided on a preferred candidate, not all of its uses would be suitable; if, for example, we decide to employ the expressions 'looks' etc., are we to accept the legitimacy of the sentence 'It looks indigestible to me' as providing us with a sense-datum sentence 'I am having an indigestible visual sense-datum'?

I shall, however, for present purposes, assume that some range of uses of locutions of the form 'It looks (feels, etc.) to X as if' has the best chance of being found suitable. I shall furthermore assume that the safest procedure for the Causal Theorist will be to restrict the actual occurrences of the term 'sense-datum' to such classificatory labels as 'sense-datum statement' or 'sense-datum sentence'; to license the introduction of a 'sense-datum terminology' to be used for the re-expression of sentences incorporating the preferred locutions seems to me both unnecessary and dangerous. I shall myself, on behalf of the CTP, often for brevity's sake talk of sense-data or sense-impressions; but I shall hope that a more rigorous, if more cumbrous, mode of expression will always be readily available. I hope that it will now be allowed that, interpreted on the lines which I have suggested, the thesis that perceiving involves having a sense-datum (involves its being the case that some sense-datum statement or other about the percipient is true) has at least a fair chance of proving acceptable.

I turn now to the special features of the CTP. The first clause of the formulation quoted above[3] from Price's *Perception* may be interpreted as representing it to be a necessary and sufficient condition of its being the case that X perceives M that X's sense-impression should be causally dependent on some state of affairs involving M. Let us first enquire whether the suggested condition is necessary. Suppose that it looks to X as if there is a clock on the shelf; what more is required for it to be true to say that X sees a clock on the shelf? There must, one might say, actually be a clock on the shelf which is in X's field of view, before X's eyes. But this does not seem to be enough. For it is logically conceivable that there should be some method by which an expert could make it look to X as if there were a clock on the shelf on occasions when the shelf was empty: there might be some apparatus by which X's cortex could be suitably stimulated, or some technique analogous to post-hypnotic suggestion. If such treatment were applied to X on an occasion when there actually was a clock on the shelf, and if X's impressions were found to continue unchanged when the clock was removed or its position altered, then I think we should be inclined to say that X did not see the clock which was before his eyes, just because we should regard the clock as playing no part in the origination of his impression. Or, to leave the realm of fantasy, it might be that it looked to me as if there were a certain sort of pillar in a certain direction at a certain distance, and there might actually be such a pillar in that place; but if, unknown to me, there were a

[3] p. 67 *supra*.

mirror interposed between myself and the pillar, which reflected a numerically different though similar pillar, it would certainly be incorrect to say that I saw the first pillar, and correct to say that I saw the second; and it is extremely tempting to explain this linguistic fact by saying that the first pillar was, and the second was not, causally irrelevant to the way things looked to me.

There seems then a good case for allowing that the suggested condition is necessary; but as it stands it can hardly be sufficient. For in any particular perceptual situation there will be objects other than that which would ordinarily be regarded as being perceived, of which some state or mode of functioning is causally relevant to the occurrence of a particular sense-impression: this might be true of such objects as the percipient's eyes or the sun. So some restriction will have to be added to the analysis of perceiving which is under consideration. Price suggested that use should be made of a distinction between 'standing' and 'differential' conditions:[4] as the state of the sun and of the percipient's eyes, for example, are standing conditions in that (roughly speaking) if they were suitably altered, all the visual impressions of the percipient would be in some respect different from what they would otherwise have been; whereas the state of the perceived object is a differential condition in that a change in it would affect only some of the percipient's visual impressions, perhaps only the particular impression the causal origin of which is in question. The suggestion then is that the CTP should hold that an object is perceived if and only if some condition involving it is a differential condition of some sense-impression of the percipient. I doubt, however, whether the imposition of this restriction is adequate. Suppose that on a dark night I see, at one and the same time, a number of objects each of which is illuminated by a different torch; if one torch is tampered with, the effect on my visual impressions will be restricted, not general; the objects illuminated by the other torches will continue to look the same to me. Yet we do not want to be compelled to say that each torch is perceived in such a situation; concealed torches may illuminate. But this is the position into which the proposed revision of the CTP would force us.

I am inclined to think that a more promising direction for the CTP to take is to formulate the required restriction in terms of the way in which a perceived object contributes towards the occurrence of the sense-impression. A conceivable course would be to

4 *Perception*, 70.

introduce into the specification of the restriction some part of the specialist's account, for example to make a reference to the transmission of light-waves to the retina; but the objection to this procedure is obvious; if we are attempting to characterize the ordinary notion of perceiving, we should not explicitly introduce material of which someone who is perfectly capable of employing the ordinary notion might be ignorant. I suggest that the best procedure for the Causal Theorist is to indicate the mode of causal connection by examples; to say that, for an object to be perceived by X, it is sufficient that it should be causally involved in the generation of some sense-impression by X in the kind of way in which, for example, when I look at my hand in a good light, my hand is causally responsible for its looking at me as if there were a hand before me, or in which . . . (and so on), *whatever that kind of way may be;* and to be enlightened on that question one must have recourse to the specialist. I see nothing absurd in the idea that a non-specialist concept should contain, so to speak, a blank space to be filled in by the specialist; that this is so, for example, in the case of the concept of seeing is perhaps indicated by the consideration that if we were in doubt about the correctness of speaking of a certain creature with peculiar sense-organs as *seeing* objects, we might well wish to hear from a specialist a comparative account of the human eye and the relevant sense-organs of the creature in question. We do not, of course, ordinarily need the specialist's contribution; for we may be in a position to say that the same kind of mechanism is involved in a plurality of cases without being in a position to say what that mechanism is.[5]

At this point an objection must be mentioned with which I shall deal only briefly. The CTP as I have so expounded it, it may be said, requires that it should be linguistically correct to speak of the causes of sense-impressions which are involved in perfectly normal perceptual situations. But this is a mistake; it is quite unnatural to talk about the cause, say, of its looking to X as if there were a cat before him unless the situation is or is thought to be in some way abnormal or delusive; this being so, when a cause can, without speaking unnaturally, be assigned to an impression, it will always

---

[5] It might be thought that we need a further restriction, limiting the permissible degree of divergence between the way things appear to X and the way they actually are. But objects can be said to be seen even when they are looked at through rough thick glass or distorting spectacles, in spite of the fact that they may then be unrecognizable.

be something other than the presence of the perceived object. There is no natural use for such a sentence as 'The presence of a cat caused it to look at X as if there were a cat before him'; yet it is absolutely essential to the CTP that there should be.

In reply to this objection I will make three points. (1) If we are to deal sympathetically with the CTP we must not restrict the Causal Theorist to the verb 'cause'; we must allow him to make use of other members of the family of causal verbs or verb-phrases if he wishes. This family includes such expressions as 'accounts for', 'explains', 'is part of the explanation of', 'is partly responsible for', and it seems quite possible that some alternative formulation of the theory would escape this objection. (2) If I regard myself as being in a position to say 'There is a cat', or 'I see a cat', I naturally refrain from making the weaker statement 'It looks to me as if there were a cat before me', and so, *a fortiori*, I refrain from talking about the cause of its looking to me thus. But to have made the weaker statement would have been to have said something linguistically correct and true, even if misleading; is there then any reason against supposing that it could have been linguistically correct and true, even if pointless or misleading, to have ascribed to a particular cause the state of affairs reported in the weaker statement? (3) X is standing in a street up which an elephant is approaching; he thinks his eyes must be deceiving him. Knowing this, I could quite naturally say to X, 'The fact that it looks to you as if there is an elephant approaching is accounted for by the fact that an elephant is approaching, not by your having become deranged.' To say the same thing to one's neighbour at the circus would surely be to say something which is true, though it might be regarded as provocative.

I have extracted from the first clause of the initial formulation of the CTP an outline of a causal analysis of perceiving which is, I hope, at least not obviously unacceptable. I have of course considered the suggested analysis only in relation to seeing; a more careful discussion would have to pay attention to non-visual perception; and even within the field of visual perception the suggested analysis might well be unsuitable for some uses of the word 'see', which would require a stronger condition than that proposed by the theory.

III

Is the CTP, as so far expounded, open to the charge that it represents material objects as being in principle unobservable, and in consequence leads to scepticism about the material world? I have some difficulty in understanding the precise nature of the accusation, in that it is by no means obvious what, in this context, is meant by 'unobservable'.

1. It would be not unnatural to take 'unobservable' to mean 'incapable of being perceived'. Now it may be the case that one could, without being guilty of inconsistency, combine the acceptance of the causal analysis of perceiving with the view that material objects cannot in principle be perceived, if one were prepared to maintain that it is in principle impossible for material objects to cause sense-impressions but that this impossibility has escaped the notice of common sense. This position, even if internally consistent, would seem to be open to grave objection. But even if the proposition that material objects cannot be perceived is consistent with the causal analysis of perceiving, it certainly does not appear to be a consequence of the latter; and the exposition of the CTP has so far been confined to the propounding of a causal analysis of perceiving.

2. The critic might be equating 'unobservable' with 'not directly observable'; and to say that material objects are not directly observable might in turn be interpreted as saying that statements about material objects lack that immunity from factual mistake which is (or is supposed to be) possessed by at least some sense-datum statements. But if 'unobservable' is thus interpreted, it seems to be *true* that material objects are unobservable, and the recognition of this truth could hardly be regarded as a matter for reproach.

3. 'Observation' may be contrasted with 'inference' as a source of knowledge and so the critic's claim may be that the CTP asserts or implies that the existence of particular material objects can only be a matter of inference. But in the first place, it is not established that the acceptance of the causal analysis of perceiving commits one to the view that the existence of particular material objects is necessarily a matter of inference (though this view is explicitly asserted by the second clause of Price's initial formulation of the CTP); and secondly, many of the critics have been phenomenalists, who would themselves be prepared to allow that the existence of particular material objects is, in some sense, a matter of inference. And if the complaint is that the CTP does not represent the inference as being of the right kind, then it looks as if the critic might in effect be complaining that the Causal Theorist is not a Phenomenalist. Apart from the fact that the criticism under discussion

could now be made only by someone who not only accepted Phenomenalism but also regarded it as the only means of deliverance from scepticism, it is by no means clear that to accept a causal analysis of perceiving is to debar oneself from accepting Phenomenalism; there seems to be no patent absurdity in the idea that one could, as a first stage, offer a causal analysis of '*X* perceives *M*', and then re-express the result in phenomenalist terms. If the CTP is to be (as it is often regarded as being) a rival to Phenomenalism, the opposition may well have to spring from the second clause of the initial formulation of the theory.

There is a further possibility of interpretation, related to the previous one. If someone has seen a speck on the horizon which is in fact a battleship, we should in some contexts be willing to say that he has seen a battleship; but we should not, I think, be willing to say that he has observed a battleship unless he has recognized what he has seen as a battleship. The criticism levelled at the CTP may then be that it asserts or entails the impossibility in principle of *knowing*, or even of being reasonably assured, that one is perceiving a particular material object, even if one is in fact perceiving it. At this point we must direct our attention to the second clause of the initial formulation of the CTP, which asserted that 'perceptual consciousness is fundamentally an inference from effect to cause'. I shall assume (I hope not unreasonably) that the essence of the view here being advanced is that anyone who claims to perceive a particular material object *M* may legitimately be asked to justify his claim; and that the only way to meet this demand, in the most fundamental type of case, is to produce an acceptable argument to the effect that the existence of *M* is required, or is probably required, in order that the claimant's current sense-impressions should be adequately accounted for. A detailed exposition of the CTP may supplement this clause by supplying general principles which, by assuring us of correspondences between causes and effects, are supposed to make possible the production of satisfactory arguments of the required kind.

It is clear that, if the Causal Theorist proceeds on the lines which I have just indicated, he cannot possibly be accused of having *asserted* that material objects are unobservable in the sense under consideration; for he has gone to some trouble in an attempt to show how we may be reasonably assured of the existence of particular material objects. But it may be argued that (in which is perhaps a somewhat special sense of 'consequence') it is an unwanted consequence of the CTP that material objects are unobservable: for if we accept the contentions of the CTP (1) that perceiving is to be analysed in causal terms, (2) that knowledge about perceived objects depends on causal inference, and (3) that the required causal inferences will be unsound unless suitable general principles of correspondence can be provided, then we shall have to admit that knowledge about perceived objects is unobtainable: for the general principles offered, apart from being dubious both in respect of truth and in respect of status, fail to yield the conclusions for which they are designed; and more successful substitutes are not available. If this is how the criticism of the CTP is to be understood, then I shall not challenge it, though I must confess to being in some doubt whether this is what actual critics have really meant. My comment on the criticism is now that it is unsympathetic in a way that is philosophically important.

There seem to me to be two possible ways of looking at the CTP. One is to suppose an initial situation in which it is recognized that, while appearance is ultimately the only guide to reality, what appears to be the case cannot be assumed to correspond with what is the case. The problem is conceived to be that of exhibiting a legitimate method of arguing from appearance to reality. The CTP is then regarded as a complex construction designed to solve this problem; and if one part of the structure collapses, the remainder ceases to be of much interest. The second way of looking at the CTP is to think of the causal analysis of perceiving as something to be judged primarily on its intrinsic merits and not merely as a part of a solution to a prior epistemological problem, and to recognize that some version of it is quite likely to be correct; the remainder of the CTP is then regarded as consisting (1) of steps which appear to be forced upon one if one accepts the causal analysis of perceiving, and which lead to a sceptical difficulty, and (2) a not very successful attempt to meet this difficulty. This way of looking at the CTP recognizes the possibility that we are confronted with a case in which the natural dialectic elicits distressing consequences (or rather apparent consequences) from true propositions. To adopt the first attitude to the exclusion of the second is both to put on one side what may well be an acceptable bit of philosophical analysis and to neglect what might be an opportunity for deriving philosophical profit from the exposure of operations of the natural dialectic. This, I suggest, is what the critics have tended to do; though, no doubt, they might plead historical justification, in that the first way of looking at the CTP may have been that of actual Causal Theorists.

It remains for me to show that the CTP can be looked upon in the second way by exhibiting a line of argument, sceptical in character, which incorporates appropriately the elements of the CTP. I offer the following example. In the fundamental type of case, a bona fide claim to perceive a particular material object M is based on sense-datum statements; it is only in virtue of the occurrence of certain sense-impressions that the claimant would regard himself as entitled to assert the existence of M. Since the causal analysis of perceiving is to be accepted, the claim to perceive M involves the claim that the presence of M causally explains the occurrence of the appropriate sense-impressions. The combination of these considerations yields the conclusion that the claimant accepts the existence of *M on the grounds that* it is required for the causal explanation of certain sense-impressions; that is, the existence of M is a matter of causal inference from the occurrence of the sense-impressions. Now a model case of causal inference would be an inference from smoke to fire; the acceptability of such an inference involves the possibility of establishing a correlation between occurrences of smoke and occurrences of fire, and this is only possible because there is a way of establishing the occurrence of a fire otherwise than by a causal inference. But there is supposed to be no way of establishing the existence of particular material objects except by a causal inference from sense-impressions; so such inferences cannot be rationally justified. The specification of principles of correspondence is of course an attempt to avert this consequence by rejecting the smoke–fire model. (If this model is rejected, recourse may be had to an assimilation of material objects to such entities as electrons, the acceptability of which is regarded as being (roughly) a matter of their utility for the purposes of explanation and prediction; but this assimilation is repugnant for the reason that material objects, after having been first contrasted, as a paradigm case of uninvented entities, with the theoretical constructs or *entia rationis* of the scientist, are then treated as being themselves *entia rationis*.)

One possible reaction to this argument is, of course, 'So much the worse for the causal analysis of perceiving'; but, as an alternative, the argument itself may be challenged, and I shall conclude by mentioning, without attempting to evaluate, some ways in which this might be done. (1) It may be argued that it is quite incorrect to describe many of my perceptual beliefs (for example, that there is now a table in front of me) as 'inferences' of any kind, if this is to be taken to imply that it would be incumbent upon me, on demand, to justify by an argument (perhaps after acquiring further data) the contention that what appears to me to be the case actually is the case. When, in normal circumstances, it looks to me as if there were a table before me, I am entitled to say flatly that there is a table before me, and to reject any demand that I should justify my claim until specific grounds for doubting it have been indicated. It is essential to the sceptic to assume that any perceptual claim may, without preliminaries, be put on trial and that innocence, not guilt, has to be proved; but this assumption is mistaken. (2) The allegedly 'fundamental' case (which is supposed to underlie other kinds of case), in which a perceptual claim is to be establishable purely on the basis of some set of sense-datum statements, is a myth; any justification of a particular perceptual claim will rely on the truth of one or more further propositions about the material world (for example, about the percipient's body). To insist that the 'fundamental' case be selected for consideration is, in effect, to assume at the start that it is conceptually legitimate for me to treat as open to question all my beliefs about the material world at once; and the sceptic is not entitled to start with this assumption. (3) It might be questioned whether, given that I accept the existence of M on the evidence of certain sense-impressions, and given also that I think that M is causally responsible for those sense-impressions it follows that I accept the existence of M *on the grounds that* its existence is required in order to account for the sense-impressions. (4) The use made of the smoke–fire model in the sceptical argument might be criticized on two different grounds. First, if the first point in this paragraph is well made, there are cases in which the existence of a perceived object is not the conclusion of a causal inference, namely those in which it cannot correctly be described as a matter of inference at all. Secondly, the model should never have been introduced; for whereas the proposition that fires tend to cause smoke is supposedly purely contingent, this is not in general true of propositions to the effect that the presence of a material object possessing property P tends to (or will in standard circumstances) make it look to particular persons as if there were an object possessing P. It is then an objectionable feature of the sceptical argument that it first treats non-contingent connections as if they were contingent, and then complains that such connections cannot be established in the manner appropriate to contingent connections. The non-contingent character of the proposition that the presence of a red (or round) object tends to make it look to particular people as if there were something red (or round) before them does not, of course, in itself preclude the particular fact that it looks to me as if there were something red before me from being explained by the presence of a particular red object; it is a non-contingent matter that corrosive substances tend to destroy surfaces to which they are applied; but it is quite legitimate to account for a particular case of surface-damage by saying that it was caused by some corrosive substance. In each case the effect might have come about in some other way.

IV

I conclude that it is not out of the question that the following version of the CTP should be acceptable: (1) It is true that X perceives M if, and only if, some present-tense sense-datum statement is true of X which reports a state of affairs for which M, in a way to be indicated by example, is causally responsible, and (2) a claim on the part of X to perceive M, if it needs to be justified at all, is justified by showing that the existence of M is required if the circumstances reported by certain true sense-datum statements, some of which may be about persons other than X, are to be causally accounted for. Whether this twofold thesis deserves to be called a Theory of Perception I shall not presume to judge; I have already suggested that the first clause neither obviously entails nor obviously conflicts with Phenomenalism; I suspect that the same may be true of the second clause. I am conscious that my version, however close to the letter, is very far from the spirit of the original theory; but to defend the spirit as well as the letter would be beyond my powers.

IV

VERIDICAL HALLUCINATION AND PROSTHETIC VISION

D. LEWIS

I

I see. Before my eyes various things are present and various things are going on. The scene before my eyes causes a certain sort of visual experience in me, thanks to a causal process involving light, the retina, the optic nerve, and the brain. The visual experience so caused more or less matches the scene before my eyes. All this goes on in much the same way in my case as in the case of other people who see. And it goes on in much the same way that it would have if the scene before my eyes had been visibly different, though in that case the visual experience produced would have been different.

How much of all this is essential to seeing?

II

It is not far wrong to say simply that someone sees if and only if the scene before his eyes causes matching visual experience. So far as I know, there are no counterexamples to this in our ordinary life. Shortly we shall consider some that arise under extraordinary circumstances.

But first, what do we mean by 'matching visual experience'? What goes on in the brain (or perhaps the soul) is not very much like what goes on before the eyes. They cannot match in the way that a scale model matches its prototype, or anything like that. Rather, visual experience has informational content about the scene before the eyes, and it matches the scene to the extent that its content is correct.

Reprinted from *Australasian Journal of Philosophy*, 58/3 (1980), 239–49, by permission of the Editor.

Visual experience is a state characterized by its typical causal role, and its role is to participate in a double causal dependence. Visual experience depends on the scene before the eyes[1] and the subject's beliefs about that scene depend in turn partly on his visual experience. The content of the experience is, roughly, the content of the belief it tends to produce.

The matter is more complicated, however. The same visual experience will have a different impact on the beliefs of different subjects, depending on what they believed beforehand. (And on other differences between them, for example differences of intelligence.) Holmes will believe more on the basis of a given visual experience than Watson; and Watson in turn will believe more than someone will who suspects that he has fallen victim to a field linguist no less powerful than deceitful.[2] We should take the range of prior states that actually exist among us, and ask what is common to the impact of a given visual experience on all these states. Only if a certain belief would be produced in almost every case may we take its content as part of the content of the visual experience. (The more stringently we take 'almost every', the more we cut down the content of the visual experience and the more of its impact we attribute to unconscious inference; for our purposes, we need not consider how that line ought to be drawn.)

Beliefs produced by visual experience are in large part self-ascriptive: the subject believes not only that the world is a certain way but also that he himself is situated in the world in a certain way. To believe that the scene before my eyes is stormy is the same as to believe that I am facing a stormy part of the world. Elsewhere I have argued that the objects of such beliefs should be taken, and that the objects of all beliefs may be taken, as properties which the subject self-ascribes.[3] Hence the content of visual experience likewise consists of properties—properties which the subject will self-ascribe if the visual experience produces its characteristic sort of belief. The content is correct, and the visual experience matches the scene before the eyes, to the extent that the subject has the properties that comprise the content of his visual experience.

[1] I shall have more to say about this dependence in what follows. So although my concern here is with the analysis of seeing in terms of visual experience, what I say would also figure in a prior analysis of visual experience in terms of its definitive causal role.

[2] The problem of the suspicious subject is raised in Frank Jackson, *Perception: A Representative Theory* (Cambridge, 1977), 37–42.

[3] 'Attitudes *De Dicto* and *De Se*', *The Philosophical Review*, 88 (1979), 513–43.

Equivalently we might follow Hintikka's scheme and take the content of visual experience as a set of alternative possibilities.[4] A modification is desirable, however, in view of the self-ascriptive character of visually produced belief. We should take these visual alternatives not as possible worlds but as possible individuals-situated-in-worlds. The visual experience characteristically produces in the subject the belief that he himself belongs to this set of alternative possible individuals. Matching then means that the subject is, or at least closely resembles, a member of his alternative set.

Not all of the content of visual experience can be characterized in terms of the beliefs it tends to produce. It is part of the content that the duck–rabbit look like a duck or a rabbit, but the belief produced is that there is no duck and no rabbit but only paper and ink. However, aspects of the content that do not show up in the produced belief also are irrelevant to our task of saying what it is for visual experience to match the scene before the eyes. We can therefore ignore them.

III

I shall not dwell on the question whether it is possible to see even if the scene before the eyes does not cause matching visual experience. Three sorts of examples come to mind. (1) Perhaps someone could see without having visual experience. He would need something that more or less played the role of visual experience; but this substitute might not be visual experience, either because it played the role quite imperfectly,[5] or because it is not what normally plays the role in human beings (or in some other natural kind to which the subject in question belongs).[6] (2) Perhaps someone could see in whom the scene before the eyes causes non-matching visual experience, provided that the failure of match is systematic and

---

[4] Jaakko Hintikka, 'On the Logic of Perception', in his *Models for Modalities: Selected Essays* (Dordrecht, 1969). The proposed modification solves (by theft rather than toil) a problem for Hintikka's important idea of perceptual cross-identification: where do we get the cross-identification of the perceiving subject himself, in relation to whom we perceptually cross-identify the things that surround him?

[5] As in cases of 'blind sight' in which the subject claims to have no visual experience and yet acquires information about the scene before his eyes just as if he did.

[6] See my 'Mad Pain and Martian Pain', in Ned Block, ed., *Readings in the Philosophy of Psychology*, i (Cambridge, Mass., 1980).

that the subject knows how to infer information about the scene before the eyes from this non-matching visual experience. (3) Perhaps someone could see in whom the scene elsewhere than before the eyes causes visual experience matching that scene, but not matching the scene before the eyes (if such there be). I do not find these examples clear one way or the other, and therefore I shall consider them no further. They will not meet the conditions for seeing that follow, wherefore I claim only sufficiency and not necessity for those conditions.

Two further preliminaries. (1) My analysandum is seeing in a strong sense that requires a relation to the external scene. Someone whose visual experience is entirely hallucinatory does not see in this strong sense. I take it that he can be said to see in a weaker, phenomenal sense—he sees what isn't there—and this is to say just that he has visual experience. (2) My analysandum is seeing in the intransitive sense, not seeing such-and-such particular thing. The latter analysandum poses all the problems of the former, and more besides: it raises the questions whether something is seen if it makes a suitable causal contribution to visual experience but it is not noticed separately from its background, and whether something is seen when part of it—for instance, its front surface—makes a causal contribution to visual experience.[7]

IV

My first stab is good enough to deal with some familiar counter-examples to causal analyses of seeing: they are not cases of seeing because they are not cases in which the scene before the eyes causes matching visual experience.[8]

Example 1: The Brain. I hallucinate at random; by chance I seem to see a brain floating before my eyes; my own brain happens to look just like the one I seem to see; my brain is causing my visual experience, which matches it. I do not see. No problem: my brain is no part of the scene before my eyes.

---

[7] Alvin Goldman considers transitive seeing in his 'Discrimination and Perceptual Knowledge', Essay II in this volume. Despite the difference of analysandum, I have followed his treatment to a considerable extent.

[8] Example 1 and an auditory version of Example 2 are due to P. F. Strawson, 'Causation in Perception', in his *Freedom and Resentment and Other Essays* (London, 1974), 77–8.

Example 2: The Memory. I hallucinate not at random; visual memory influences the process; thus I seem to see again a scene from long ago; this past scene causes visual experience which matches it. I do not see. No problem: the past scene is not part of the scene before my eyes.[9]

However, more difficult cases are possible. They are cases of *veridical hallucination,* in which the scene before the eyes causes matching visual experience, and still one does not see. They show that what I have said so far does not provide a sufficient condition for seeing.

Example 3: The Brain Before the Eyes. As in Example 1, I hallucinate at random, I seem to see a brain before my eyes, my own brain looks just like the one I seem to see, and my brain is causing my visual experience. But this time my brain is before my eyes. It has been carefully removed from my skull. The nerves and blood vessels that connect it to the rest of me have been stretched somehow, not severed. It is still working and still hallucinating.

Example 4: The Wizard. The scene before my eyes consists mostly of a wizard casting a spell. His spell causes me to hallucinate at random, and the hallucination so caused happens to match the scene before my eyes.

Example 5: The Light Meter. I am blind; but electrodes have been implanted in my brain in such a way that when turned on they will cause me to have visual experience of a certain sort of landscape. A light meter is on my head. It is connected to the electrodes in such a way that they are turned on if and only if the average illumination of the scene before my eyes exceeds a certain threshold. By chance, just such a landscape is before my eyes, and its illumination is enough to turn on the electrodes.

v

Ordinarily, when the scene before the eyes causes matching visual experience, it happens as follows. Parts of the scene reflect or emit

[9] However, it seems that some past things are part of the scene now before my eyes: distant stars as they were long ago, to take an extreme case. It would be circular to say that they, unlike the past scene in Example 2, are visible now. Perhaps the best answer is that the stars, as I now see them, are not straightforwardly past; for lightlike connection has as good a claim as simultaneity-in-my-rest-frame to be the legitimate heir to our defunct concept of absolute simultaneity. (I owe the problem to D. M. Armstrong and the answer to Eric Melum.)

light in a certain pattern; this light travels to the eye by a more or less straight path, and is focused by the lens to form an image on the retina; the retinal cells are stimulated in proportion to the intensity and spectral distribution of the light that falls on them; these stimulated cells stimulate other cells in turn, and so on, and the stimulations comprise a signal which propagates up the optic nerve into the brain; and finally there is a pattern of stimulation in the brain cells which either is or else causes the subject's visual experience.

That is not at all what goes on in our three examples of veridical hallucination. Rather, the scene before the eyes causes matching visual experience by peculiar, non-standard causal processes. Perhaps, as has been proposed by Grice[10] and others, seeing requires the standard causal process. That would explain why Examples 3, 4, and 5 do not qualify as cases of seeing.

(The proposal faces a technical dilemma. If the standard process is defined as the process in which light is reflected or emitted, etc. (as above), then it seems to follow that few of us now (and none in the not-too-distant past) know enough to have the concept of seeing; whereas if the standard process is defined as the most common process by which the scene before the eyes causes matching visual experience, whatever that may be, then it seems to follow that any of our examples of veridical hallucination might have been a case of seeing, and what I am doing now might not have been, if only the frequencies had been a bit different. Either conclusion would be absurd. However, the dilemma can be avoided by appeal to the recent idea of fixing reference by rigidified descriptions.)[11]

Unfortunately, requiring the standard process would disqualify good cases along with the bad. Some cases in which the scene before the eyes causes matching visual experience by a non-standard process seem fairly clearly to be cases of genuine seeing, not veridical hallucination.

Example 6: The Minority. It might be found that a few of us have visual systems that work on different principles from other peoples'. The differences might be as extreme as the difference between AM versus FM transmission of signals; analogue versus

---

[10] H. P. Grice, 'The Causal Theory of Perception', Essay III in this volume.

[11] See the discussion of the metre and the metre bar in Saul A. Kripke, 'Naming and Necessity', in Donald Davidson and Gilbert Harman, *Semantics of Natural Language* (Dordrecht, 1972), 274–5, 288–9.

digital processing; or point-by-point measurement of light versus edge detection. If so, would we be prepared to say that the minority do not really see? Would those who belong to the minority be prepared to say it? Surely not.

I anticipate the reply that the abnormal process in the minority is not different enough; the boundaries of the standard process should be drawn widely enough to include it. But I think this puts the cart before the horse. We know which processes to include just because somehow we already know which processes are ones by which someone might see.

Example 7: The Prosthetic Eye. A prosthetic eye consists of a miniature television camera mounted in, or on, the front of the head; a computer; and an array of electrodes in the brain. The computer receives input from the camera and sends signals to the electrodes in such a way as to produce visual experience that matches the scene before the eyes. When prosthetic eyes are perfected, the blind will see. The standard process will be absent, unless by 'standard process' we just mean one that permits seeing; but they will see by a non-standard process.

Some prosthetic eyes are more convincing than others as means for genuine seeing. (1) It seems better if the computer is surgically implanted rather than carried in a knapsack, but better if it is carried in a knapsack rather than stationary and linked by radio to the camera and electrodes. (2) It seems better if the prosthetic eye contains no parts which can be regarded as having wills of their own and co-operating because they want to. (3) It seems better if the prosthetic eye works in some uniform way, rather than dealing with different sorts of inputs by significantly different means. (4) It seems better if it does not use processes which also figure in the standard processes by which we sometimes hallucinate. But if these considerations influence us, presumably it is because they make the prosthetic eye seem a little more like the natural eye. (Or so we think —but we just might be wrong about the natural eye, and these properties of a prosthetic eye just might detract from the resemblance.) Why should that matter, once we grant that the standard process is not required? I see no real need for any limits on how a prosthetic eye might work. Even the least convincing cases of prosthetic vision are quite convincing enough.

If you insist that 'strictly speaking' prosthetic vision is not really seeing, then I am prepared to concede you this much. Often we do leave semantic questions unsettled when we have no practical need to settle them. Perhaps this is such a case, and you are resolving a genuine indeterminacy in the way you prefer. But if you are within your rights, so, I insist, am I. I do not really think my favoured usage is at all idiosyncratic. But it scarcely matters: I would like to understand it whether it is idiosyncratic or not.

VI

The trouble with veridical hallucination is not that it involves a non-standard causal process. Is it perhaps this: that the process involved produces matching visual experience only seldom, perhaps only this once?

No; someone might go on having veridical hallucinations for a long time. Veridical hallucinations are improbable, and a long run of them is still more improbable, but that does not make it impossible. No matter how long they go on, the sorts of occurrences I have classified as cases of veridical hallucination still are that and not seeing.

On the other hand, a process that permits genuine seeing might work only seldom, perhaps only this once.

Example 8: The Deathbed Cure. God might cure a blind man on his deathbed, granting him an instant of sight by means of some suitable non-standard process. For an instant he sees exactly as others do. Then he is dead. The scene before his eyes produces matching visual experience by a suitable process, namely the standard one, but only this once.

Example 9: The Loose Wire. A prosthetic eye has a loose wire. Mostly it flops around; and when it does the eye malfunctions and the subject's visual experience consists of splotches unrelated to the scene before the eyes. But sometimes it touches the contact it ought to be bonded to; and as long as it does, the eye functions perfectly and the subject sees. Whether he sees has nothing to do with whether the wire touches the contact often, or seldom, or only this once.

The proposal isn't far wrong. It asks almost the right question: when the scene before the eyes causes matching visual experience this time, is that an isolated case or is it part of a range of such cases? The mistake is in asking for a range of actual cases, spread out in time. Rather, we need a range of counterfactual alternatives to the case under consideration.

VII

What distinguishes our cases of veridical hallucination from genuine seeing—natural or prosthetic, lasting or momentary—is that there is no proper counterfactual dependence of visual experience on the scene before the eyes. If the scene had been different, it would not have caused correspondingly different visual experience to match that different scene. Any match that occurs is a lucky accident. It depends on the scene being just right. In genuine seeing, the fact of match is independent of the scene. Just as the actual scene causes matching visual experience, so likewise would alternative scenes. Different scenes would have produced different visual experience, and thus the subject is in a position to discriminate between the alternatives.

This is my proposal: if the scene before the eyes causes matching visual experience as part of a suitable pattern of counterfactual dependence, then the subject sees; if the scene before the eyes causes matching visual experience without a suitable pattern of counterfactual dependence, then the subject does not see.

An ideal pattern of dependence would be one such that any scene whatever would produce perfectly matching visual experience. But that is too much to require. Certainly one can see even if the match, actual and counterfactual, is close but imperfect and the content of visual experience is mostly, but not entirely correct. Perhaps indeed this is our common lot. Further, one can see even if there are some alternative scenes that would fail altogether to produce matching visual experience, so long as the actual scene is not one of those ones.

Example 10: The Laser Beam. I see now; but if the scene before my eyes had included a powerful laser beam straight into my eyes, I would have been instantly struck blind and would not have had matching visual experience even for a moment.

Example 11: The Hypnotic Suggestion. I must do business with Martians and I can't stand the sight of them. The remedy is hypnotic suggestion: when a Martian is before my eyes I will seem to see not a Martian but a nice black cat. Thus when there are Martians around, the scene before my eyes causes visual experience that does not match the scene very closely. But when there are no Martians, I see perfectly well. [12]

[12] Adapted from an olfactory example in Robert A. Heinlein, *Double Star* (Garden City, NY, 1956), ch. 3.

We cannot require that any two different scenes would produce different visual experience; for they might differ in some invisible respect, in which case the same visual experience would match both equally well. Its content would concern only those aspects of the scene in which both are alike. For one who sees, *visibly* different scenes would (for the most part) produce different visual experience; but that is unhelpful unless we say which differences are the visible ones, and that seems to be an empirical matter rather than part of the analysis of seeing. What can be required analytically is that there be plenty of visible differences of some sort or other; that is, plenty of different alternative scenes that would produce different visual experience and thus be visually discriminable.

That would almost follow from a requirement of match over a wide range of alternative scenes. But not quite. Most of our visual experience is rich in content; but some is poor in content and would match a wide range of alternative scenes equally well. Any pitch-dark scene would produce matching visual experience—what content there is would be entirely correct—but it would be the same in every case. Seeing is a capacity to discriminate, so this sort of match over a wide range of alternatives will not suffice.

I conclude that the required pattern of counterfactual dependence may be specified as follows. There is a large class of alternative possible scenes before the subject's eyes, and there are many mutually exclusive and jointly exhaustive subclasses thereof, such that (1) any scene in the large class would cause visual experience closely matching that scene, and (2) any two scenes in different subclasses would cause different visual experience.

The requirement admits of degree in three ways. How large a class? How many subclasses? How close a match? The difference between veridical hallucination and genuine seeing is not sharp, on my analysis. It is fuzzy; when the requirement of suitable counterfactual dependence is met to some degree, but to a degree that falls far short of the standard set by normal seeing, we may expect borderline cases. And indeed it is easy to imagine cases of partial blindness, or of rudimentary prosthetic vision, in which the counterfactual dependence is unsatisfactory and it is therefore doubtful whether the subject may be said to see.

VIII

A further condition might also be imposed: that in the actual case the subject's visual experience must be rich in content, that it must not be the sort of visual experience that would match a wide range of scenes equally well. For instance, it must not be the sort of visual experience that we have when it is pitch dark. This condition of rich content is needed to explain why we do not see in the dark, even though the scene before the eyes causes matching visual experience as part of a suitable pattern of counterfactual dependence.

But we are of two minds on the matter. We think we do not see in the dark; but also we think we find things out by sight only when we see; and in the pitch dark, we find out by sight that it is dark. How else—by smell? By the very fact that we do not see?—No, for we also do not see in dazzling light or thick fog, and it is by sight that we distinguish various situations in which we do not see.

In a sense, we do see in the dark when we see that it is dark. In a more common sense, we never see in the dark. There is an ambiguity in our concept of seeing, and the condition of rich content is often but not always required. When it is, it admits of degree and thus permits still another sort of borderline case of seeing.

IX

Given a suitable pattern of counterfactual dependence of visual experience on the scene before the eyes (including both the actual case and its counterfactual alternatives) it is redundant to say as I did that the scene causes, or would cause, the visual experience. To make the explicit mention of causation redundant, according to my counterfactual analysis of causation, we need not only a suitable battery of scene-to-visual-experience counterfactuals but also some further counterfactuals. Along with each counterfactual saying that if the scene were S the visual experience would be E, we need another saying that if the scene S were entirely absent, the visual experience would not be E. Counterfactuals of the latter sort may follow from the battery of scene-to-visual-experience counter-factuals in some cases, but they do not do so generally. According to the counter-factual analysis of causation that I have defended elsewhere,[13] any such counterfactual dependence among distinct occurrences is causal dependence, and implies causation of the dependent occurrences by those on which they depend. It would suffice if our counterfactuals said just that if the scene before the eyes were so-and-so, then the visual experience would be such-and-such.

[13] 'Causation', *Journal of Philosophy*, 70 (1973), 556–67.

If we leave the causation implicit, however, then we must take care that the counterfactuals from scene to visual experience are of the proper sort to comprise a causal dependence. We must avoid backtrackers: those counterfactuals that we would support by arguing that different effects would have to have been produced by different causes.[14] Backtracking counterfactual dependence does not imply causal dependence and does not suffice for seeing.

Example 12: The Screen. I am hallucinating at random. My hallucinations at any moment are determined by my precursor brain states a few seconds before. My brain states are monitored, and my hallucinations are predicted by a fast computer. It controls a battery of lights focused on a screen before my eyes in such a way that the scene before my eyes is made to match my predicted visual experience at the time. It is true in a sense—in the backtracking sense—that whatever might be on the screen, my visual experience would match it. But my visual experience does not depend causally on the scene before my eyes. Rather, they are independent effects of a common cause, namely my precursor brain states. Therefore I do not see.

The same example shows that it would not suffice just to require that the laws of nature and the prevailing conditions imply a suitable correspondence between visual experience and the scene before the eyes. That could be so without the proper sort of counterfactual, and hence causal, dependence; in which case one would not see.

X

The following case (Example 11 carried to extremes) is a hard one. It closely resembles cases of genuine seeing, and we might well be tempted to classify it as such. According to my analysis, however, it is a case of veridical hallucination. The scene before the eyes causes matching visual experience without any pattern of counterfactual dependence whatever, suitable or otherwise.

Example 13: The Censor. My natural or prosthetic eye is in perfect condition and functioning normally, and by means of it the scene before my eyes causes matching visual experience. But if the scene were any different my visual experience would be just the same. For

---

[14] This is circular in the context of a counterfactual analysis of causation; but in 'Counterfactual Dependence and Time's Arrow', *Noûs*, 13 (1979), 455–76, I have proposed a way to distinguish backtrackers without the circular reference to causation, at least under determinism.

there is a censor standing by, ready to see to it that I have precisely that visual experience and no other, whatever the scene may be. (Perhaps the censor is external, perhaps it is something in my own brain.) So long as the scene is such as to cause the right experience, the censor does nothing. But if the scene were any different, the censor would intervene and cause the same experience by other means. If so, my eye would not function normally and the scene before my eyes would not cause matching visual experience.

The case is one of causal pre-emption.[15] The scene before my eyes is the actual cause of my visual experience; the censor is an alternative potential cause of the same effect. The actual cause pre-empts the potential cause, stopping the alternative causal chain that would otherwise have gone to completion.

The argument for classifying the case as seeing is that it is just like a clear case of seeing except for the presence of the censor; and, after all, the censor does not actually do anything; and if the scene before the eyes were different and the censor nevertheless stood idly by—as in actuality—then the different scene would indeed cause suitably different visual experience.

My reply is that the case is really not so very much like the clear case of seeing to which it is compared. The censor's idleness is an essential factor in the causal process by which matching visual experience is produced, just as the censor's intervention would be in the alternative process. No such factor is present in the comparison case. If the scene were different this factor would not be there, so it is wrong to hold it fixed in asking what would happen if the scene were different. We cannot uniformly ignore or hold fixed those causal factors which are absences of interventions. The standard process might be riddled with them. (Think of a circuit built up from exclusive-or-gates: every output signal from such a gate is caused partly by the absence of a second input signal.) Who knows what would happen in an ordinary case of natural (or prosthetic) vision if the scene were different and all absences of interventions were held fixed? Who cares? We do not in general hold fixed the absences of intervention, and I see no good reason to give the censor's idleness special treatment.

The decisive consideration, despite the misleading resemblance of this case to genuine cases of seeing, is that the censor's potential victim has no capacity at all to discriminate by sight. Just as in any other case of veridical hallucination, the match that occurs is a lucky accident.

[15] See my discussion of pre-emption in 'Causation'.

V

PERCEPTION AND ITS OBJECTS

P. F. STRAWSON

I

Ayer has always given the problem of perception a central place in his thinking. Reasonably so; for a philosopher's views on this question are a key both to his theory of knowledge in general and to his metaphysics. The movement of Ayer's own thought has been from phenomenalism to what he describes in his latest treatment of the topic as 'a sophisticated form of realism'.[1] The epithet is doubly apt. No adequate account of the matter can be simple; and Ayer's account, while distinguished by his accustomed lucidity and economy of style, is notably and subtly responsive to all the complexities inherent in the subject itself and to all the pressures of more or less persuasive argument which have marked the course of its treatment by philosophers. Yet the form of realism he defends has another kind of sophistication about which it is possible to have reservations and doubts; and, though I am conscious of being far from clear on the matter myself, I shall try to make some of my own doubts and reservations as clear as I can. I shall take as my text Chapters 4 and 5 of *The Central Questions of Philosophy*; and I shall also consider a different kind of realism—that advocated by J. L. Mackie in his book on Locke.[2] There are points of contact as well as of contrast between Ayer's and Mackie's views. A comparison between them will help to bring out the nature of my reservations about both.

According to Ayer, the starting-point of serious thought on the matter of perception consists in the fact that our normal perceptual judgements always 'go beyond' the sensible experience which gives

Reprinted by permission of the author and Macmillan, London and Basingstoke, from G. McDonald (ed.), *Perception and Identity: Essays presented to A. J. Ayer* (1979), 41–60.

[1] A. J. Ayer, *The Central Questions of Philosophy* (London, 1973) chs. 4 and 5, pp. 68–111.

[2] J. L. Mackie, *Problems from Locke* (Oxford, 1976) chs. 1 and 2, pp. 7–71.

rise to them; for those judgements carry implications which would not be carried by any 'strict account' of that experience.[3] Ayer sees ordinary perceptual judgements as reflecting or embodying what he calls the common-sense view of the physical world, which is, among other things, a realist view; and he sees that view itself as having the character of 'a theory with respect to the immediate data of perception'.[4] He devotes some space to an account of how the theory might be seen as capable of being developed by an individual observer on the basis of the data available to him; though he disavows any intention of giving an actual history of the theory's development. The purpose of the account is, rather, to bring out those features of sensible experience which make it possible to employ the theory successfully and which, indeed, justify acceptance of it. For it is, he holds, by and large an acceptable theory, even though the discoveries of physical science may require us to modify it in certain respects.

Evidently no infant is delivered into the world already equipped with what Ayer calls the common-sense view of it. That view has to be acquired; and it is open to the psychologist of infant learning to produce at least a speculative account of the stages of its acquisition. Ayer insists, as I have remarked, that his own account of a possible line of development or construction of the common-sense view is not intended as a speculative contribution to the theory of infant learning. It is intended, rather, as an analysis of the nature of mature or adult perceptual experience, an analysis designed to show just how certain features of mature sensible experience vindicate or sustain the common-sense view which is embodied or reflected in mature perceptual judgements. Clearly the two aims here distinguished—the genetic-psychological and the analytic-philosophical—are very different indeed, and it will be of great importance not to confuse them. In particular it will be important to run no risk of characterizing mature sensible experience in terms adequate at best only for the characterization of some stage of infantile experience. It is not clear that Ayer entirely avoids this danger.

What is clear is that if we accept Ayer's starting-point, if we agree that our ordinary perceptual judgements carry implications not carried by a 'strict account' of the sensible experience which gives rise to them, then we must make absolutely sure that our account of that experience, in the form it takes in our mature life, is indeed strict—in

[3] Ayer, *Central Questions*, 81, 89.
[4] Ibid. 88.

the sense of strictly correct. Only so can we have any prospect of making a correct estimate of the further doctrines that the common-sense view of the world has the status of a *theory* with respect to a type of sensible experience which provides *data* for the theory; that this experience supplies the *evidence* on which the theory is based;[5] that the common-sense view can be regarded as *inferred* or at least inferrable from this evidence; and that our ordinary perceptual judgements have the character of *interpretations*,[6] in the light of theory, of what sensible experience actually presents us with.

But can we—and should we—accept Ayer's starting-point? I think that, suitably interpreted, we both can, and should, accept it. Two things will be required of a strict account of our sensible experience or of any particular episode or slice of sensible experience: first, as I have just remarked, that it should in no way distort or misrepresent the character of that experience as we actually enjoy it, that is, that it should be a true or faithful account; secondly, that its truth, in any particular case, should be independent of the truth of the associated perceptual judgement, that is, that it should remain true even if the associated perceptual judgement is false. It is the second requirement on which Ayer lays stress when he remarks that those judgements carry implications which would not be carried by any strict account of sensible experience; or, less happily in my opinion, that in making such judgements we take a step beyond what our sensible experience actually presents us with. But it is the first requirement to which I now wish to give some attention.

Suppose a non-philosophical observer gazing idly through a window. To him we address the request, 'Give us a description of your current visual experience', or 'How is it with you, visually, at the moment?' Uncautioned as to exactly what we want, he might reply in some such terms as these: 'I see the red light of the setting sun filtering through the black and thickly clustered branches of the elms; I see the dappled deer grazing in groups on the vivid green grass . . .' and so on. So we explain to him. We explain that we want him to amend his account so that, without any sacrifice of fidelity to the experience as actually enjoyed, it nevertheless sheds all that heavy load of commitment to propositions about the world which was carried by the description he gave. We want an account which confines itself strictly within the limits of the subjective

---

5 Ibid. 89.
6 Ibid. 81.

episode, an account which would remain true even if he had seen nothing of what he claimed to see, even if he had been subject to total illusion.

Our observer is quick on the uptake. He does not start talking about lights and colours, patches and patterns. For he sees that to do so would be to falsify the character of the experience he actually enjoyed. He says, instead, 'I understand. I've got to cut out of my report all commitment to propositions about independently existing objects. Well, the simplest way to do this, while remaining faithful to the character of the experience as actually enjoyed, is to put my previous report in inverted commas or oratio obliqua and describe my visual experience as such as it would have been natural to describe in these terms, had I not received this additional instruction. Thus: "I had a visual experience such as it would have been natural to describe by saying that I saw, etc. . . . [or, to describe in these words, 'I saw . . . etc.'] were it not for the obligation to exclude commitment to propositions about independently existing objects." In this way [continues the observer] I *use* the perceptual claim—the claim it was natural to make in the circumstances—in order to characterize my experience, without actually making the claim. I render the perceptual judgement internal to the characterization of the experience without actually asserting the content of the judgement. And this is really the best possible way of characterizing the experience. There are perhaps alternative locutions which might serve the purpose, so long as they are understood as being to the same effect—on the whole, the more artificial the better, since their artificiality will help to make it clearer just to what effect they are intended to be. Thus we might have: "It sensibly seemed to me just as if I were seeing such-and-such a scene" or "My visual experience can be characterized by saying that I saw what I saw, supposing I saw anything, *as* a scene of the following character . . ."'

If my observer is right in this—and I think he is—then certain general conclusions follow. Our perceptual judgements, as Ayer remarks, embody or reflect a certain view of the world, as containing objects, variously propertied, located in a common space and continuing in their existence independently of our interrupted and relatively fleeting perceptions of them. Our making of such judgements implies our possession and application of concepts of such objects. But now it appears that we cannot give a veridical characterization even of the sensible experience which these judgements, as Ayer expresses it, 'go beyond', without reference to those judgements themselves; that our sensible experience itself is thoroughly permeated with those concepts of objects which figure in such judgements. This does not mean, that is, it does not follow directly from this feature of sensible experience, that the general view of the world which those judgements reflect must be true. That would be too short a way with scepticism. But it does follow, I think, that our sensible experience could not have the character it does have unless—at least before philosophical reflection sets in— we unquestioningly *took* that general view of the world to be true. The concepts of the objective which we see to be indispensable to the veridical characterization of sensible experience simply would not be in this way indispensable unless those whose experience it was initially and unreflectively took such concepts to have application in the world.

This has a further consequence: the consequence that it is quite inappropriate to represent the general, realist view of the world which is reflected in our ordinary perceptual judgements as having the status of a *theory* with respect to sensible experience; that it is inappropriate to represent that experience as supplying the *data* for such a theory or the *evidence* on which it is based or from which it is *inferred* or *inferrable*; that it is inappropriate to speak of our ordinary perceptual judgements as having the character of an *interpretation*, in the light of theory, of the content of our sensible experience. The reason for this is simple. In order for some belief or set of beliefs to be correctly described as a theory in respect of certain data, it must be possible to describe the data on the basis of which the theory is held in terms which do not presuppose the acceptance of the theory on the part of those for whom the data *are* data. But this is just the condition we have seen not to be satisfied in the case where the so-called data are the contents of sensible experience and the so-called theory is a general realist view of the world. The 'data' are laden with the 'theory'. Sensible experience is permeated by concepts unreflective acceptance of the general applicability of which is a condition of its being so permeated, a condition of that experience being what it is; and these concepts are of realistically conceived objects.

I must make it quite clear what I am saying and what I am not saying here. I am talking of the ordinary non-philosophical man. I am talking of us all before we felt, if ever we did feel, any inclination to respond to the solicitations of a general scepticism, to regard it as raising a problem. I am saying that it follows from the character of sensible experience as we all actually enjoy it that a common-sense realist view of the world does not in general have the status of a theory in respect of that experience; while Ayer, as I understand him, holds that it does. But I am not denying that to one who has seen, or thinks he has seen, that sensible experience might have the character it does have and *yet* a realist view of the world be false, to *him* the idea may well present itself that the best way of accounting for sensible experience as having that character is to accept the common realist view of the world or some variant of it. *He* might be said to adopt, as a theory, the doctrine that the common realist view of the world is, at least in some basic essentials, true. But this will be a philosopher's theory, designed to deal with a philosopher's problem. (I shall not here discuss its merits as such.) What I am concerned to dispute is the doctrine that a realist view of the world has, for any man, the status of a theory in relation to his sensible experience, a theory in the light of which he interprets that experience in making his perceptual judgements.

To put the point summarily, whereas Ayer says we take a step beyond our sensible experience in making our perceptual judgements, I say rather that we take a step back (in general) from our perceptual judgements in framing accounts of our sensible experience; for we have (in general) to include a reference to the former in framing a veridical description of the latter.

It may seem, on a superficial reading, that Ayer had anticipated and answered this objection. He introduces, as necessary for the characterization of our sensible experience, certain concepts of types of pattern, the names for which are borrowed from the names of ordinary physical objects. Thus he speaks of visual leaf patterns, chair patterns, cat patterns, and so on.[7] At the same time, he is careful, if I read him rightly, to guard against the impression that the use of this terminology commits him to the view that the employment of the corresponding physical-object concepts themselves is necessary to the characterization of our sensible experience.[8] The terminology is appropriate (he holds) simply because those features of sensible experience to which the terminology is applied are the features which govern our identifications of the physical objects we think we see. They are the features, 'implicitly noticed',[9] which provide the main clues on which our everyday judgements of perception are based.

[7] Ibid. 91.　　　　　　　　[8] Ibid. 96.　　　　　　　　[9] Ibid. 91

This is ingenious, but I do not think it will do. This we can see more clearly if we use an invented, rather than a derived, terminology for these supposed features and then draw up a table of explicit correlations between the invented names and the physical-object names. Each artificial feature name is set against the name of a type of physical object: our perceptual identifications of seen objects as of that type are held to be governed by implicit noticings of that feature. The nature and significance of the feature names is now quite clearly explained and we have to ask ourselves whether it is these rather than the associated physical-object terms that we ought to use if we are to give a quite strict and faithful account of our sensible experience. I think it is clear that this is not so; that the idea of our ordinary perceptual judgements as being invariably based upon, or invariably issuing from, awareness of such features is a myth. The situation is rather, as I have already argued, that the employment of our ordinary, full-blooded concepts of physical objects is indispensable to a strict, and strictly veridical, account of our sensible experience.

Once again, I must make it clear what I am, and what I am not, saying. I have been speaking of the typical or standard case of mature sensible and perceptual experience. I have no interest at all in denying the thesis that there also occur cases of sensible experience such that the employment of full-blooded concepts of physical objects would not be indispensable, and may be inappropriate, to giving a strict account of the experience. Such cases are of different types, and there is one in particular which is of interest in the present connection. An observer, gazing through his window, may perhaps, by an effort of will, bring himself to see, or even will-lessly find himself seeing, what he knows to be the branches of the trees no longer *as* branches at all, but as an intricate pattern of dark lines of complex directions and shapes and various sizes against a background of varying shades of grey. The frame of mind in which we enjoy, if we ever do enjoy, this kind of experience is a rare and sophisticated, not a standard or normal, frame of mind. Perhaps the fact, if it is a fact, that we can bring ourselves into this frame of mind when we choose may be held to give a sense to the idea of our 'implicitly noticing' such patterns even when we are not in this frame of mind. If so, it is a sense very far removed from that which Ayer's thesis requires. For that thesis requires not simply the possibility, but the actual occurrence, in all cases of perception, of sensible experience of this kind. One line of retreat may seem to lie open at this point: a retreat to the position of saying that the occurrence of such experiences may be *inferred*, even though we do not, in the hurry of life, generally notice or recall their occurrence. But such a retreat would be the final irony. The items in question would have changed their status radically: instead of data for a common-sense theory of the world, they would appear as consequences of a sophisticated theory of the mind.

This concludes the first stage of my argument. I have argued that mature sensible experience (in general) presents itself as, in Kantian phrase, an *immediate* consciousness of the existence of things outside us. (*Immediate*, of course, does not mean *infallible*.) Hence, the common realist conception of the world does not have the character of a 'theory' in relation to the 'data of sense'. I have not claimed that this fact is of itself sufficient to 'refute' scepticism or to provide a philosophical 'demonstration' of the truth of some form of realism; though I think it does provide the right starting-point for reflection upon these enterprises. But that is another story and I shall not try to tell it here. My point so far is that the ordinary human commitment to a conceptual scheme of a realist character is not properly described, even in a stretched sense of the words, as a theoretical commitment. It is, rather, something given with the given.

II

But we are philosophers as well as men; and so must examine more closely the nature of the realist scheme to which we are pre-theoretically committed and then consider whether we are not rationally constrained, as Locke and Mackie would maintain we are, to modify it quite radically in the light of our knowledge of physics and physiology. Should we not also, as philosophers, consider the question of whether we can rationally maintain any form of realism at all? Perhaps we should; but, as already remarked, that is a question I shall not consider here. My main object, in the present section, is to get a clear view of the main features of our pre-theoretical scheme before considering whether it is defensible, as it stands, or not, I go in a somewhat roundabout way to work.

I have spoken of our pre-theoretical scheme as realist in character. Philosophers who treat of these questions commonly distinguish different forms of realism. So do both Ayer and Mackie. They both mention, at one extreme, a form of realism which Mackie calls 'naïve' and even 'very naïve', but which might more appropriately be called 'confused realism'. A sufferer from confused realism fails to draw any distinction between sensible experiences (or 'perceptions') and independently existing things (or 'objects perceived') but is said (by Mackie expounding Hume) to credit the former with persistent unobserved existence.[10] It should be remarked that, if this is an accurate way of describing the naïve realist's conception of the matter, he must be very confused indeed, since the expression 'unobserved' already implies the distinction which he is said to fail to make. Speaking in his own person, Mackie gives no positive account of the naïve realist's view of things, but simply says that there is, historically, in the thought of each of us, a phase in which we fail to make the distinction in question.[11] It may indeed be so. The point is one to be referred to the experts on infantile development. But in any case the matter is not here of any consequence. For we are concerned with mature perceptual experience and with the character of the scheme to which those who enjoy such experience are pre-theoretically committed. And it seems to me as certain as anything can be that, as an integral part of that scheme, we distinguish, naturally and unreflectively, between our seeings and hearings and feelings—our perceivings—of objects and the objects we see and hear and feel; and hence quite consistently accept both the interruptedness of the former and the continuance in existence, unobserved, of the latter.

At the opposite extreme from naïve realism stands what may be called scientific or Lockian realism. This form of realism credits physical objects only with those of their properties which are mentioned in physical theory and physical explanation, including the causal explanation of our enjoyment of the kind of perceptual experience we in fact enjoy. It has the consequence that we do not, and indeed cannot, perceive objects as they really are. It might be said that this consequence does not hold in an unqualified form. For we perceive (or seem to perceive) objects as having shape, size, and position; and they really do have shape, size, and position and more or less such shape, size, and position as we seem to perceive them as having. But this reply misconstrues the intended force of the alleged consequence. We cannot in sense perception—the point is an old one—become aware of the shape, size and position of

---

[10] Mackie, *Problems*, 67.
[11] Ibid. 68.

physical objects except by way of awareness of boundaries defined in some sensory mode—for example, by visual and tactile qualities such as scientific realism denies to the objects themselves; and no change in, or addition to, our sensory equipment could alter this fact. To perceive physical objects as, according to scientific realism, they really are would be to perceive them as lacking any such qualities. But this notion is self-contradictory. So it is a necessary consequence of this form of realism that we do not perceive objects as they really are. Indeed, in the sense of the pre-theoretical notion of perceiving—that is, of immediate awareness of things outside us—we do not, on the scientific-realist view, perceive physical objects at all. We are, rather, the victims of a systematic illusion which obstinately clings to us even if we embrace scientific realism. For we continue to enjoy experience *as of* physical objects in space, objects of which the spatial characteristics and relations are defined by the sensible qualities we perceive them as having; but there are no such physical objects as these. The only true physical objects are items systematically correlated with and causally responsible for that experience; and the only sense in which we *can* be said to perceive them is just that they cause us to enjoy that experience.

These remarks are intended only as a *description* of scientific realism. I do not claim that they show it to be untenable. I shall return to the topic later.

In between the 'naïve' and the 'scientific' varieties, Ayer and Mackie each recognize another form of realism, which they each ascribe to 'common sense'. But there is a difference between Ayer's version of common-sense realism and Mackie's. For Mackie's version, unlike Ayer's, shares one crucial feature with scientific realism.

The theory of perception associated with scientific or Lockian realism is commonly and reasonably described as a representative theory. Each of us seems to himself to be perceptually aware of objects of a certain kind: objects in space outside us with visual and tactile qualities. There are in fact, on this view, no such objects; but these object appearances can in a broad sense be said to be representative of those actual objects in space outside us which are systematically correlated with the appearances and causally responsible for them. The interesting feature of Mackie's version of common-sense realism is that the theory of perception associated with it is no less a representative theory than that associated with

Lockian realism. The difference is simply that common sense, according to Mackie, views object appearances as more faithful representatives of actual physical objects than the Lockian allows: in that common sense, gratuitously by scientific standards, credits actual objects in space outside us with visual and tactile as well as primary qualities. As Mackie puts it, common sense allows 'colours-as-we-see-them to be *resemblances* of qualities actually in the things'.[12] On both views, sensible experience has its own, sensible objects; but the common-sense view, according to Mackie, allows a kind of resemblance between sensible and physical objects which the scientific view does not.

I hope it is already clear that this version of common-sense realism is quite different from what I have called our pre-theoretical scheme. What we ordinarily take ourselves to be aware of in perception are not resemblances of physical things themselves. This does not mean, as already remarked, that we have any difficulty in distinguishing between our experiences of seeing, hearing and feeling objects and the objects themselves. That distinction is as firmly a part of our pre-theoretical scheme as is our taking ourselves, in general, to be immediately aware of those objects. Nor does it mean that we take ourselves to be immune from illusion, hallucination, or mistake. We can, and do, perfectly adequately describe such cases without what is, from the point of view of the pre-theoretical scheme, the quite gratuitous introduction of sensible objects interposed between us and the actual physical objects they are supposed to represent.

The odd thing about Mackie's presentation is that at one point he shows himself to be perfectly well aware of this feature of the real realism of common sense; for he writes, 'What we seem to see, feel, hear and so on . . . *are seen as real things without us*—that is, outside us. We just see things as being simply there, of such-and-such sorts, in such-and-such relations. . . .'[13] He goes on, of course, to say that 'our seeing them so is logically distinct from their being so', that we might be, and indeed are, wrong. But he would scarcely dispute that what is thus *seen as* real and outside us is also *seen as* coloured, as possessing visual qualities; that what is *felt as* a real thing outside us is also felt as hard or soft, smooth or rough-surfaced—as possessing tactile qualities. The real realism of common sense, then, does indeed credit physical things with visual and tactile properties; but it does so not in the spirit of a notion of

___

[12] Ibid. 64.   [13] Ibid. 61.

representative perception, but in the spirit of a notion of direct or immediate perception.

Mackie's version of common-sense realism is, then, I maintain, a distortion of the actual pre-theoretical realism of common sense, a distortion which wrongly assimilates it, in a fundamental respect, to the Lockian realism he espouses. I do not find any comparable distortion in Ayer's version. He aptly describes the physical objects we seem to ourselves, and take ourselves, to perceive as 'visuo-tactual continuants'. The scheme as he presents it allows for the distinction between these items and the experiences of perceiving them and for the causal dependence of the latter on the former; and does so, as far as I can see, without introducing the alien features I have discerned in Mackie's account. It is perhaps debatable whether Ayer can consistently maintain the scheme's freedom from such alien elements while continuing to represent it as having the status of a 'theory' in relation to the 'data' of sensible experience. But, having already set out my objections to that doctrine, I shall not pursue the point.

Something more must be said, however, about the position, in the common-sense scheme, of the causal relation between physical object and the experience of perceiving it. Although Ayer admits the relation to a place in the scheme, he seems to regard it as a somewhat sophisticated addition to the latter, a latecomer, as it were, for which room has to be made in an already settled arrangement.[14] This seems to me wrong. The idea of the presence of the thing as accounting for, or being responsible for, our perceptual awareness of it is implicit in the pre-theoretical scheme from the very start. For we think of perception as a way, indeed the basic way, of informing ourselves about the world of independently existing things: we assume, that is to say, the general reliability of our perceptual experiences; and that assumption is the same as the assumption of a general causal dependence of our perceptual experiences on the independently existing things we take them to be of. The thought of my fleeting perception as a *perception* of a continuously and independently existing thing implicitly contains the thought that if the thing had not been there, I should not even have *seemed* to perceive it. It really should be obvious that with the distinction between independently existing objects and perceptual awareness of objects we already have the general notion of causal dependence of the latter on the former, even if this is not a matter

[14] Ayer, *Central Questions*, 87–8.

to which we give much reflective attention in our pre-theoretical days.

Two things seem to have impeded recognition of this point. One is the fact that the correctness of the description of a perceptual experience as the perception of a certain physical thing *logically* requires the existence of that thing; and the *logical* is thought to exclude the *causal* connection, since only logically distinct existences can be causally related. This is not a serious difficulty. The situation has many parallels. Gibbon would not be the historian of the decline and fall of the Roman Empire unless there had occurred some actual sequence of events more or less corresponding to his narrative. But it is not enough, for him to merit that description, that such a sequence of events should have occurred and he should have written the sentences he did write. For him to qualify as the *historian* of these events, there must be a causal chain connecting them with the writing of the sentences. Similarly, the memory of an event's occurrence does not count as such unless it has its causal origin in that event. And the recently much canvassed 'causal theory of reference' merely calls attention to another instance of the causal link which obtains between thought and independently (and anteriorly) existing thing when the former is rightly said to have the latter as its object.

The second impediment is slightly more subtle. We are philosophically accustomed—it is a Humean legacy—to thinking of the simplest and most obvious kind of causal relation as holding between types of item such that items of both types are observable or experienceable and such that observation or experience of either term of the relation is distinct from observation or experience of the other: that is, the causally related items are not only distinct existences, but also the objects of distinct observations or experiences. We may then come to think of these conditions as constituting a requirement on all primitive belief in causal relations, a requirement which could be modified or abandoned only in the interests of theory. Since we obviously cannot distinguish the observation of a physical object from the experience of observing it—for they are the same thing—we shall then be led to conclude that the idea of the causal dependence of perceptual experience on the perceived object cannot be even an implicit part of our pretheoretical scheme, but must be at best an essentially theoretical addition to it.

But the difficulty is spurious. By directing our attention to causal relations between *objects* of perception, we have simply been led to overlook the special character of perception itself. Of course, the requirement holds for causal relations between distinct objects of perception; but not for the relation between perception and its object. When x is a physical object and y is a perception of x, then x is *observed* and y is *enjoyed*. And in taking the enjoyment of y to be a perception of x, we *are* implicitly taking it to be caused by x.

This concludes the second phase of my argument. I have tried to bring out some main features of the real realism of common sense and of the associated notion of perception. From the standpoint of common-sense realism we take ourselves to be immediately aware of real, enduring physical things in space, things endowed with visual and tactile properties; and we take it for granted that these enduring things are causally responsible for our interrupted perceptions of them. The immediacy which common sense attributes to perceptual awareness is in no way inconsistent either with the distinction between perceptual experience and thing perceived or with the causal dependence of the former on the latter or the existence of other causally necessary conditions of its occurrence. Neither is it inconsistent with the occurrence of perceptual mistake or illusion—a point, like so many others of importance, which is explicitly made by Kant. [15] Both Ayer and Mackie, explicitly or implicitly, acknowledge that the common-sense scheme includes this assumption of immediacy—Mackie in a passage I have quoted, Ayer in his description of the common-sense scheme. Unfortunately, Mackie's acknowledgement of the fact is belied by his describing common-sense realism as representative in character and Ayer's acknowledgement of it is put in doubt by his describing the common-sense scheme as having the status of a theory in relation to sensible experience.

III

It is one thing to describe the scheme of common sense; it is another to subject it to critical examination. This is the third and most difficult part of my task. The main question to be considered, as already indicated, is whether we are rationally bound to abandon, or radically to modify, the scheme in the light of scientific knowledge.

Before addressing ourselves directly to this question, it is worth stressing—indeed, it is essential to stress—the grip that common-

[15] Kant, 'The Refutation of Idealism', in *Critique of Pure Reason*, B274-9.

sense non-representative realism has on our ordinary thinking. It is a view of the world which so thoroughly permeates our conscious-ness that even those who are intellectually convinced of its falsity remain subject to its power. Mackie admits as much, saying that, even when we are trying to entertain a Lockian or scientific realism, 'our language and our natural ways of thinking keep pulling us back' to a more primitive view.[16] Consider the character of those ordinary concepts of objects on the employment of which our lives, our transactions with each other and the world, depend: our concepts of cabbages, roads, tweed coats, horses, the lips and hair of the beloved. In using these terms we certainly intend to be talking of independent existences and we certainly intend to be talking of immediately perceptible things, bearers of phenomenal (visuo-tactile) properties. If scientific or Lockian realism is correct, we cannot be doing both at once; it is confusion or illusion to suppose we can. If the things we talk of really have phenomenal properties, then they cannot, on this view, be physical things continuously existing in physical space. Nothing perceptible—I here drop the qualification 'immediately', for my use of it should now be clear—is a physically real, independent existence. No two persons can ever, in this sense, perceive the same item: nothing at all is publicly perceptible.

But how deep the confusion or the illusion must go! How radically it infects our concepts! Surely we mean by a cabbage a kind of thing of which most of the specimens we have encountered have a characteristic range of colours and visual shapes and felt textures; and not something unobservable, mentally represented by a complex of sensible experiences which it causes. The common consciousness is not to be fobbed off with the concession that, after all, the physical thing has—in a way—a shape. The way in which scientific realism concedes a shape is altogether the wrong way for the common consciousness. The lover who admires the curve of his mistress's lips or the lover of architecture who admires the lines of a building takes himself to be admiring features of those very objects themselves; but it is the visual shape, the visually defined shape, that he admires. Mackie suggests that there is a genuine *resemblance* between subjective representation and objective reality as far as shape is concerned;[17] but this suggestion is quite unaccept-able. It makes no sense to speak of a phenomenal property as

---

[16] Mackie, *Problems*, 68.
[17] Ibid., chs. 1 and 2, *passim*.

resembling a non-phenomenal, abstract property such as physical shape is conceived to be by scientific realism. The property of looking square or round can no more resemble the property, so conceived, of being physically square or round that the property of looking intelligent or looking ill can resemble the property of being intelligent or being ill. If it seems to make sense to speak of a resemblance between phenomenal properties and physical properties, so conceived, it is only because we give ourselves pictures— phenomenal pictures—of the latter. The resemblance is with the picture, not the pictured.

So, then, the common consciousness lives, or has the illusion of living, in a phenomenally propertied world of perceptible things in space. We might call it the lived world. It is also the public world, accessible to observation by all: the world in which one man, following another's pointing finger, can see the very thing that the other sees. (Even in our philosophical moments we habitually contrast the colours and visual shapes of things, as being publicly observable, with the subjective contents of consciousness, private to each of us, though not thereby unknowable to others.)

Such a reminder of the depth and reality of our habitual commitment to the common-sense scheme does not, by itself, amount to a demonstration of that scheme's immunity from philosophical criticism. The scientific realist, though no Kantian, may be ready, by way of making his maximum concession, with a reply modelled on Kant's combination of empirical realism with transcendental idealism. He may distinguish between the uncritical standpoint of ordinary living and the critical standpoint of philosophy informed by science. We are humanly, or naturally—he may say—constrained to 'see the world' in one way (that is, to think of it as we seem to perceive it) and rationally, or critically, constrained to think of it in quite another. The first way (being itself a causal product of physical reality) has a kind of validity at its own level; but it is, critically and rationally speaking, an inferior level. The second way really is a correction of the first.

The authentically Kantian combination is open to objection in many ways; but, by reason of its very extravagance, it escapes one specific form of difficulty to which the scientific realist's soberer variant remains exposed. Kant uncompromisingly declares that space is in us; that it is 'solely from the human standpoint that we can speak of space, of extended things etc.',[18] that things as they

---

[18] Kant, 'Refutation of Idealism', in *Critique*, B42.

are in themselves are not spatial at all. This will not do for the scientific realist. The phenomenally propertied items which we take ourselves to perceive and the apparent relations between which yield (or contribute vitally to yielding) our notion of space, are indeed declared to have no independent reality; but, when they are banished from the realm of the real, they are supposed to leave behind them—as occupants, so to speak, of the evacuated territory —those spatially related items which, though necessarily unobservable, nevertheless constitute the whole of physical reality. Ayer refers in several places to this consequence; and questions its coherence.[19] He writes, for example, 'I doubt whether the notion of a spatial system of which none of the elements can be observed is even intelligible.'

It is not clear that this difficulty is insuperable. The scientific realist will claim to be able to abstract the notion of a position in physical space from the phenomenal integuments with which it is originally and deceptively associated; and it is hard to think of a conclusive reason for denying him this power. He will say that the places where the phenomenally propertied things we seem to perceive seem to be are, often enough, places at which the correlated physically real items really are. Such a claim may make us uneasy; but it is not obvious nonsense.

Still, to say that a difficulty is not clearly insuperable is not to say that it is clearly not insuperable. It would be better to avoid it if we can. We cannot avoid it if we embrace unadulterated scientific realism and incidentally announce ourselves thereby as the sufferers from persistent illusion, however natural. We can avoid it, perhaps, if we can succeed in combining elements of the scientific story with our common-sense scheme without downgrading the latter. This is the course that Ayer recommends,[20] and, I suspect, the course that most of us semi-reflectively follow. The question is whether it is a consistent or coherent course. And at bottom this question is one of identity. Can we coherently identify the phenomenally propertied, immediately perceptible things which common sense supposes to occupy physical space with the configurations of unobservable ultimate particulars by which an unqualified scientific realism purports to replace them?

I approach the question indirectly, by considering once again Mackie's version of common-sense realism. According to this

---

[19] Ayer, *Central Questions*, 84, 86–7, 110.
[20] Ibid. 110–11.

version, it will be remembered, physical things, though not directly perceived, really possess visual and tactile qualities which resemble those we seem to perceive them as possessing; so that if, *per impossibile*, the veil of perception were drawn aside and we saw things in their true colours, these would turn out to be colours indeed and, on the whole, just the colours with which we were naïvely inclined to credit them. Mackie does not represent this view as absurd or incoherent. He just thinks that it is, as a matter of fact, false. Things *could* really be coloured; but, since there is no scientific reason for supposing they are, it is gratuitous to make any such supposition.

Mackie is surely too lenient to his version of common-sense realism. That version effects a complete logical divorce between a thing's being red and its being red-looking. Although it is a part of the theory that a thing which is, in itself, red has the power to cause us to seem to see a red thing, the logical divorce between these two properties is absolute. And, as far as I can see, that divorce really produces nonsense. The ascription of colours to things becomes not merely gratuitous, but senseless. Whatever may be the case with shape and position, colours are visibilia or they are nothing. I have already pointed out that this version of common-sense realism is not the real realism of common sense: *that* realism effects no logical divorce between being red and being red-looking; for it is a perceptually direct and not a perceptually representative realism. The things seen as coloured are the things themselves. There is no 'veil past which we cannot see'; for there is no veil.

But this does not mean that a thing which is red, that is, red-looking, has to look red all the time and in all circumstances and to all observers. There is an irreducible relativity, a relativity to what in the broadest sense may be called the perceptual point of view, built in to our ascriptions of particular visual properties to things. The mountains are red-looking at this distance in this light; blue-looking at that distance at that light; and, when we are clambering up them, perhaps neither. Such-and-such a surface looks pink and smooth from a distance; mottled and grainy when closely examined; different again, perhaps, under the microscope.

We absorb this relativity easily enough for ordinary purposes in our ordinary talk, tacitly taking some range of perceptual conditions, some perceptual point of view (in the broad sense) as standard or normal, and introducing an explicit acknowledgement of relativity only in cases which deviate from the standard. 'It looks purple in this light,' we say, 'but take it to the door and you will see that it's really green.' But sometimes we do something else. We shift the standard. Magnified, the fabric appears as printed with tiny blue and yellow dots. So those are the colours it really is. Does this ascription contradict 'it's really green'? No; for the standard has shifted. Looking at photographs, in journals of popular science, of patches of human skin, vastly magnified, we say, 'How fantastically uneven and ridgy it really is.' We study a sample of blood through a microscope and say, 'It's mostly colourless.' But skin can still be smooth and blood be red; for in another context we shift our standard back. Such shifts do not convict us of volatility or condemn us to internal conflict. The appearance of both volatility and conflict vanishes when we acknowledge the relativity of our 'reallys'.

My examples are banal. But perhaps they suggest a way of resolving the apparent conflict between scientific and common-sense realism. We can shift our point of view within the general framework of perception, whether aided or unaided by artificial means; and the different sensible-quality ascriptions we then make to the same object are not seen as conflicting once their relativity is recognized. Can we not see the adoption of the viewpoint of scientific realism as simply a more radical shift—a shift to a viewpoint from which no characteristics are to be ascribed to things except those which figure in the physical theories of science and in 'the explanation of what goes on in the physical world in the processes which lead to our having the sensations and perceptions that we have'?[21] We can say that this is how things really are so long as the relativity of this 'really' is recognized as well; and, when it is recognized, the scientific account will no more conflict with the ascription to things of visual and tactile qualities than the assertion that blood is really a mainly colourless fluid conflicts with the assertion that it is bright red in colour. Of course, the scientific point of view is not, in one sense, a point of *view* at all. It is an intellectual, not a perceptual, standpoint. We could not occupy it at all, did we not first occupy the other. But we can perfectly well occupy both at once, so long as we realize what we are doing.

This method of reconciling scientific and common-sense realism requires us to recognize a certain relativity in our conception of the real properties of physical objects. Relative to the human perceptual standpoint the grosser physical objects are visuo-tactile

---

[21] Mackie, *Problems*, 18.

continuants (and within that standpoint the phenomenal properties they possess are relative to particular perceptual viewpoints, taken as standard). Relative to the scientific standpoint, they have no properties but those which figure in the physical theories of science. Such a relativistic conception will not please the absolute-minded. Ayer recommends a different procedure. He suggests that we should conceive of perceptible objects (that is, objects perceptible in the sense of the common-sense scheme) as being literally composed of the ultimate particles of physical theory, the latter being imperceptible, not in principle, but only empirically, as a consequence of their being so minute.[22] I doubt, however, whether this proposal, which Ayer rightly describes as an attempt to *blend* the two schemes, can be regarded as satisfactory. If the impossibility of perceiving the ultimate components is to be viewed as merely empirical, we can sensibly ask what the conceptual consequences would be of supposing that impossibility not to exist. The answer is clear. Even if there were something which we counted as perceiving the ultimate particles, this would still not, from the point of view of scientific realism, count as perceiving them as they really are. And nothing could so count; for no phenomenal properties we seemed to perceive them as having would figure in the physical explanation of the causal mechanisms of our success. But, so long as we stay at this point of view, what goes for the parts goes for any wholes they compose. However gross those wholes, they remain, from this point of view, imperceptible in the sense of common sense.

Ayer attempts to form one viewpoint out of two discrepant viewpoints: to form a single, unified description of physical reality by blending features of two discrepant descriptions, each valid from its own viewpoint. He can seem to succeed only by doing violence to one of the two viewpoints, the scientific. I acknowledge the discrepancy of the two descriptions, but claim that, once we recognize the relativity in our conception of the real, they need not be seen as in contradiction with each other. Those very things which from one standpoint we conceive as phenomenally propertied we conceive from another as constituted in a way which can only be described in what are, from the phenomenal point of view, abstract terms. 'This smooth, green, leather table-top', we say, 'is, considered scientifically, nothing but a congeries of electric charges widely separated and in rapid motion.' Thus we combine the two standpoints in a single sentence. The standpoint of

22 Ayer, *Central Questions*, 110.

common-sense realism, not explicitly signalled as such, is reflected in the sentence's grammatical subject phrase, of which the words are employed in no esoteric sense. The standpoint of physical science, explicitly signalled as such, is reflected in the predicate. Once relativity of description to standpoint is recognized, the sentence is seen to contain no contradiction; and, if it contains no contradiction, the problem of identification is solved.

I recognize that this position is unlikely to satisfy the determined scientific realist. If he is only moderately determined, he may be partially satisfied, and may content himself with saying that the scientific viewpoint is *superior* to that of common sense. He will then simply be expressing a preference, which he will not expect the artist, for example, to share. But, if he is a hard-liner, he will insist that the common-sense view is wholly undermined by science; that it is shown to be false; that the visual and tactile properties we ascribe to things are nowhere but in our minds; that we do not live in a world of perceptible objects, as understood by common sense, at all. He must then accept the consequence that each of us is a sufferer from a persistent and inescapable illusion and that it is fortunate that this is so, since, if it were not, we should be unable to pursue the scientific enterprise itself. Without the illusion of perceiving objects as bearers of sensible qualities, we should not have the illusion of perceiving them as space-occupiers at all; and without that we should have no concept of space and no power to pursue our researches into the nature of its occupants. Science is not only the offspring of common sense; it remains its dependant. For this reason, and for others touched on earlier, the scientific realist must, however ruefully, admit that the ascription to objects of sensible qualities, the standard of correctness of such ascription being (what we take to be) intersubjective agreement, is something quite securely rooted in our conceptual scheme. If this means, as he must maintain it does, that our thought is condemned to incoherence, then we can only conclude that incoherence is something we can perfectly well live with and could not perfectly well live without.

THE EXISTENCE OF MENTAL OBJECTS

F. JACKSON

I

The mental objects I will be concerned with in this paper are such things as pains, itches, and throbs—that is, the bodily sensations; and such things as after-images and mirages—that is, the visual hallucinations. There is a very widespread view that, while there may be things like the *having* of bodily sensations and the *experiencing* of after-images, there are, strictly speaking, no such things as bodily sensations and after-images. What exists includes the experiencing of pains and after-images, but not the pains and after-images themselves.

I will argue that there are considerable problems facing this denial of mental objects, and to this extent support the view that there are mental objects and the associated act–object account of having sensations and after-images. (The view that sensations and images exist, is just that. It is not that they exist *independently* of sentient creatures. It is an open question whether everything (that exists) exists independently, one to be settled by looking at cases—including ours of sensations and images.)

II

We talk as if there were mental objects: '*There is* a pain in my foot', '*This* after-image is brighter than *that* one', and so on.

This settles nothing as it stands. We once talked as if there were demons, and we now often talk about the average family or the next waltz; yet there are no demons, average families, or waltzes. These three examples illustrate three ways to show that there are no *A*s. We were wrong about demons, because certain statements we took to be true turned out false (epilepsy is *not* caused by demons).

Reprinted from *American Philosophical Quarterly*, 13 (1976), 23–40, by permission of the Editor.

There is no average family because statements that appear to be about this family can be given a reductive style of analysis in terms of the many non-average families that there are. The case with waltzes is different. No doubt, 'The waltz is about to start' can be given a reductive analysis in which 'waltz' does not appear. But it is sufficient to observe that 'The waltz is about to start' can be construed as 'People are about to start waltzing.' We don't need a full-scale analysis of waltzing, we only need to know enough about the meaning of 'waltz' to know that statements putatively about waltzes can be, and are best, recast as about people waltzing.

Likewise, there are three ways we might seek to show that there are no mental objects: by showing that all statements of the form '*S* has a pain (itch, after-image, etc.)' are false; by producing a reductive analysis of such statements, for example, of a behaviourist or topic-neutral kind, which eliminates the relevant psychological terms; or, finally, by offering a partial analysis (a recasting which better displays logical form) of these psychological statements, and which, while not eliminating all mentalist vocabulary, shows that these statements are not really about mental objects.

Of the first strategy, I will just say that I am sure it is mistaken, but do not know how to prove that it is. For I do not know of any premisses which are more obvious than that it is sometimes true that we are in pain, having a red after-image, and so on, from which a proof might be constructed. The second strategy has been much discussed in connection with the translation versions of materialism advanced by J. J. C. Smart and D. M. Armstrong. I don't find the analysis they give of psychological statements plausible for reasons that are familiar and which will be taken as read.

I will concentrate on the third strategy in this paper. I am sure the popularity of the denial of mental objects is due to the belief that it can be sustained by a relatively simple recasting of visual image and sensation statements without recourse to either a wholesale rejection of their truth or a full-scale, reductive analysis.

III

With one exception, our discussion of the third strategy applies equally to bodily sensations and visual images. The exception arises from Bruce Aune's suggestion that sensations can be regarded as relations between persons and their bodies. His ground for this is that ' "I have a pain *in my arm*" . . . may be rephrased as, "My arm pains me" or 'My arm hurts".'[1] But it is impossible for a relation to hold in the absence of its relata. Hence, if sensation statements essentially related persons to parts of their body, they could not be true in the absence of appropriate parts of the body. But the phantom limb phenomenon shows that they can be; and a statement that I have a pain 'in a phantom limb' cannot be regarded by Aune as relating me to my phantom limb, because either phantom limbs don't exist or else they are a species of mental object (part of the 'body-image'). Moreover, even if—as has sometimes been maintained—a pain in my phantom limb is really in my stump, the statement cannot be rephrased as 'My stump pains me', because this is the translation of a quite different statement according to the view in question, namely 'I have a pain in my stump.'

VI

I now turn to examples of strategy three which are equally applicable to sensations and images. I will start by talking in terms of the sensation case and switch later, for variety, to the image case.

The following passage from Thomas Nagel's paper, 'Physicalism', makes a convenient starting-point:

we may regard the ascription of properties to a sensation simply as part of the specification of a psychological state's being ascribed to the person. When we assert that a person has a sensation of a certain description B, this is not to be taken as asserting that there exist an x and a y such that x is a person and y is a sensation and $B(y)$ and x has y. Rather we are to take it as asserting the existence of only one thing, x, such that x is a person, and moreover $C(x)$, where C is the attribute 'has a sensation of description B.'[2]

Nagel's general idea is to switch from predicates on or descriptions of sensations, to predicates on or descriptions of persons: strictly, nothing is painful, but many things are persons with painful sensations, But how does the switch he recommends dispose of sensations?

Every description of my brother can be transposed to a description of me without meaning loss: 'My brother is tall', for instance, goes to 'I have a tall brother.' But the possibility of switching from 'is tall' as a predicate on my brother to 'has a tall brother' as a

---

[1] *Knowledge, Mind and Nature* (New York, 1967), 130.
[2] *The Philosophical Review*, 74 (1965), 342.

predicate on me is irrelevant to the question of my brother's existence. What matters is how we ought to understand the predicate 'has a tall brother'; the answer in this case being that it is to be understood as formed from a relation by filling an argument place with a singular term. Likewise, what is crucial for whether sensations exist, is not just that a statement like 'My pain is severe' can be rendered as 'I have a severe pain'; but whether or not it can be so rendered with the predicate 'has a severe pain' understood other than as containing 'a pain' functioning as a singular term filling an argument place in the relation 'x has y'.

V

Can we, then, view the semantic structure of 'has a painful sensation' and the like so as not to commit ourselves to there being painful sensations?

The simplest such view would be the view which sees nothing; the view, that is, that sensation predicates on persons have no semantic structure at all; they have meaning only as wholes; a view we might express by writing 'has-a-painful-sensation' or 'hasapainfulsensation'.

This is holism gone mad. It is perfectly obvious, for example, that the meanings of 'has a burning pain' and 'has a burning itch' are related, and that this relation is a function of the common term 'burning': if they did not have this term in common, the relation would not be the same. But to concede that the appearance of 'burning' in *both* is semantically significant is to concede that its appearance in *either* is, which is to concede that the predicates are semantically structured.

Given the unacceptability of this no-structure theory, what theories are open to one who denies that there are mental objects? Just two seem to have either currency or plausibility: the first I will call the state theory, the second the adverbial theory.

VI

Those who deny that there are mental objects commonly make considerable use of terms like 'state' and 'condition'. For instance, Nagel urges that to say that a person has a pain 'describes a *condition* of one entity, the person', and again 'we may regard the ascription of properties to a sensation simply as part of the specification of a psychological *state's* being ascribed to the person.'[3]

This suggests a state theory of the following kind. 'I have a throbbing, painful sensation in my knee' does not relate me to my sensation, saying of it that it is throbbing, painful, and in my knee. rather it is about me and a state (or condition) of mine: it says that I am in a throbbing, painful, in my knee sensation-state. The sensing, not the sensation has the properties.

Does this really achieve anything? On the act–object theory, 'I have a painful sensation' is explicated as '($\exists x$) [I have x & x is painful & x is a sensation]', while on the state theory we get '($\exists x$)[I am in x & x is a sensation state & x is painful].' The gain appears to be verbal rather than ontological.

The state theorist has some sort of reply if he distinguishes *unitary* states from *relational* states. A unitary state of a person is a state of that person not essentially involving anything over and above that person. My being happy, to take a psychological example, and my being warm, to take a physical example, are both unitary states of mine. There is a natural, if philosophically difficult, sense in which my being happy or being warm at some time are not things over and above and distinct from me at that time. This is essentially linked to the connection between the counting principles for persons and their unitary states: for a given person at a time, there cannot be more than one unitary state of a given kind. For instance, there cannot be more cases of persons being warm (happy) in a room than there are persons. If this were not so, if there might be two unitary states of a given kind for one person at one time, there would be no sense to the claim that such states were, in some substantial sense, nothing over and above the one subject in these states. Therefore, if the state theorist insists that the sensation states—the sensings—are unitary, rather than relational states like being happy *at* or being warmed *by*, it appears he has a theory distinct from the act–object theory.

He also has a theory exposed to two serious objections. I will call the first, the many property objection, and the second, the complement objection.

VII

The many property objection arises from the fact that we ascribe many things to our sensations: a sensation may be painful *and* burning *and* in the foot. How can a state theorist handle this?

---

[3] Ibid. 342. My emphasis.

The state theorist transcribes 'I have an F sensation' as 'I am in an F sensation-state.' Hence, the obvious account for him to give of 'I have a sensation which is F and G' is 'I am in a sensation-state which is F and G.'

This account faces a decisive difficulty. Suppose I have a sensation which is F and a sensation which is G, then, on the state theory, I am in a sensation-state which is F and in one which is G. But there may at a given time be only one such unitary state for a given person; therefore, I am in a sensation-state which is F and G. But the latter is the preferred account of 'I have a sensation which is F and G.' Hence, we have 'I have a sensation which is F and a sensation which is G' entailing 'I have a sensation which is F and G', which is quite wrong. For I may have one sensation which is F and, at the same time, another which is G. That is, having, for example, a burning, painful sensation is being conflated with having a burning sensation and a painful sensation.

The state theorist must, therefore, give a different account of statements that a particular sensation is F and G and . . . It turns out that the various possibilities are essentially the same as those that arise in the discussion of the corresponding objection to the adverbial theory, so I will postpone the matter until then.

VIII

The complement objection to the state theory is a special case of a general way of showing that some term does not qualify a given thing, the way which proceeds by showing that if the term did, so might its complement.

The view that truth is a property of sentence *types* may be refuted by noting that 'is true' and its complement 'is not true' may apply to one and the same sentence type depending on the meanings given to the constituent terms of that type. A second example is the view that 'school-age' in 'I have a school-age child' qualifies having a child rather than the child; that is, that being of school-age is, strictly, a property of having children rather than of children. But 'I have a school-age child' and 'I have a non-school-age child' are both true. And nothing, including the having of children, can be both F and non-F, hence it is the children which are or are not of school-age.

Likewise, it may be the case that 'I have a painful sensation' and 'I have a non-painful sensation' are both true at the one time, hence we cannot construe being painful or not as a characteristic of the having of the pain rather than the pain. For if we did, we would have a state being both F and non-F. As with the first objection, the possible replies are essentially the same as those to the corresponding objection to the adverbial theory, and will thus be discussed then.

(A digression: the possibility of having different kinds of sensations at the one time also seems to me to undermine Descartes's suggestion that we view sensations on the model of impressions in wax: 'I allow only so much difference between the soul and its ideas as there is between a piece of wax and the various shapes it can assume.'[4] But it is impossible for one thing to be two different shapes at the same time; hence the analogy fails at a crucial point.)

IX

The most widely canvassed theory which denies that there are mental objects is the so-called adverbial theory.[5] Our discussion will be couched principally in terms of visual images (after-images, for example) rather than bodily sensations.

This theory utilizes the fact that after-images, sensations, and the like, cannot exist when not sensed by some person (sentient creature), in order to reconstrue statements which purport to be about sensations, after-images, and so on, as being about the way or mode in which some person is sensing. Thus, 'I have a red after-image' becomes 'I sense red-ly', and 'I have a pain' becomes 'I sense painfully.' A parallel is often drawn with the elimination of talk about smiles in favour of talk about the manner of smiling ; as in the recasting of 'Mary wore a seductive smile' as 'Mary smiled seductively.'

My two objections parallel the two brought against the state theory.

X

Our statements about visual images are not just to the effect that an image is red, or square, or whatever; they are also to the effect that

---

[4] *Descartes: Philosophical Writings*, tr. Elizabeth Anscombe and P. T. Geach (London, 1954), 288.
[5] Advanced in e.g. C. J. Ducasse, *Nature, Mind, and Death* (Illinois, 1951); R. M. Chisholm, *Perceiving* (Ithaca, 1957); Aune, *Knowledge, Mind, and Nature.*

an image is red *and* square *and* . . . As with the state theory, I will refer to this as the many property problem.

Adverbial theorists have been rather reticent about how they handle this problem. It is clear that their view is that to have an image which is *F*, is to sense *F*-ly—the attribute, *F*, goes to the mode or manner, *F*-ly. But it is not clear just what account would be offered of having an image which is *F* and *G*. Do both of the (in their view, apparent) attributes go to separate modes, so that to have an image which is *F* and *G* is analysed as sensing *F*-ly and *G*-ly; or do we have a new, compound mode, *F-G*-ly? It seems to me that both of these answers, and the variants on them, face substantial difficulties.

Suppose having an *F*, *G* image is analysed as sensing *F*-ly and *G*-ly.[6] This conjunctive style of answer has the advantage of explaining the entailment from 'I have a red, square image' to 'I have a red image'; for it will correspond to the entailment from 'I sense red-ly and square-ly' to 'I sense red-ly.'

But if it is adopted, it will be impossible for the adverbial theorist to distinguish the two very different states of affairs of having a red, square after-image at the same time as having a green, round one, from that of having a green, square after-image at the same time as having a red, round one; because both will have to be accounted the same, namely, as sensing red-ly and round-ly and square-ly and green-ly. In essence, the point is that we must be able to distinguish the statements: 'I have an *F* and a *G* image', and 'I have an *F*, *G* image.'

In discussion it has been suggested to me that the adverbial theorist might have recourse to the point that when I have a red, square after-image at the same time as a green, round one, they must (as we say) be in different places in my visual field: the red one will be, for instance, to the left of the green one. But how can this help the adverbial theorist? For 'I have a red after-image to the left of a green one' raises the same problem; namely, that it cannot be analysed conjunctively as 'I sense red-ly and to-the-left-ly and green-ly'; for that is equivalent to 'I sense green-ly and to-the-left-ly and red-ly' which would be the analysis of 'I have a green after-image to the left of a red one.'

Perhaps the thought is that 'red' and 'square' when applied to images are *incomplete*, they demand supplementation with a term indicating location in a visual field. But this can't be right. I can

[6] This is the obvious reading of Ducasse, *Nature, Mind, and Death*, ch. 13, §22.

know perfectly well what saying someone has a red or a square after-image means without having any idea at all of its location. Moreover, it is evidently not possible to give an exhaustive list, p_1, ..., p_n of all the parts of a person's visual field that might be occupied by one of his after-images. So that 'I have a red after-image' cannot be analysed as 'I sense red-p_1-ly or . . . or red-p_n-ly.' *The best that can be done is '($\exists x$) [x is a part of my visual field and I sense red-x-ly]'*, which—leaving aside the question of interpreting quantification into adverbial modification—commits the adverbial theorist to the existence of a species of mental object, namely, parts of visual fields, and so undermines the whole rationale behind his theory.

XI

An alternative approach would be to translate 'I have an *F, G* image' as 'I sense *F*-ly *G*-ly', and model the latter on 'He wrote astonishingly slowly': '*F*-ly' being taken to modify '*G*-ly' rather than 'sense', just as 'astonishingly' modifies 'slowly' rather than 'spoke' in the model.

But the two essential features of 'He wrote astonishingly slowly' are, first, that it is evidently not equivalent to 'He wrote slowly astonishingly', and, second, that it does not entail 'He wrote astonishingly': it is these two features which lead us to distinguish it sharply from 'He wrote astonishingly and slowly.'

The adverbial theorist, however, cannot attribute either feature to his translations. He must allow that 'I sense red-ly square-ly' is equivalent to 'I sense square-ly red-ly', for they are, respectively, his translations of the evidently equivalent 'I have a red, square image' and 'I have a square, red image.' He must also allow that 'I sense red-ly square-ly' entails 'I sense red-ly', for 'I have a red, square image' entails 'I have a red image.' Having a red, square image is a special case of having a red image, while writing astonishingly slowly is not a special case of writing astonishingly (just as writing very quickly is not a special case of writing very).

XII

When talking of having a red, triangular sense-impression, Wilfrid Sellars talks of sensing red-triangular-ly.[7] The hyphenation suggests

---

[7] In e.g. *Science and Metaphysics* (London, 1968). Sellars ties his view to a topic-neutral analysis of the kind I have said (without arguing) is implausible.

an interpretation according to which red-triangular-ly is not a mode of sensing having red-ly as a component; it is, rather, a quite new mode of sensing; and so, the meaning of 'red-triangular-ly' is not to be viewed as being built out of independently semantically significant components like 'red' and 'triangular'; and likewise for 'green-square-ly', etc.[8]

Put thus, this view obviously faces the difficulty just considered. Having a red, triangular after-image is a special case of having a red after-image, hence any adverbial theorist must treat sensing red-triangular-ly as a special case of sensing red-ly. But sensing red-triangular-ly fails to have sensing red-ly as even a component on this view.

It might, however, be refined. In discussions of the step from 'This is a horse's head' to 'This is a head', it is sometimes suggested that the latter should be read as 'This is a head of something.' In similar vein, it might be suggested that 'I have a red image' should be expanded to 'I have a red image of some shape', and consequently its adverbial translation should be expanded to 'I sense red-some-shape-ly.' On this view, red-ly is not a mode of sensing at all. The modes of sensing are red-triangular-ly, green-round-ly, and so on; and sensing red-ly is to be understood as sensing red-squarely or red-round-ly or red- . . . -ly.

There are two serious difficulties facing this suggestion (apart from that of giving a precise construal of the dots). The first is that the modification appears to undermine the adverbial theorist's claim to be offering a philosophically perspicuous account of after-images. When I have a red, square after-image, the redness and the squareness appear as discriminable elements in my experience; and hence elements that it is desirable to have reflected in distinct elements of any offered analysis. But, on the modification in question, having a red, square after-image is accounted as sensing red-square-ly, where the hyphenation indicates that this mode of sensing is not to be further broken up into distinct elements. Indeed, on this view, someone who remarks on the common feature in having a red, square after-image and having a red, round after-image is making a plain mistake. But, far from being a plain mistake, the remark looks like an evident truth.

The second objection derives from the point that there are indefinitely many things that may be said about one's images. An

---

[8] Such a view is explicitly advanced by George Pitcher, 'Minds and Ideas in Berkeley', *American Philosophical Quarterly*, 6 (1969), 198–207.

after-image may be red, red and square, red and square and fuzzy at the edges, red and square and fuzzy at the edges and to the left of a blue after-image, and so on. Now consider how the adverbial theory should handle 'I have a red, square, fuzzy after-image.' It cannot analyse this as 'I sense red-square-ly and fuzzy-ly', for the same reason the conjunctive account had to be rejected. In brief, such a treatment would conflate 'I have a red, square, fuzzy after-image' with 'I have a red, square after-image and a fuzzy after-image.' Should the theory then abandon the view that red-square-ly is a fundamental mode of sensing, and adopt the view that red-square-fuzzy-ly is a fundamental mode of sensing? On this further modification, 'I have a red, square fuzzy after-image' would go to 'I sense red-square-fuzzy-ly'; and 'I have a red, square after-image' would be analysed as, roughly, 'I sense red-square-fuzzy-ly or I sense red-square-sharp-ly.' Thus, on this further modification, red-square-ly, green-round-ly, and so on, are no longer modes of sensing; rather red-square-fuzzy-ly, green-round-sharp-ly, and so on, will be the various ways of sensing.

However, in view of the point this objection started with, this process of modification will continue without end. For any n that the adverbial theorist offers an analysis of 'I have an $F_1, \ldots, F_n$ after-image' as 'I sense F_1- $\ldots$ -F_n-ly', he can be challenged for his analysis of 'I have an $F_1, \ldots, F_{n+1}$ after-image'; and so, for the reasons above, be forced to abandon F_1- $\ldots$ -F_n-ly in favour of F_1-$\ldots$ -F_n-F_{n+1}-ly as a basic mode of sensing. This means that the adverbial theorist cannot ever give even a single example of a basic mode of sensing, and thus cannot ever complete even one of his adverbial analyses; and even if he could, would, moreover, end up with a theory no better than the no-structure one rejected earlier.

I suspect that some adverbial theorists who have written down expressions like 'red-square-ly', have meant by the hyphenation no more than that mode of sensing associated with what we normally, and in their view misleadingly, call having a red, square after-image. But this is not to give us a theory we can oppose to the act–object theory, it is merely to express the hope that such a theory may be forthcoming. It is not to argue or show that we can do without mental objects, it is just to say that we can; for the central question of how to interpret the hyphenation is left unanswered except for a reference to the very theory being denied.

XIII

My second objection to the adverbial theory is the complement objection transferred from the state theory to the adverbial. Just as it is not possible for something to be F and non-F at the same time, it is not possible for a person at a given time to V both F-ly and non-F-ly. I can sing badly easily enough, but I cannot sing both well and badly at the same time; I can run quickly, but not both quickly and slowly; and I can inspect carefully, but not both carefully and carelessly; and so on and so forth.

Therefore, to have an image which is F cannot be to sense F-ly; for it is manifestly possible to have an image which is F at the same time as one which is non-F: I may have a red and a green after-image at the same time, or a square and a round one at the same time; while it is not possible to sense F-ly and non-F-ly at the same time.

The only reply which appears to have any real plausibility here is to urge that, though one cannot V both F-ly and non-F-ly at a given time, one can V F-ly with respect to A and V non-F-ly with respect to B: I can, during a concerto, listen happily to the strings and unhappily to the piano. And that when I have a red and non-red after-image together, I am sensing red-ly with respect to one thing and non-red-ly with respect to another. But what are these things with respect to which I am sensing, for there need, of course, be no appropriate physical thing in the offing? It is hard to see what they could be other than the mental objects of the act–object theory.

XIV

Two matters in conclusion.

1. Terence Parsons claims that

> (1) John wrote painstakingly and illegibly.
>
> and
>
> (2) John wrote painstakingly and John wrote illegibly.

are not equivalent because—though (1) entails (2)—(2) does not entail (1). He gives two cases which he claims show (2) may be true when (1) is false:

if there were two separate past occasions on which John wrote, on one of which he wrote painstakingly, and on the other of which he wrote illegibly, but no past occasion on which he did both at once . . . Also if on one and the same occasion he wrote painstakingly with one hand and illegibly with the other.[9]

This might appear to threaten my arguments in two ways. First, in my discussion of the conjunctive reply in Section X I was clearly working under the general assumption that there is no significant distinction between a statement like (1) and the corresponding statement like (2). Second, Parson's second case where (2) may be true while (1) is false, could easily be modified to threaten the principle that one cannot V F-ly and non-F-ly at the same time, and so my discussion of complementation *vis-à-vis* the adverbial theory. The modification would be to consider a case where John wrote illegibly with his left hand while writing legibly with his right; would he then be writing legibly and illegibly at the same time?

The threat, however, is more apparent than real. This is obvious in the first case Parsons gives, because it involves considering *different* times of writing; and our discussion of the conjunctive reply involved just *one* time—we noted the possibility of having different visual images at the *same* time. In short, it is sufficient for us if 'John is writing painstakingly and illegibly' is equivalent to 'John is writing painstakingly and John is writing illegibly', and the first case does not threaten this equivalence.

With the second case we must remember that we are dealing with something that can be judged both overall and in a particular aspect. Normally, when we say that Jones wrote illegibly, we mean that overall the writing was illegible, not that every word was illegible (likewise, a speech may be impressive without every part of it being impressive). In this sense, 'Jones wrote illegibly with one hand (his left, say)', does not entail that Jones wrote illegibly, for most of the writing may have been with his right hand in elegant copperplate; and similarly for 'painstakingly'. And in this sense Parsons will be right that it is possible that Jones wrote painstakingly with one hand and illegibly with the other without (1) being true, but equally this is possible without (2) being true, so the case fails to establish that (2) may be true without (1) being true.

On the other hand, if we take 'Jones wrote illegibly' to count as true if any part or aspect of Jones's writing was illegible, and likewise for 'painstakingly'; then if Jones wrote painstakingly with one

[9] 'Some Problems Concerning the Logic of Grammatical Modifiers', *Synthese*, 21 (1970), 131.

hand and illegibly with the other, (2) must be true, but so will (1); and so there is still no case for denying that (2) entails (1).

Parallel remarks apply to the possibility of writing illegibly and legibly. It is not, in the overall sense, possible to write, on a given occasion, both legibly and illegibly (though it is possible to write in a manner which deserves neither epithet). It is possible that one aspect of one's writing be legible and *another* be illegible. But we noted in Section XIII that the possibility of *V-ing F*-ly with respect to *A* while *V*-ing non-*F*-ly with respect to *B* is of no use to the adverbial theory; for the only plausible candidates for *A* and *B* in the sensing case are mental objects.

In general, whether or not one agrees with my discussion of (1) and (2), there is little comfort for the adverbial theorist in Parsons's remarks. The case for distinguishing (1) and (2) rests heavily on there being something *more* involved than just the person (John's hand as well as John); and the adverbial theorist's aim is to effect an ontic reduction to the person alone in his account of sensing.

2. The second matter concerns the 'predicate modifier' formal semantics for adverbs given by Parsons. By contrast with Davidson's event-predicate treatment,[10] these semantics view adverbs as functions on predicates; and it might be thought that they could be appealed to by the adverbial theorist to elucidate 'green-triangular-ly' and so on in a way which acknowledged structure without facing the problems of the conjunctive treatment.

The 'predicate-modifier' theorist must, however, see a certain *intensionality* in *all* adverbs. '*X* senses' and '*x* breathes' are (we may suppose) co-extensional. But John doesn't breathe slowly if and only if he senses slowly, and the adverbial theorist won't allow that he breathes red-ly when he senses red-ly. Without going into the details,[11] this means that possible worlds (and beings) other than the actual must be invoked in predicate-modifier semantics. Hence, they achieve nothing for the adverbial theory. Perhaps (perhaps) we need possibilia for the elucidation of modal statements, but 'I have a pain' and 'I have a red image' are statements about the actual world, if any are. Moreover, appeal to possibilia would make a mockery of any claim of the adverbial theory to greater ontological economy than the act–object theory.

[10] In 'The Logical Form of Action Sentences', *Logic of Action and Preference*, ed. Nicholas Rescher (Pittsburgh, 1967). Adoption of this treatment would make the adverbial and state theories virtually indistinguishable.

[11] But see David Lewis, 'General Semantics', *Synthese*, 22 (1970), esp. p. 28.

PERCEPTION AND BELIEF

D. M. ARMSTRONG

I. PERCEPTION AS ACQUIRING OF BELIEF

It is clear that the biological function of perception is to give the organism information about the current state of its own body and its physical environment, information that will assist the organism in the conduct of life. This is a most important clue to the *nature* of perception. It leads us to the view that perception is nothing but the acquiring of true or false beliefs concerning the current state of the organism's body and environment. 'True belief', here, is meant to cover both knowledge and *mere* true belief. Veridical perception is the acquiring of true beliefs, sensory illusion the acquiring of false beliefs.

The beliefs involved must be conceived of as sub-verbal beliefs. Animals can perceive, sometimes, we believe, better than we can, but they lack words entirely. And we ourselves are often hard put to translate our perceptions into words. If we think of the wealth and subtlety of the information that we gain by our eyes, to take one example only, we see that much of it eludes the relatively coarse mesh of the net of language.

The word 'belief' is a stumbling-block. To talk of beliefs may seem to be to talk in a very sophisticated and self-conscious way, quite unsuited to such an unsophisticated thing as perception. Do animals have beliefs? It may seem a strange way to talk about them. But the difficulty is to find another word. 'Judgement' is even worse than 'belief'. A word like 'awareness' would be nearer the mark in some ways, but it has the most serious disadvantage that it is linguistically improper to speak of false awareness. Yet any theory of perception must cover both veridical perception and sensory illusion. Perhaps one could say that perception is a

Reprinted by permission of Humanities Press International, Inc., Atlantic Highlands, NJ, and Routledge & Kegan Paul, Ltd., from *A Materialist Theory of the Mind* (1968).

continuous 'mapping' of what is going on in our body or our environment, for mapping can be correct or incorrect. It is certainly useful to think of our sensory field at any one time as a partial and sometimes faulty map of our body and its environment. But to talk of mapping may be to err in an opposite way to talking of believing. It suggests that it is just a matter of our body and our environment registering upon, or making an impression upon, our minds. A map, after all, is just a physical object which we have to *use* to tell us where things are. But perceptions are not like that. If they are maps, they are maps that essentially refer beyond themselves to the objects they claim to map. Unlike ordinary maps, perceptions have intentionality.

One useful alternative to the word 'belief' is the word 'information'. It has in fact already been employed in this section, and will be employed again in future. It has the advantage that we can then speak of sensory illusion as 'misinformation'. However, the word does have one misleading association. It is often natural to think of information or misinformation as something distinct from the true or false beliefs one acquires as a result of the information or misinformation. Spoken or written words are often naturally spoken of as information, and they are distinct from the beliefs which the words create in hearer or reader. But when perception is spoken of in this work as the acquiring of information, it must be clearly understood that no distinction at all is intended between the information and the beliefs to which it gives rise. Information and beliefs are identical. Given this warning, the term 'information' will often be convenient.

If perception is the acquiring of beliefs or information then clearly it must involve the possession of concepts. For to believe that A is B entails possessing the concepts of A and B. But since perception can occur in the total absence of the ability to speak, we are committed to the view that there can be concepts that involve no linguistic ability.

I have spoken of perception as the acquiring of true or false beliefs about the *current* state of our body and environment. It may be objected that it is possible to see, in the literal sense of 'see', that somebody came in with muddy boots last night. However, such a case can always be regarded as a case of inference, even if quite unselfconscious inference, an inference based upon perception of some current state of the environment (the bootmarks). I acquire the belief that there is a certain muddy pattern of marks on the floor now, and this causes me to acquire the further belief that somebody came in with muddy boots last night. It is significant that in such cases we speak only of seeing *that*. It would be improper to say we saw the person or the muddy boots.

If perceptions are acquirings of beliefs, then the correspondence or failure of correspondence of perceptions to physical reality is simply the correspondence or failure of correspondence of beliefs to the facts. And the intentionality of perception reduces to the intentionality of the beliefs acquired.

II. THE ROLE OF THE SENSE-ORGANS

It is tempting to include a reference to the sense-organs: the eyes, ears, nose, etc., in the logical analysis of perception. That is to say, it is tempting to say that seeing is the acquiring of true or false beliefs as the causal result of the operation of the eyes, hearing is the acquiring of true or false beliefs as the causal result of the operation of the ears, and so on.

But the suggestion involves a number of difficulties. In the first place, it is difficult to say what is the organ of *touch*. Most of the body is tactually sensitive. Perhaps this difficulty can be met by saying that touch does not involve a special organ but rather a special procedure: objects coming into contact with the flesh. This procedure causes certain sorts of beliefs to be acquired, and we call such acquirings of beliefs tactual perceptions.

In the second place, there is one form of perception where it does not seem possible to specify even such a procedure for acquiring beliefs. This is bodily perception. Where I perceive the motion or position of my limbs and body, or the heating up or cooling down of parts or the whole of my body, there is no process, and still less no organ, that I can point to from my ordinary knowledge as causally responsible for such perceptions. Of course, there are in fact mechanisms in the body which are involved in bodily perception, but only physiologists know anything about them. There is nothing we ordinarily say we perceive the motion of our limbs with.

In the third place, it is possible to have experiences resembling ordinary perceptions which do not involve stimulation of sense-organs, known or unknown. If the central nervous system is acted upon in various ways (for instance, by continuous drinking or by a probe being stuck in certain brain-areas), the subject may have visual or other sorts of hallucination without any stimulation of the sense-organs.

In the fourth place, even if we waive all these objections, it is imaginable that we should have much the same perceptual experiences that we have now, even although we could discover nothing that we could identify as sense-organs. Again, we can imagine that stimulation of particular sense-organs might produce quite different perceptual experiences from those that are actually produced. Stimulation of the ears, for instance, might lead to what we now call visual experiences.

But even when all these points have been admitted, it still remains true that the sense-organs play a part in our concept of perception, or, perhaps it would be better to say, in our 'picture' of perception. Quite early in life we learn that the acquiring of certain very complex and idiosyncratic patterns of information about the current state of the world is bound up with the operation of certain organs or combination of organs. In a loose sense of the word 'presuppose' our concept of perception comes to presuppose such knowledge. If we started to acquire beliefs about the current state of our body and environment in a way that did not conform to established patterns, we might start talking of a new sense, or even of a new faculty different from sense-perception.

It is this knowledge that the acquiring of certain patterns of information about the environment is bound up with the operation of certain organs that makes us talk, for example, of *visual* hallucinations even when no stimulation of the eyes is involved. Macbeth, while considering the hypothesis that the dagger is a mere hallucination, says 'It is the bloody business which informs thus to *mine eyes*' in the very process of putting forward the suggestion that it is *not* any stimulation of his eyes that is responsible! His way of talking strikes us as natural. The pattern of misinformation involved is so like the patterns of true and false belief actually acquired as a result of the stimulation of the eyes that it is easy to think of it as caused by stimulation of the eyes.

We can therefore say, if we like, that perception is the acquiring of true or false beliefs about the current state of our body and environment *by means of the senses*. But we must remember that the final phrase, although helpful, has not a full right to appear in a definition.

What is our concept of a sense-organ? One mark of a sense-organ is obvious: it is a portion of our body which when stimulated produces a characteristic range of perceptions. A further important mark has been pointed out by Anthony Kenny in his *Action, Emotion, and Will* (p. 57). It is a portion of our body which we habitually move at will with the object of perceiving what is going on in our body and environment. The two criteria seem to be jointly necessary and sufficient for calling something a sense-organ.

The receptors involved in bodily perception fulfil the first criterion for being sense-organs, but not the second. In this work, however, it will sometimes be convenient to talk about the 'stimulation of the sense-organs' in contexts where bodily perception is included. In that case we will be using a relaxed test for 'sense-organ' where only the first criterion is required.

The second criterion has the interesting consequence that not all perceptions can arise as a result of the use (as opposed to the mere stimulation) of our sense-organs. The operation of the will is logically bound up with the occurrence of perceptions acting as 'information' which suitably modify the direction of the causal influence of the will. Now this entails that if we are to move our sense-organs at will we must be able to become perceptually aware of what happens to them during the time that they are being moved. If this perceptual awareness is gained as a result of the use, as opposed to the mere stimulation, of a sense-organ we are faced with an incipient vicious infinite regress. So there must be some perceptions that do not arise as the result of the *use* of the sense-organs.

This result consorts well with, although it does not actually entail, the point that there are no organs of bodily perception in the *full* sense of the word 'organ'. For normally, at any rate, we become aware of a change in the state of our sense-organs by bodily perception. We should therefore expect that there was no organ we *use* when we come to have bodily perceptions themselves.

III. BELIEF IS DISPOSITIONAL, BUT PERCEPTION IS AN EVENT

To say that A believes p does not entail that there is anything going on in A's mind, or that A is engaged in any behaviour, which could be called a manifestation of A's belief. It makes sense to say that A believes p, but that A is asleep, or unconscious. It is true that there must be some difference in A's state of mind if he believes p from his state of mind if he does not believe *p*. But we need not know what that difference of state is, any more than we need know what is the difference in state between brittle glass and glass that is not brittle. Belief is a dispositional state of mind which endures for a greater or lesser length of time, and that may or may not manifest itself (either in consciousness or in behaviour) during that time. But perceptions are definite events that take place at definite instants and are then over. How, then, can perceptions be beliefs?

The answer is that perceptions are not beliefs, and so not dispositional states, because they are *acquirings* of belief. The acquiring of a dispositional state is not a state, nor a process, but an event. If a glass becomes brittle at t_1, that is an event even although brittleness is a dispositional state.

Now perception is an event, in this sense of the word 'event'. It is not a process which happens to occupy a very short stretch of time (an event in another sense of the word). Up to a certain moment the perceiver has not yet perceived a certain state of affairs, from that moment on he has perceived it. This we interpret as meaning that up to a certain moment the subject has not yet acquired a certain belief, and that after that moment he has acquired it.

We owe the recognition that perception is an event to Gilbert Ryle. He put the point, rather unhappily as we shall see in a moment, by saying that verbs of perception are 'achievement-words'. His view is sometimes attacked by pointing out that we can perceive an unchanging scene for a period of time. To espy a robin may be an achievement, but where, it is asked, is the achievement involved in going on staring at the robin? However, if we think of perception as the acquiring of beliefs, and if we remember that we cannot look at a robin without time passing, this objection is easily met. At t_1 we acquire the information that the robin is there at t_1. At t_2 we acquire the information that the robin is still there at t_2. This is new, even if monotonous, information. And so for the whole stretch of time that we are looking at the robin.

It may still be objected that looking at a robin is a continuous performance, quite unlike spotting one. However, some achievements are continuous. If I hold a heavy weight aloft for some time, this is a continuous performance which is also a continuous achievement: keeping the weight there. Each new instant is, in a way, a new achievement. Looking at the robin is also a continuous achievement, continually yielding new, although monotonous, information.

But to talk of verbs of perception as 'achievement-words' is to invite us to conflate the notion that perception is an event with no less than three other notions.

In the first place, an achievement is ordinarily thought of as the outcome of some train of purposive activity. Now although many perceptions are the outcome of trains of purposive activity, in particular trains of activity involving the use, as opposed to the mere stimulation, of sense-organs, this is not the case with all perception. Some perceptions simply occur, without our having done anything to bring them about.

In the second place, to talk of achievement implies that what is brought about, or comes about, is some sort of *success*. Now we do normally use the phrase 'perceive that' and its determinates 'see that', 'hear that', etc., to imply that the perception reported is veridical. If I perceive that *x* is *y*, then indeed *x is y*. We might call this the 'success-grammar' of these phrases. So to perceive that *x* is *y*, might be called an achievement, even if it is not the outcome of a train of purposive activity, because it is the coming to be of a success. But although all perceptions are events, that is, they are the coming to be of states, they are not all the coming to be of *success*-states. For some perceptions are illusory. When we perceive, we do not always 'perceive that . . .'.

This point about the 'success-grammar' of 'perceive that' is in turn easily confused with another point. When verbs of perception are followed by the name of an object, process, or event (as *opposed* to a 'that' clause) they normally have what we might call 'existence-grammar'. If *A* is said to see a bush, then there must be a bush to be seen. This is *not* the point about 'success-grammar' because to say that *A* sees a bush does not entail that his perception is veridical. *A* may see the bush, but quite fail to see *that* it is a bush. (In passing, it may be noted that not *all* perceptions logically imply the existence of something perceived. In hallucinatory perception there need be no existent object that can be said to be perceived.) This feature of the grammar of verbs of perception is easily, but mistakenly, assimilated to the notion of achievement or success.

In view of these ambiguities we do best not to say that verbs of perception are 'achievement-words'. But it is important to see that all perceptions, of whatever sort, are *events*. These events, we have said, are acquirings of true or false beliefs.

IV. PERCEPTION WITHOUT BELIEF

But there are cases where perception occurs, but there is no acquiring of true or false beliefs.

In the first place, as has often been pointed out, it is possible to have perceptions that do not correspond to physical reality yet quite fail to be deceived by them, that is, quite fail to acquire false beliefs. In the case of visual perception, this is a familiar experience. When we look into a mirror, the visual appearance that we are presented with is that of a mirror-*doppelgänger* behind the glass. Yet, whatever may be the case for anybody unfamiliar with mirrors, mirror-images do not normally deceive us.

The same thing can happen, although it is rarer, in the case of veridical perception. If I am told that the conditions under which I am viewing a certain pond are such that, although it is in fact round, it looks elliptical to me, then I may believe it is round although it looks elliptical. It may nevertheless be the case that viewing conditions are perfectly normal, and the pond really is elliptical. Here we have veridical perception, but no acquiring of true belief.

In the second place, there are cases where we cannot speak of *acquiring* true or false belief because we already have that true or false belief. Here the normal cases are those involving veridical perception. Thus if I am looking at a red book, I may know with perfect certainty that it will continue to be red in the next instant. So when my eyes still rest upon the book during that instant, I cannot be said to acquire the true belief that it is now red, because I already knew it would be red during that instant.

It is possible, although less common, to have the same sort of thing occur in the case of sensory illusion. If a pond looks to me to be elliptical, and I believe it to be elliptical, although in fact it is not, I may be perfectly certain that it will be elliptical the next instant. And if I look at the pond at that instant, I cannot be said to acquire a false belief because I already falsely believed that it would be elliptical during that instant.

The first set of cases may be called 'perception without belief', the second 'perception without acquiring of belief'.

All these cases seem to show that we ought to make a distinction between the beliefs that we acquire in perception, and the perceptual experience on which these beliefs are based.

How is this perceptual experience to be conceived? Suppose I have the perceptions that we associate with looking at a red ball. It is clear that I might have had exactly the same perceptions without there being any red ball in physical reality. When we reflect on this point it is very tempting to say that what is involved is some relationship between my mind and a non-physical red item: a sense-impression or sense-datum. Now it is clear that if there are such items involved in perception, then it is false that perception is simply a state of the person apt for the bringing about of certain physical behaviour or a state of the person apt to be brought about by certain physical stimuli. The 'causal' analysis of the concept of perception would be false. We must therefore give an account of perception, and in particular of 'perception without belief' and 'perception without acquiring of belief', which does not involve non-physical sensory items.

One way to do this would be to admit the notion of perceptual experience as something quite distinct from the acquiring of beliefs about the environment, but go on to give an account of perceptual experience that was compatible with a causal analysis of all the mental concepts. I have been unable to see how this can be done, and so I will attempt to give an account of perception in terms of the acquiring of beliefs.

But before this task is attempted, those who accept the existence of sensory items may fairly demand that cause be shown why their intuitively plausible view should be rejected. What justification is there for proposing elaborate analyses where a straight-forward and simple account in terms of sensory items is available?

In the first place, as has been shown again and again, the view that all perceptual acquiring of belief is based upon some relation-ship that the mind has to non-physical sensory items leads to one of two very unsatisfactory alternatives. In the representative theory, the mind is confined to non-inferential knowledge of its own sensory items, and has to make an inference to the existence of physical things. The phenomenalist alternative, which gives an account of physical reality as nothing but an elaborate construction out of the sensory items themselves, is even less satisfactory.

Some modern philosophers, aware of these difficulties, have tried to reduce non-physical sensory items to mere phenomeno-logical facts, mere accompaniments to our acquiring beliefs about the current state of our body and its physical environment. Yet surely this is a thoroughly artifical view? If there are non-physical sensory items, they surely could not stand in this quite external relation to our perceptual beliefs. If one espouses sensory items at all, does one not want to say that we believe there is a red ball before us *because* there is a certain non-physical item in a certain relation to our mind?

These objections to the postulation of sensory items are rather general. So now let us consider a much more specific difficulty. It is the paradox about the non-transitivity of the relation 'exact similarity in a given respect' with regard to the alleged sensory items.

If A is exactly similar to B in respect X, and B is exactly similar to C in respect X, then it follows of logical necessity, that A is exactly similar to C in respect X. 'Exact similarity in a particular respect' is necessarily a transitive relation. Now suppose that we have three samples of cloth, A, B, and C, which are exactly alike except that they differ very slightly in colour. Suppose further, however, that A and B are *perceptually* completely indistinguishable in respect of colour, and B and C are *perceptually* completely indistinguishable in respect of colour. Suppose, however, that A and C can be perceptually distinguished from each other in this respect.

Now consider the situation if we hold a 'sensory item' view of perception. If the pieces of cloth A and B are perceptually indistinguishable in colour, it will seem to follow that the two sensory items A_1 and B_1 that we have when we look at the two pieces *actually are identical in colour*. For the sensory items are what are supposed to make a perception the perception it is, and here, by hypothesis, the *perceptions* are identical. In the same way B_1 and C_1 will be sensory items that are identical in colour. Yet, by hypothesis, sensory items A_1 and C_1 are not identical in colour!

There are two ways in which a defender of sensory items might try to deal with this paradox. In the first place he might take the heroic course adopted by Bertrand Russell, and say that this only shows that exact similarity in a certain respect is not necessarily a transitive relation. I think this is a somewhat staggering defence. It is nearly as bad as if we had demonstrated to a philosopher that there was a contradiction in his argument, and he had asked, 'What is so wrong about a contradiction?' If it is not obvious that exact similarity in a certain respect is transitive, what is obvious?

A more hopeful line of escape is open if the upholder of sensory items is prepared to abandon the view that we have incorrigible knowledge of the nature of the items at the time of having them. He can then say that in the case described it cannot really be true that sensory items A_1 and B_1 are identical in colour, so are B_1 and C_1, but A_1 and C_1 are not identical in colour. We must have made an error concerning the nature of our perceptions at some point, and so made an error in the nature of the sensory item present.

But although this way of escape is not logically absurd as Russell's suggestion seems to be, it is nevertheless most implausible. The phenomenological facts seem clear: piece of cloth A looks to be exactly the same colour as piece of cloth B, which looks to be exactly the same colour as piece of cloth C. But A looks to be a slightly different colour from C. There seems to be no reason to suggest that any phenomenological error has occurred, except the fact that the case clashes with a certain theory of the nature of perception. It seems rational to back the case against the theory. After all, those who support the analysis of perception as involving sensory items, regularly allege that it is their view, and their view alone, that does phenomenological justice to the perceptual facts. It will be ironic if they, faced with a difficult case, turn round and assert that there is a phenomenological error involved in the case!

It seems, then, that the defender of sensory items has no easy escape from this paradoxical case involving the apparent non-transitivity of the relation of 'exact similarity in a certain respect' in the case of sensory items. We shall see shortly that an analysis in terms of belief deals with this case with the utmost ease.

A second difficulty for an analysis of perception as involving non-physical sensory items is provided by the indeterminacy of perceptions. The classical case is that of the speckled hen. I may be able to see that it has quite a number of speckles, but unable to see exactly how many speckles it has. The hen has a definite number of speckles, but the perception is a perception of an indeterminate number of speckles. However, this indeterminacy is present in perception generally, perhaps in all perception. For instance, when I see or feel that one object is larger than another, I do not perceive exactly how much larger the first object is. The first object's size bears a perfectly definite relation to the second object's size, but the perception does not yield that definite relation. It yields something much less determinate. What is being referred to here is not simply what can be *verbalized* in our perceptions. If we completely abstract from the way we verbally describe our perceptions, they still remain indeterminate.

Now the difficulty that this indeterminacy of perception creates for a theory of sensory items is that it seems to imply that the items will have to be indeterminate in nature. The non-physical item that exists when we perceive the physical speckled hen will have to have an indeterminate number of speckles. Again, of the non-physical items that exist when we perceive that one physical object is larger than the other, one will have to be larger than the other without being any determinate amount larger. And how can any object be indeterminately larger than another?

Once again, there are two lines of escape available to the defender of sensory items. In the first place, he may argue that, although in the physical sphere to be is to be perfectly determinate in character, this rule does not hold for non-physical sensory items. Among sensory items, there can be speckled surfaces with a non-definite number of speckles, or one item can be larger than another without being any definite amount larger, and so on.

This reply seems to have something of the same character as Russell's reply to the difficulty concerning the transitivity of 'exact similarity in a certain respect'. It simply proposes to suspend the rules for objects in the case of mental objects. It asserts that in the sphere of mental objects there can be determinables without determinates. Against this no more can be said except that it is obvious that to be is to be determinate.

The alternative reply would be to say that the sensory items do have perfectly determinate characteristics, but that we are only *aware* of something less. The sensory item has a perfectly definite number of speckles, but we are only aware that it has *a large number* of speckles. But this has the paradoxical consequence that objects specially postulated to do phenomenological justice to perception are now credited with characteristics that lie quite outside perceptual awareness. The theory is now postulating (i) speckled physical surfaces with perfectly determinate characteristics; (ii) speckled sensory items with perfectly determinate characteristics; (iii) indeterminate awareness of the speckled sensory items. But have not items (ii) become redundant? Why not simply postulate the speckled physical surfaces and indeterminate awareness (perception) of those surfaces? It is hard to see that the sensory items are now doing any work in the theory.

We shall see shortly that, by contrast, an analysis of perception in terms of the acquiring of belief accounts for the indeterminacy of perception with the greatest ease.

Now I do not claim that these difficulties for the analysis of perception as involving sensory items are quite conclusive. But they do show that the theory is involved in strange paradoxes. The first move in the analysis may seem simple and obvious, but the consequences are far from simple or obvious. Since this is so, the attempt we are about to embark on of explaining cases of 'perception without belief' and 'perception without the acquiring of belief' in terms of those cases where belief *is* acquired cannot be rejected out of hand as a quite artificial manoeuvre. It will emerge, incidentally, that our own analysis does not reject the notion that perception involves the having of sense-impressions. All it rejects is the notion that sense-impressions are perceived items or objects.

We shall now attempt a positive account of 'perception without belief'.

In the first place, in cases where such perceptions occur there may still be an inclination to 'believe our senses'. If a thing looks to be a certain way, although we know on independent grounds that it cannot actually be that way, we may still half-believe, or be inclined to believe, that it is as it looks. And this inclination to believe can persist even when we clearly recognize that the inclination is irrational. What is an inclination to believe? I think it is nothing but a belief that is held in check by a stronger belief. We acquire certain beliefs about the world by means of our senses, but these beliefs are held in check by stronger beliefs that we already possess. So there is nothing here that is recalcitrant to an analysis of perception in terms of the acquiring of beliefs.

But, it will be objected, there are plenty of cases where 'perception without belief' occurs and no inclination to believe is acquired. One case already mentioned is the perceptions normally involved in looking at a mirror.

Nevertheless, we may reply, in such cases of perception without belief and even without inclination to believe, it is possible to formulate a true counter-factual statement of the form 'But for the fact that the perceiver had other, independent, beliefs about the world, he would have acquired certain beliefs—the beliefs corresponding to the content of his perception.' We do not believe that our mirror-double stands before us *only* because we have a great deal of other knowledge about the world which contradicts the belief that there is anything like the object we seem to see behind the surface of the glass. When our vision blurs, it is *only* because of our knowledge of the ways of the world that we do not acquire the belief that our environment is actually becoming misty and that the outlines of objects are actually beginning to waver. And so on for other cases of 'perception without belief'.

It is to be noticed here that only in a relatively small number of cases are we actually moved to *utter* such counter-factual statements. We might actually say, among high mountains: 'If I had not been told of the effects of a clear and rarefied atmosphere I should have believed the mountain was quite near.' The corresponding remark about a mirror-image will not be made in ordinary contexts. However, this seems to be of little importance. The situations in which a certain remark would be true form a much wider class than the situations in which the remark would be natural or called-for. We actually *assert* such counter-factual statements in cases where we think it was a relatively near thing that we were not deceived. But such counter-factual statements might still be true in cases where there was absolutely no risk of deception, even if there was no point in asserting them in the course of ordinary chat.

Now, we argued earlier for what we called a 'realist' as opposed to a 'phenomenalist' account of dispositions. This means that we are committed to saying that, if up to t_1 a certain counter-factual statement is not true of A, but after t_1 it is true, then some actual event took place at t_1. We may not know the nature of this event, but we know that such an event must have occurred. We have also argued that ordinary perception is the acquiring of a belief, which is a mental event as opposed to a process or a state. In cases of 'perception without belief', we can now argue, an event still occurs in our mind, an event which can be described as one that would be the acquiring of belief but for the existence of other, contrary, beliefs that we already hold. The event might perhaps be called the acquiring of a *potential belief*. We come to be in a certain state which would be a belief-state but for the inhibiting effect of other, contrary, beliefs. In this way, perception without belief or inclination to believe might be fitted into our analysis. Introspective awareness of such perception would be awareness of the acquiring of such potential beliefs.

But dissatisfaction may remain. It may be objected that it is at best a contingent fact of psychology that 'perception without belief' is an event that would be the acquiring of belief but for the possession of other, independent, beliefs. We can quite well imagine the occurrence of perceptions that involve no acquiring of belief at all, even although contrary beliefs about the world are quite absent. Now if this is so, the objection goes on, it does not pertain to the essence of perceptual experiences that they involve either belief or even 'potential belief'. So perception is something more than our analysis allows.

In answer to this I say that, if perceptions did occur which were not even the acquiring of potential beliefs, we could only describe such perceptions by reference to the central cases where beliefs are acquired. They would be events *like* the acquiring of beliefs or potential beliefs about the world. What is the force of 'like' here? We have already discussed the problem in connection with wants and wishes. We compared purposes that we actually act from with those central cases of perception where true or false beliefs are acquired. Desires which press towards action, but which we do not act from, were compared with perceptions which involve the acquiring of inclinations to believe held in check by stronger contrary beliefs. Then we argued that wants and wishes which do not press towards any fulfilling action were nevertheless potentially action-producing. If circumstances were to occur that seemed to the agent to give some promise of fulfilling the want or wish by the action of the agent, there would be at least some pressure in the agent's mind to take such action. These we may compare with those cases of 'perception without belief' which are acquirings of 'potential beliefs'.

Finally we called attention to the possibility that there might be 'idle' wants and wishes which neither pressed towards action nor were even potentially pressures towards action. Such mental states, we said, might be described as *like* real wants and wishes although lacking even the potential power to initiate action. In order to understand the force of 'like' here an imaginary case was envisaged. In this case a man had the power to say truly when he tasted a liquid, on the basis of no evidence at all, that it 'contained poison, but in insufficient quantity to poison'. It was then suggested that introspective apprehension of the likeness of 'idle' and ordinary, real, wants and wishes was parallel to the taster's apprehension of the likeness between this liquid and genuinely poisonous liquid.

Our account of the nature of perception without even the acquiring of potential belief should now be clear. It is exactly parallel to the account of 'idle' wants and wishes. The event involved is of the belief-acquiring sort, but, like the poison insufficiently concentrated to poison, not even potential belief is acquired. It is an 'idle' perception.

If our account of 'perception without belief' has been correct, it will be easy to give an account of 'perception without *acquiring* of belief'. It is clear that in all normal cases here a true counter-factual will hold. If I had not already known 'that the book would be red at t_2', then I would have acquired the belief 'that the book was red at t_2'. The event is one that would have been the acquiring of belief if belief had not already been acquired. Like the case where we discover good reasons for what we already know, the perception is like a seal stamped on wax that already bears the impression of that seal. Nothing further is done, because the seal simply fits into an imprint already made. Information is duplicated. And if it is said that it is imaginable that in some cases this counter-factual may not hold true of the perceptual event, then it is an 'idle' perception, and we can give an account of it like that given in the previous paragraph.

In considering 'perception without belief' and 'perception without the acquiring of belief' it is particularly helpful to think of perception as the acquiring of true or false *information*. A perception which involves an inclination, but no more than an inclination, to believe, may be conceived of as the acquiring of information which we have some tendency, but no more than some tendency, to accept. A perception which involves mere potential belief may be conceived of as the acquiring of information that, because of other information that we already possess, we completely discount. An 'idle' perception may be conceived of as information that is completely disregarded, but, incredibly, not because of any other information that we already possess. 'Perception without the acquiring of belief' may be conceived of as a case where the information received simply duplicates information that is already at our disposal.

It must now be shown that our account of perception can deal with the paradoxes about the non-transitivity of exact similarity in a given respect with respect to perceptions, and with the indeterminacy of perceptions.

Consider first the problem about similarity. Looking at samples of cloth A and B, I acquire the belief that they are the same colour. Looking at B and C, I acquire the same belief. But looking at A and C I acquire the belief that they are slightly different in colour. This forces me to realize that A and B cannot really be exactly the same colour, and neither can B and C. These two beliefs become mere 'potential beliefs'. There is no difficulty at all here, no question of the rules for the transitivity of exact similarity in a certain respect having broken down. The reason why we prefer the third perception to the first two is that we have discovered by experience that where we seem to perceive small differences between things the differences are usually real, but that where we can perceive no difference there often are small unperceived differences all the same. So we acquire the belief that all three colour-samples differ slightly in colour.

Again, there is nothing puzzling about beliefs being indeterminate. I may believe, and believe truly, that Jupiter has a number of satellites, yet not have any belief about their exact number. My belief is indeterminate in that respect. Equally, when I turn my eyes towards the speckled hen, I acquire the belief that it has a great number of speckles, but I do not acquire any belief that it has, say, ninety-three speckles. My belief is indeterminate in that respect. When I compare two objects in size by means of the hand or the eye, I acquire the belief that one is larger than the other. I do not acquire any belief about their exact proportion. My belief is indeterminate in that respect.

It seems, then, that when we are introspectively aware of our perceptions, we are aware of a stream of mental events: acquirings of beliefs about the current state of the world, or events which resemble such acquirings. Perception is a flow of information, a flow that goes on the whole time that we are not completely unconscious. Perceptual *experience*, as opposed to mere perception, is simply this flow in so far as we are conscious of it, that is to say, are introspectively aware of it. The content of our perceptions, which so many philosophers want to turn into a non-physical object, is simply the content of the beliefs involved.

Our perceptions, then, are not the basis for our perceptual judgements, nor are they a mere phenomenological accompaniment of our perceptual judgements. They are simply the acquirings of these judgements themselves. Our perceptions do not stand between our mind and physical reality, because they *are* our apprehensions of that reality.

It may be objected that ordinary discourse provides evidence for saying that we treat our perceptions as evidence or grounds on which we base conclusions about the physical world. 'How do you know that there is a mouse in the cupboard?' 'I saw it just then.' Here I seem to be appealing to my visual data to support a judgement about the contents of the cupboard.

However, this dialogue can be understood quite differently, and in a way compatible with our analysis. In saying I *saw* the mouse I am (besides begging the question by using the word 'see', thus assuming the mouse was there) indicating that I acquired the belief that there was a mouse in the cupboard *by using my eyes*. Now it is a known fact that beliefs of that sort acquired as a causal result of the use of the eyes are pretty reliable beliefs. So I have provided my questioner with a reason for believing that there was a mouse in the cupboard. The position is the same as that of the man who estimates a distance by eye, and then defends his claim to knowledge of the distance by pointing out that he regularly gets such estimates right. The only difference is that the ability to gather reasonably reliable information about mice by using the eyes, as in the first case, is an almost universal ability.

VIII

SENSATION AND PERCEPTION

F. DRETSKE

Information-processing models of mental activity tend to conflate perceptual and sensory phenomena on the one hand with cognitive and conceptual phenomena on the other. Perception is concerned with the pickup and delivery of information, cognition with its utilization. But these, one is told, are merely different stages in a more or less continuous information-handling process. Recognition, identification, and classification (cognitive activities) occur at every phase of the perceptual process. Seeing and hearing are low-grade forms of knowing.

I think this is a confusion. It obscures the distinctive role of *sensory experience* in the entire cognitive process. In order to clarify this point, it will be necessary to examine the way information can be delivered and made available *to* the cognitive centres without itself qualifying for cognitive attributes—without itself having the kind of structure associated with knowledge and belief. For this purpose we must say something about the different ways information can be coded.

I. ANALOG AND DIGITAL CODING

It is traditional to think of the difference between an analog and a digital encoding of information as the difference between a continuous and a discrete representation of some variable property at the source. So, for example, the speedometer on an automobile constitutes an analog encoding of information about the vehicle's speed because different speeds are represented by different positions of the pointer. The position of the pointer is (more or less) continuously variable, and each of its different positions represents a different value for the quantity being represented. The light on the dashboard that registers oil pressure, on the other hand, is a

Abridged from *Knowledge and the Flow of Information* (1981), ch. 6, pp. 135–53, 254–8, by permission of Basil Blackwell Publ. and MIT Press, Cambridge, Mass.

digital device, since it has only two informationally relevant states (on and off). These states are discrete because there are no informationally relevant intermediate states. One could, of course, exploit the fact that lights have a variable intensity. This continuous property of the signal could be used to represent the *amount* of oil pressure: the brighter the light, the lower the oil pressure. Used in this way the light would be functioning, in part at least, as an analog representation of the oil pressure.

The analog–digital distinction is usually used to mark a difference in the way information is carried about a variable property, magnitude, or quantity: time, speed, temperature, pressure, height, volume, weight, distance, and so on. Ordinary household thermometers are analog devices: the variable height of the mercury represents the variable temperature. The hands on a clock carry information about the time in analog form, but alarm clocks convert a pre-selected part of this into digital form.

I am interested, however, not in information about properties and magnitudes and the various ways this might be encoded, but in information about the instantiation of these properties and magnitudes by particular items at the source. I am interested, in other words, not in how we might encode information about temperature, but in how we might represent the *fact* that the temperature is too high, over 100°, or exactly 153°. What we want is a distinction, similar to the analog–digital distinction as it relates to the representation of properties, to mark the different way *facts* can be represented. Can we say, for example, that one structure carries the information that *s* is *F* in digital form, and another carries it in analog form?

For the purpose of marking an important difference in the way information can be encoded in a signal or structure, I propose to use the familiar terminology—analog vs. digital—in a slightly unorthodox way. The justification for extending the old terminology to cover what is basically a different distinction will appear as we proceed.

I will say that a signal (structure, event, state) carries the information that *s* is *F* in *digital* form if and only if the signal carries no additional information about *s*, no information that is not already nested in *s*'s being *F*. If the signal *does* carry additional information about *s*, information that is *not* nested in *s*'s being *F*, then I shall say that the signal carries this information in analog form. When a signal carries the information that *s* is *F* in analog form, the signal

always carries more specific, more determinate, information about
s than that it is *F*. Every signal carries information in both analog
and digital form. The most specific piece of information the signal
carries (about *s*) is the only piece of information it carries (about *s*)
in digital form.[1] All other information (about *s*) is coded in analog
form.

To illustrate the way this distinction applies, consider the difference between a picture and a statement. Suppose a cup has coffee in
it, and we want to communicate this piece of information. If I
simply *tell* you, 'The cup has coffee in it', this (acoustic) signal
carries the information that the cup has coffee in it in digital form.
No more specific information is supplied about the cup (or the
coffee) than that there is some coffee in the cup. You are not told
how much coffee there is in the cup, how large the cup is, *how dark*
the coffee is, what the shape and orientation of the cup are, and so
on. If, on the other hand, I photograph the scene and show you the
picture, the information that the cup has coffee in it is conveyed in
analog form. The picture tells you that there is some coffee in the
cup by telling you, roughly, how much coffee is in the cup, the
shape, size, and colour of the cup, and so on.

I can say that *A* and *B* are of different size without saying how
much they differ in size or which is larger, but I cannot picture *A*
and *B* as being of different size without picturing one of them as
larger and indicating, roughly, how much larger it is. Similarly, if a
yellow ball is situated between a red and a blue ball, I can *state* that
this is so without revealing where (on the left or on the right) the
blue ball is. But if this information is to be communicated pic-
torially, the signal is necessarily more specific. Either the blue or
the red ball must be pictured on the left. For such facts as these a
picture is, of necessity, an analog representation. The corresponding statements ('*A* and *B* are of different size', 'The yellow ball is
between the red and the blue balls') are digital representations of
the same facts.

As indicated, a signal carrying information in analog form will
always carry some information in digital form. A sentence expressing
all the information a signal carries will be a sentence expressing
the information the signal carries in digital form (since this will be the
most specific, most determinate, piece of information the signal

---

[1] The parenthetical 'about *s*' is necessary at this point since information *about s*
that is coded in digital form may none the less be nested in information about some
other item.

carries). This is true of pictures as well as other analog representations. The information a picture carries in digital form can be rendered only by some enormously complex sentence, a sentence that describes every detail of the situation about which the picture carries information. To say that a picture is worth a thousand words is merely to acknowledge that, for most pictures at least, the sentence needed to express all the information contained in the picture would have to be very complex indeed. Most pictures have a wealth of detail, and a degree of specificity, that makes it all but impossible to provide even an approximate *linguistic* rendition of the information the picture carries in digital form. Typically, when we describe the information conveyed by a picture, we are describing the information the picture carries in analog form—abstracting, as it were, from its more concrete embodiment in the picture.

This is not to say that we cannot develop alternative means of encoding the information a picture carries in digital form. We could build a device (a buzzer system, say) that was activated when and only when a situation occurred at the source that was *exactly* like that depicted in the picture (the only variations permitted being those about which the picture carried no information). The buzzer, when it sounded, would then carry exactly the same information as the picture, and both structures (the one pictorial, the other not) would carry this information in digital form. Computer recognition programs that rely on whole-template matching routines approximate this type of transformation. The incoming information is supplied in pictorial form (letters of the alphabet or geometric patterns). If there is an exact match between the input pattern and the stored template, the computer 'recognizes' the pattern and labels it appropriately. The label assigned to the input pattern corresponds to our buzzer system. The output (label) carries the same information as the input pattern. The information the picture carries in digital form has merely been physically transformed.

As everyone recognizes, however, such template-matching processes have very little to do with genuine recognition. As long as what comes out (some identificatory label) carries *all* the information contained in the input pattern, we have nothing corresponding to stimulus generalization, categorization, or classification. What we want, of course, is a computer program that will 'recognize', not just a letter A in *this* type fount, in *this* orientation, and of *this* size (the only thing the stored template will *exactly* match), but the letter A in a variety of type founts, in a variety of orientations, and a variety of different sizes. For this purpose we need something that will extract information the input pattern carries in *analog* form. We want something that will disregard irrelevant features of this particular A (irrelevant to its being an instance of the letter A) in order to respond to those particular features relevantly involved in the pattern's being an instance of the letter A. We want, in other words, a buzzer system that is responsive to pieces of information the pictures (patterns) carry in analog form.

To understand the importance of the analog-to-digital conversion, and to appreciate its significance for the distinction between perceptual and cognitive processes, consider the following simple mechanism. A variable source is capable of assuming 100 different values. Information about this source is fed into an information-processing system. The first stage of this system contains a device that accurately registers the state of the source. The reader may think of the source as the speed of a vehicle (capable of going from 0 to 99 m.p.h.), and the first stage of our information-processing system as a speedometer capable of registering (in its mobile pointer) the vehicle's speed. This information is then fed into a converter. The converter consists of four differently pitched tones, and a mechanism for activating these different tones. If the source is in the range 0 to 14, the lowest-pitched tone is heard. A higher-pitched tone occurs in the range 15 to 24, a still higher pitch from 25 to 49, and the highest at 50 to 99. These different ranges may be thought of as the approximate ranges in which one should be in first, second, third, and fourth gear, and the converter a device for alerting novice drivers (by the differently pitched tones) of the need to shift gears. The flow of information looks something like Fig. 1. What I have labelled the 'Analog Representation' (the speedometer) carries all the information generated by the variable

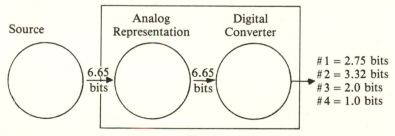

Fig. 1

source. Since the source has 100 different possible states (all equally likely), the speedometer carries 6.65 bits of information about the source. It carries the information that the vehicle is going, say, 43 m.p.h. This information is fed into a converter, and (assuming a speed of 43 m.p.h.) the third tone is activated. Since the third tone is activated when, and only when, the vehicle has a speed in the range 25 to 49, this tone carries 2 bits of information about the speed of the vehicle (a reduction of 100 equally likely possibilities to 25).

The output of this system is always less, quantitatively, than the input. Although 6.65 bits of information get in, something less than this comes out. What is gained by this loss of information is a *classification* (in the various tones) of the *significant ranges* of the input variable. This is a form, albeit a fairly primitive form, of *stimulus generalization*. The output of this system ignores the difference between 43 m.p.h. and 32 m.p.h. Both these values are treated as essentially the same. Both activate tone 3. From the point of view of the information the system is designed to communicate, the internal speedometer is an analog representation of the source because it carries more specific, more determinate information about the source than is required to control the system's output. The speedometer 'says' that the vehicle is going 43 m.p.h. Nested within this piece of information is the information that the vehicle is going *between* 25 and 50 m.p.h. The digital converter is interested only in the latter piece of information. It 'throws away' the more specific piece of information and passes along a piece of information (that the vehicle is going somewhere between 25 and 50 m.p.h.) that the speedometer carries in analog form. Of course, the speedometer carries the information that the vehicle is going 43 m.p.h. in digital form (since it carries no more specific information about the vehicle's speed), but relative to the information this system is designed to communicate (for example, whether the speed is between 15 and 24 or between 25 and 49) the speedometer constitutes an analog representation of the state of the source. It is the information the speedometer carries in analog form that the system is *acting* on, that *drives* its motor centres (the various buzzers). The more specific pieces of information it carries are systematically ignored in order to achieve a uniform response to *relevant similarities*.

To describe a process in which a piece of information is converted from analog to digital form is to describe a process that necessarily involves the *loss* of information. Information is lost because we pass from a structure (the speedometer) of greater informational content to one of lesser information content. Digital conversion is a process in which irrelevant pieces of information are pruned away and discarded. Until information has been lost, or discarded, an information-processing system has failed to treat *different* things as essentially the *same*. It has failed to classify or categorize, failed to generalize, failed to 'recognize' the input as being an instance (token) of a more general type. The simple system just described carries out this process in a completely mechanical way. Nevertheless, although it lacks some of the essential features of a genuine perceptual-cognitive system, it illustrates the information-theoretic processes underlying *all* forms of stimulus generalization, classification, and recognition.

II. SENSORY VS. COGNITIVE PROCESSES

The contrast between an analog and a digital encoding of information (as just defined) is useful for distinguishing between sensory and cognitive processes. Perception is a process by means of which information is delivered within a richer matrix of information (hence in *analog* form) *to* the cognitive centres for their selective use. Seeing, hearing, and smelling are different ways we have of getting information about *s* to a digital-conversion unit whose function it is to extract pertinent information from the sensory representation for purposes of modifying output. It is the successful conversion of information into (appropriate)[2] digital form that constitutes the essence of cognitive activity. If the information that *s* is *F* is never converted from a sensory (analog) to a cognitive (digital) form, the system in question has, perhaps, seen, heard, or smelled an *s* which is *F*, but it has not *seen that* it is *F*—does not *know* that it is *F*. The traditional idea that knowledge, belief, and thought involve *concepts* while sensation (or sensory experience) does not is reflected in this coding difference. Cognitive activity is the *conceptual* mobilization

---

[2] It is not *merely* the conversion of information from analog to digital form that qualifies a system as a perceptual–cognitive system. The speedometer–buzzer system described above neither *sees* nor *knows* that the vehicle is going between 25 and 49 m.p.h. when the third tone is activated. To qualify as a genuine perceptual system, it is necessary that there *be* a digital-conversion unit in which the information can be given a cognitive embodiment, but the cognitive embodiment of information is not *simply* a matter of digitalization. Additional conditions must be satisfied to qualify a structure as a *cognitive* structure (besides digitalization).

of incoming information, and this conceptual treatment is fundamentally a matter of ignoring differences (as irrelevant to an underlying sameness), of going from the concrete to the abstract, of
passing from the particular to the general. It is, in short, a matter of
making the analog–digital transformation.

Sensation, what the ordinary man refers to as the look (sound,
smell, etc.) of things, and what the psychologist refers to as the
percept or (in some contexts) the sensory information store (SIS), is
informationally profuse and specific in the way a picture is. Knowledge and belief, on the other hand, are selective and exclusive in the
way a statement is. 'The tapestry of awareness is rich, but the pattern
recognition process, dependent on classification, is relatively
impoverished in the detail with which it operates.'[3] Our sensory
experience embodies information about a variety of details that, if
carried over *in toto* to the cognitive centres, would require
gigantically large storage and retrieval capabilities.[4] There is more
information in the sensory store than can be extracted, a limit on how
much of this information can be exploited by the cognitive
mechanisms.

I do not mean to suggest by my comparison of sensory experience
to pictures (or cognitive structures with statements) that our sensory
experience is always (or *ever*) pictorial or imagistic in character—that
the perception of things involves having little images (sounds, smells,
tastes) in the head, or that cognitive activity is a linguistic
phenomenon. It may be that the acquisition of language is essential
to an organism's having the capacity to convert sensory information
into digital form (hence the capacity to have beliefs and knowledge),
but this, if so, is an empirical question. For the moment I merely wish
to develop the idea that the difference between our perceptual experience, the experience that constitutes our seeing and hearing things,
and the knowledge (or belief) that is normally consequent upon that
experience is, fundamentally, a coding difference. In this respect the
relation between sensory processes and cognitive processes is like
the relation between the preliminary analog representation and the
subsequent digital representation described in Fig. 1. The speedometer carries the information that the vehicle is going between 25
and 50 m.p.h., and it carries this information in analog form
(embedded in the more specific information that the vehicle is

[3] Karl H. Pribram, *Languages of the Brain* (Englewood Cliffs, NJ, 1971), 136.
[4] See John R. Anderson and Gordon H. Bower, *Human Associative Memory*
(Washington, DC 1973), 453.

going 43 m.p.h.), but the particular state of the system that carries this information (the position of the pointer) is not a picture of the vehicle's speed. It does not *resemble* the state of affairs about which it carries information. And the third tone, the one that carries (in digital form) the information that the vehicle is going between 25 and 50 m.p.h., is not a *statement* or *linguistic represen-tation* of the vehicle's speed. The conversion of information from analog to digital form *may* involve a conversion from picture to statement, but it need not. From a neurological point of view the transformation from sensory to cognitive coding takes place in the complete absence of either pictures or statements.

Unlike the simple, mechanical converter described in Fig. 1, however, living systems (most of them anyhow) are capable of modifying their digital-conversion units. As the needs, purposes, and circumstances of an organism change, it becomes necessary to alter the characteristics of the digital converter so as to exploit *more*, or *different*, pieces of information embedded in the sensory structures. Shifts of attention need not (although they may) involve a change in the kind of information made available in the sensory representation. There need not be any change in the way things look, sound, or smell. It may only involve a change in what pieces of information (carried in analog form) are extracted from the sensory representation.

Similarly, learning a concept is a process in which there is a more or less permanent modification of a system's ability to extract analogically coded information from the sensory store. What the simple mechanical system already described lacks is the capacity to change its response characteristics so as to exploit more, or different, pieces of information embodied in the speedometer's registration. It cannot *learn*. There is no way for it to modify the way it digitalizes information so as to respond, say, with tone 3 (or an altogether different tone) when and only when the vehicle is going between 30 and 35 m.p.h. This more specific piece of infor-mation *is* being picked up, processed, and fed into the converter (by the speedometer), but the system is incapable of 'attending to' this fact, incapable of extracting this piece of information and 'acting' on it. Contrast this with a young child, one whose receptor systems are fully matured and in normal working order, learning to recognize and identify items in her environment. Learning to recognize and identify daffodils, say, is not a process that requires the pickup of more information from (or about) the daffodils.

Given the child's keen eyesight, she may already (before learning) be receiving more information from daffodils than her more experienced, but near-sighted, teacher. Still, the teacher *knows* that the flower is a daffodil and the child does not. The child knows only that it is a flower of some sort (perhaps not even this much). What the pupil needs is not more information of the sort that could be supplied by the use of a magnifying glass. She is not *perceptually* deficient. The requisite information (requisite to identifying the flower *as* a daffodil) is getting in. What is lacking is an ability to extract this information, an ability to decode or interpret the sensory messages. What the child needs is not more information about the daffodil but a change in the way she codes the information she has been getting all along. Until this information (namely, that they are daffodils) is recoded in digital form, the child *sees* daffodils but neither knows nor believes that they are daffodils.

Our concern here is not with the process of digitalization, and how it is related to learning and cognitive activity in general, but with the perceptual delivery systems—those systems whose function it is to make available, in our sensory experience, the information on which such cognitive activity depends.

It should perhaps be noted that I am greatly oversimplifying the process by means of which sensory information is extracted from the physical stimulus, integrated with collateral information, and coded in sensory form. I ignore the details of this process in order to highlight an important *difference* in the way this information is coded: a sensory (analog) form and a cognitive (digital) form. In particular, I simply ignore the fact that much of the information embodied in the sensory representation (our sensory experience) is the result of a temporal integration:

evolution has tuned the human perceptual system to register not the low-grade information in momentary retinal images but rather the high-fidelity information in *sequences of images* [my emphasis] or in simultaneous complexes of images—the kind of information given by motion parallax and binocular parallax.[5]

James Gibson has argued persuasively that much of the information we manage to extract from our environment depends on a strategy of detecting higher-order invariants in a temporal series of

[5] T. G. R. Bower, 'The Visual World of Infants', in *Perception: Mechanisms and Models* (San Francisco, 1972), 357.

signals—the kind of information we are able to pick up by *moving around* and registering the systematic alteration in patterns, textures, and relative positions.[6] To understand how certain sorts of information are registered, it is important to understand the way a sensory representation may be the result of a temporal summation of signals. To think of the processing of sensory information in static terms, in terms of the kind of information embodied in the stimulus *at a particular time*, is to completely miss the extent to which our sensory representations depend on an integrative process *over time*. Even a simple tachometer (depending, as it does, on the *frequency* of pulses) can be used to illustrate the importance of this phenomenon.

I am also ignoring the fact that our sensory representations often carry information derived from a number of different sensory channels. If we considered *only* the stimulus reaching the eyes (even if understood relative to some *temporal interval*), the conclusion would be inevitable that the stimulus is (very often at least) *equivocal*. It would be a mistake, however, to conclude from this that the sensory representation of the source is itself equivocal. For there is no reason to think that our visual experience of the source relies exclusively on the information arriving in the light reaching our *visual* receptors. Quite the contrary. Information about the gravitational orientation of objects is available in the sensory experience because the visual input is processed *jointly* with body-tilt information from proprioceptive sources. Signals specifying the position of the head in relation to gravity, the angular position and movement of the eyes in relation to the head, and the relative position and movement of all other relevant body parts play a role in determining *how* we experience what we experience. The wealth of information available in our sensory experience is to be explained, in part at least, by the fact that this experience embodies information gleaned *over time* from a *variety* of sources.

Important as it is for understanding the actual processes by means of which our sensory experience is produced, and the sorts of mechanisms responsible for the information to be found therein,[7] the details are not directly relevant to our characterization

[6] See Gibson's *The Senses Considered as Perceptual Systems* (London, 1966), and the earlier *The Perception of the Visual World* (Boston, 1950).

[7] The underlying sensory mechanisms may even involve what some investigators (following Helmholtz) are pleased to describe as *computational* or *inferential* processes. Although I see nothing wrong with using this terminology to describe sensory processes, I think it a mistake to be (mis)led by it into assigning *cognitive*

of the result—the sensory experience itself—and the manner in which it codes information. It will be necessary later to look more closely at the machinery for delivering information in order to clarify the nature of the perceptual object and, in particular, the way the constancy mechanisms help to determine *what* we see, hear, and smell. But for present purposes these details can be set aside. Our immediate concern is with the analog character of our sensory experience.

Consider vision. You are looking at a fairly complex scene—a crowd of youngsters at play, a shelf full of books, a flag with all the stars and stripes visible. A reaction typical of such encounters, especially when they are brief, is that one has seen more than was (or perhaps *could be*) consciously noticed or attended to. There were (as it turns out) 27 children in the playground, and though you, perhaps, *saw them all*, you are unaware of how many you saw. Unless you had the time to count, you do not *believe* you saw 27 children (although you may certainly believe something less specific—for example, that you saw *many* children or *over a dozen* children). You saw 27 children, but this information, precise numerical information, is not reflected in what you know or believe. There is no cognitive representation of this fact. To say one *saw* this many children (without realizing it) is to imply that there was *some* sensory representation of each item. The information *got in*. It was *perceptually* coded. Why else would it be true to say you saw 27 children rather than 26 or 28? Therefore, the information that *is* cognitively extracted from the sensory representation (the information, namely, that there are *many* children in the yard, or *over a dozen* children) is information that the sensory structure codes in *analog* form. The relationship between your *experience of* the children and your *knowledge of* the children is the same as that between the speedometer and the tone in Fig. 1.

I do not mean to be suggesting that there is a psychophysical correspondence between the information contained in the physical stimulus (or temporal sequence of stimuli) and the information contained in the sensory experience to which that stimulus gives rise. There is obviously a *loss* of information between the receptor

structure to such processes. We may describe sensory phenomena in informational terms, in terms that involve (to this extent at least) a structure's having a *propositional content*, but a structure's having a propositional content should not be confused with its having the sort of content we associate with knowledge, belief, and judgement.

surfaces and the internal representation. And conversely, there occurs something that is called 'restoration'—an insertion into the sensory experience of representationally significant features that have no counterpart in the physical stimulus (closure of boundaries, restoration of missing sounds, etc.).[8] If, for example, one saw all 27 children but saw some of them only peripherally (or at dusk), it seems unlikely that information about the colour of their clothes would be available in the visual experience. If such colour information, contained in the stimulus (light reaching the retina), does not fall on the colour-sensitive cones of the fovea, it will obviously not be available in the resulting sensory experience. But even with these peripherally seen children, information about their (rough) relative location, size, spacing, and number *will* be perceptually coded. We may suppose, along with many psychologists, that the preliminary operations associated with the pre-attentive processes (those which occur prior to the more elaborate perceptual processing associated with focal attention) yield only segregated figural units, units that lack the richness of information available in those portions of the visual field to which attention is given.[9] Still, there is certainly more information embodied in this configuration of 'figural units' than we normally extract—information about the spacing, relative size, and position of the objects represented. Typically, the sensory systems overload the information-handling capacity of our cognitive mechanisms so that not all that is given to us in perception can be digested. What *is* digested are bits and pieces—information the sensory structure carries in analog form.

There is a rule of seven which tells us that there is a certain limit to the rate at which human subjects can process information.[10] When information arrives at a rate that exceeds this 'capacity', the organism fails to process it. I have shown that the idea of 'channel capacity' has no direct application to the amount of information that can be carried by a *particular* signal. It applies only to the *average* amount of information an ensemble of signals can carry. Nevertheless, understood in the correct way, this rule seems to have some rough empirical validity. Its significance should not be

[8] R. M. Warren, 'Perceptual Restoration of Missing Speech Sounds', *Science* (1970), 167.

[9] See e.g. Ulric Neisser, *Cognitive Psychology* (New York, 1967), 94–104.

[10] George A. Miller, 'The Magical Number Seven, Plus or Minus Two: Some Limits on Our Capacity for Processing Information', *The Psychological Review*, 63 (Mar. 1956).

misinterpreted, however. If the rule applies at all, it must be understood as applying to our capacity for *cognitively* processing information. It does not apply, and there is no evidence to suggest that it applies (quite the reverse), to our *perceptual* coding of information. The rule represents some kind of limit to how much information we can extract *from* our sensory experience, not a limit to how much information can be contained *in* this experience. It assigns a limit to our capacity to convert information from analog to digital form. Recall the speedometer–buzzer system. A similar limitation applies to this system considered as a whole. Although the input contains 6.65 bits of information about the speed of the vehicle, the output contains, at most, 3.32 bits. The average output is something less than this. But this limit on the information-processing capabilities of this system is a limit that arises as a result of the analog-to-digital conversion mechanism. A full 6.65 bits of information *gets in*. There is an *internal representation* of the speed of the vehicle at all times. Nevertheless, this information is selectively utilized in order to obtain, in the output, a digital representation of certain relevant features of the input. If the rule of seven applies at all, it applies to the input–output relationship. It does not apply to that stage in the process which occurs prior to digital conversion. It does not apply to the sensory coding of information.

J. R. Pierce makes the same point in discussing the informational processing capacity of human subjects.[11]

Now, Miller's law and the reading rate experiments have embarrassing implications. If a man gets only 27 bits of information from a picture, can we transmit by means of 27 bits of information a picture which, when flashed on a screen, will satisfactorily imitate any picture? If a man can transmit only about 40 bits of information per second as the reading rate experiments indicate, can we transmit TV or voice of satisfactory quality using only 40 bits per second? In each case I believe the answer to be no. What is wrong? What is wrong is that we have measured what gets *out* of the human being, not what goes *in*. Perhaps a human being can in some sense only notice 40 bits/second worth of information, but he has a choice as to what he notices. He might, for instance, notice the girl or he might notice the dress. Perhaps he notices more, but it gets away from him before he can describe it.

Pierce is making the point that to measure the amount of information that can flow *through* a subject is to measure the limitation on the *joint* operation of the perceptual and the cognitive mechan-

11 J. R. Pierce, *Symbols, Signals and Noise* (New York, 1961), 248–9.

isms (not to mention the performative mechanisms). Whatever limits are arrived at by this technique will tell us nothing about the informational limits of our sensory mechanisms. It will give us, at best, the capacity of the *weakest link* in the communication chain, and there is no reason to think that sensation constitutes the weakest link. As Pierce notes, we cannot imitate a picture with only 27 bits of information even though 27 bits of information is about the most that one can *cognitively* process. Our own perceptual experience testifies to the fact that there is more information *getting in* than we can manage to *get out*.

The same point is revealingly illustrated by a set of experiments with brief visual displays.[12] Subjects are exposed to an array of nine or more letters for a brief period (50 milliseconds). It is found that after removal of the stimulus there is a persistence of the 'visual image'. Subjects report that the letters appear to be visually present and legible at the time of a tone occurring 150 milliseconds *after* removal of the stimulus. Neisser has dubbed this iconic memory—a temporary storage of sensory information in perceptual form.[13] We need not, however, think of this as the persistence of *an image*. What persists is a structure in which incoming information *about* a pictoral array is coded in preparation for its cognitive utilization. For it turns out that although subjects can identify only three or four letters under brief exposure, *which* letters they succeed in identifying depends on the nature of a later stimulus, a stimulus that appears only 150 milliseconds after removal of the original array of letters. The later stimulus (a marker appearing in different positions) has the effect of 'shifting the subject's attention to different parts of the lingering icon'. The later stimulus changes the analog-to-digital conversion process: different pieces of information are extracted from the lingering sensory representation.

What these experiments show is that although there is a limit to the rate at which subjects can *cognitively* process information (*identify* or *recognize* letters in the stimulus array), the same limitation does not seem to apply to sensory processes by means of which this information is made available to the cognitive centres. Although the subjects could identify only three or four letters, information about *all* the letters (or at least *more* of the letters) was embodied in the persisting 'icon'. The sensory system has information

[12] G. Sperling, 'The Information Available in Brief Visual Presentations', *Psychological Monographs*, 74/11 (1960).

[13] Neisser, *Cognitive Psychology*, ch. 2.

about the character of all nine letters in the array while the subject has information about at most four. The availability of this information is demonstrated by the fact that after removal of the stimulus the subject can (depending on the nature of later stimulation) still extract information about *any* letter in the array. Hence, information about *all* the letters in the array must be available in the lingering icon. The visual system is processing and making available a quantity of information far in excess of what the subject's cognitive mechanisms can absorb (that is, convert to digital form). Our sensory experience is informationally rich and profuse in a way that our cognitive utilization of it is not. Relative to the information we manage to *extract* from the sensory representation (whatever beliefs may be occasioned by having this kind of sensory experience), the sensory representation itself qualifies as an *analog* representation of the source. It is this fact that makes the sensory representation more like a *picture* of, and the consequent belief a *statement about*, the source.

Consider, finally, an example from developmental studies. Eleanor Gibson in reporting Klüver's studies with monkeys describes a case in which the animals were trained to the larger of two rectangles.[14] When the rectangles were altered in size, the monkeys continued to respond to the larger of the two—whatever their absolute size happened to be. In the words of Klüver: 'If a monkey reacts to stimuli which can be characterized as belonging to a large number of different dimensions, and if in doing so he reacts consistently in terms of one relation, let us say in terms of the "larger than" relation, he may be said to "abstract".

Klüver's monkeys succeeded in abstracting the larger-than relation. But how shall we describe the perceptual situation *before* they learned to abstract this relation? Did the rectangles *look* different to the monkeys? If not, how could they ever learn to distinguish between them? What possible reinforcement schedule could get them to react differently to perceptually indistinguishable elements? It seems most natural to say in a situation of this sort (and the situation is typical of learning situations in general) that prior to learning, prior to successful abstraction of the appropriate relation, the monkey's perceptual experience contained the information that it only later succeeded in extracting. It is possible, I suppose, that the rectangles only *began* to look different to the monkeys after repeated exposures, that the reinforcement schedule

---

[14] *Principles of Perceptual Learning and Development* (New York, 1969), 284.

actually brought about a perceptual (as well as a cognitive) change. This would then be a remarkable case of perceptual learning (change in the *percept* or sensory representation as a result of training). [15] Perceptual learning may certainly take place, especially with the very young and the newly sighted, and in mature subjects with ambiguous figures, [16] but there is no reason to suppose that it is occurring in *every* learning situation with mature subjects. What is taking place here is very much like what takes place with the young child learning to recognize daffodils. The flowers do not look any different; the subject merely learns how to organize (recode) the information already available in its sensory experience.

The situation becomes even clearer if we present the monkeys with three rectangles and try to get them to abstract the 'inter-mediate-size' relation. This more difficult problem proves capable of solution by chimpanzees, but the monkeys find it extremely difficult. [17] Let us suppose that they are incapable of this more sophisticated type of learning. What shall we say about the perceptual situation with respect to the monkeys? Since they have already abstracted the larger-than relation, it may be assumed that they are receiving, and perceptually coding, the information that rectangle A is larger than B, and that B is larger than C. In ordinary terms this is a way of saying that the intermediate rectangle (B) *looks* smaller than the larger (A) and larger than the smaller (C). But information about which rectangle is intermediate, though obviously embedded (in analog form) in the perceptual experience itself, is not (and apparently cannot be) cognitively extracted by the animal. To say that the monkey cannot abstract the intermediate-size relation, therefore, is *not* to say anything about the way it perceptually codes information about figures. Rather, it is to say something about its cognitive limitations. The information is available in analog form in the experience the animal is having of the three rectangles, but the animal is unable to generate an appropriate on–off response, the kind of response characteristic of recognition or identification, to this piece of information. It does not *know* (think, believe, judge) that B is of intermediate size, even though this information is available in its sensory representation of A, B, and C.

[15] William Epstein, *Varieties of Perceptual Learning* (New York, 1967).

[16] See e.g. George J. Steinfeld, 'Concepts of Set and Availability and Their Relation to the Reorganization of Ambiguous Pictorial Stimuli', *Psychological Review*, 74/6 (1967), 505–22.

[17] Gibson, *Principles of Perceptual Learning and Development*, 292.

Although our speedometer-tone system cannot learn, its limitations can be usefully compared with those of the monkey. This simple mechanical system can receive, process, and generate an internal (analog) representation of the fact that the vehicle is going between 30 and 35 m.p.h. The speedometer's registration of (say) 32 m.p.h. is an analog encoding of this information. As originally conceived, however, the system as a whole cannot be made to 'respond' to this piece of information. We get the same tone whether the vehicle is going between 30 and 35 m.p.h., slower (down to 25 m.p.h.), or faster (up to 49 m.p.h.). The problem lies in the system's built-in limitation for converting information from analog to digital form. It can 'recognize' a speed as between 25 and 50 m.p.h. because this fact, the fact that the speed is within this interval, is information the system is designed to convert into digital form (a distinctive tone).[18] But the system is unable to 'recognize' finer details, unable to make more subtle discriminations. It has no *concept* of something's being between 30 and 35 m.p.h., no *beliefs* with this content, no internal structure with this kind of *meaning*.

To summarize, then, our perceptual experience (what we ordinarily refer to as the look, sound, and feel of things) is being identified with an information-carrying structure—a structure in which information about a source is coded in analog form and made available to something like a digital converter for cognitive utilization. This sensory structure or representation is said to be an analog encoding of incoming information because it is always information *embedded in* this sensory structure (embedded within a richer matrix of information) that is subjected to the digitalizing processes characteristic of the cognitive mechanisms. Until information has been *extracted from* this sensory structure (digitilization), nothing corresponding to recognition, classification, identification, or judgement has occurred—nothing, that is, of any *conceptual* or *cognitive* significance.

If perception is understood as a creature's *experience* of his surroundings, then, perception itself is cognitively neutral.[19] Neverthe-

---

[18] I put the word 'recognition' in scare quotes because this is *not* a genuine cognitive achievement. No *beliefs* are produced by this simple mechanical system— nothing having the intentional structure of *knowledge*.

[19] The word 'perception' is often reserved for those sensory transactions in which there is some cognitive uptake (identification, recognition, etc.). The sense of the term I allude to here is the sense in which we can see, hear, and smell objects or events (be aware or conscious *of* them) without necessarily categorizing them in any way.

less, although one can see (hear, etc.) an *s* which is *F* (sensorily encode information about *s* and, in particular, the information that *s* is *F*) without believing or knowing that it is *F* (without even having the concepts requisite to such beliefs), perception itself depends on there *being* a cognitive mechanism able to utilize the information contained in the sensory representation. In this sense, a system that cannot know cannot see; but if the system is capable of knowing, if it has the requisite cognitive mechanisms, then it can see without knowing. A sensory structure that carries the information that *s* is *F* is not to be confused with a belief about *s*, a belief to the effect that *s* is *F*, but to qualify as a *sensory* representation of *s* (an experience of *s*), this structure must have a certain function within the larger information-processing enterprise. It must make this information available to a suitable converter for possible cognitive utilization.

IX

COHERENCE, CERTAINTY, AND EPISTEMIC PRIORITY

R. FIRTH

Near the end of his annual lectures on epistemology at Harvard, Lewis used to tell his students that they must ultimately choose between the theory of justification that he had been defending—or something very similar to it—and a coherence theory like that of Bosanquet. These two alternatives may not seem to confront each other quite so directly in Lewis's books on epistemology, but in his paper entitled 'The Given Element in Empirical Knowledge' he again offers us this same choice.[1] He explicitly defends his own theory of the given as one of 'two alternatives for a plausible account of knowledge' (p. 168), the other alternative being an 'unabridged probabilism' like that of Reichenbach—'a modernized coherence theory' (p. 171). Although 'logical and systemic relationships are important for assuring credibility', such a 'probabilistic conception' of knowledge is incompatible with the fact that 'no logical relationship, by itself, can ever be sufficient to establish the truth, or the credibility even, of any synthetic judgment' (p. 169). 'Crudely put,' Lewis asserts, it 'strikes me as supposing that if enough probabilities can be got to lean against one another they can all be made to stand up. . . . I think the whole system of such could provide no better assurance of anything in it than that which attaches to the contents of a well-written novel' (p. 173).

The issue outlined here is apparently one which Lewis continued to take very seriously, for in a letter written to me as recently as three years ago he expressed the fear that contemporary philosophers are, in his words, 'headed back toward Bosanquet'. My intention therefore is to consider some of the problems that arise when we

Reprinted from the *Journal of Philosophy*, 61/19 (15 Oct. 1964), 545–57, by permission of the author and Managing Editor.
    [1] In a symposium with Hans Reichenbach and Nelson Goodman, in *The Philosophical Review*, 61/2 (Apr., 1952), 168–75.

attempt to formulate a precise definition of the issue Lewis had in mind. What kind of coherence theory did Lewis want to avoid, and what are the alternatives to it? I am convinced that we can ask no questions more important than these if we wish to understand Lewis's philosophical motivation and the full implications of his theory of knowledge.

It is possible to distinguish at least three theories (or perhaps I should say three types of theory) which can appropriately be labelled 'coherence theories', and which can be defined, I believe, in such a way that none of them logically entails either of the others. These are (1) the coherence theory of truth, (2) the coherence theory of concepts, and (3) the coherence theory of justification. I shall say nothing about the coherence theory of truth except that the arguments offered in its support all seem to me to presuppose the coherence theory of justification. And I shall comment on the coherence theory of concepts only to suggest that it might be quite acceptable to Lewis even though he rejects the coherence theory of justification. It is clearly this last theory, the coherence theory of justification, which Lewis is primarily concerned to refute in his epistemological writings.

I

The coherence theory of concepts is the doctrine that all our concepts are related to one another in such a way that we cannot be said fully to have grasped any one of them unless we have grasped all the others: they form an organic conceptual scheme, it is said, a system of meanings which cohere in such a way that introducing a new concept at any one point in the system has repercussions which are felt throughout the system. It is easy to illustrate this doctrine by restricting it to the technical concepts of some particular science and tracing the changes produced by the introduction of a new concept of space, matter, or energy. But the broader implications of the doctrine can better be suggested by appealing to some commonplace concept like that of 'mirror image'. It can plausibly be argued that the young child who has not yet acquired the concept of 'mirror image' cannot yet use the words 'see', 'touch', 'same', 'real', 'thing', 'space', 'coloured', 'myself', 'left', and 'right'—or perhaps *any* words in his vocabulary—to mean quite what they mean to his older brother. And once the pattern of this argument has been accepted, it can easily be extended to any other concept we may select.

Now it might seem at first thought that this coherence theory of concepts is incompatible with Lewis's analysis of the 'sense meaning' of statements about physical objects—and incompatible, indeed, even with the more moderate view of Locke and many other philosophers that some material-object *predicates* (e.g. 'red') can be analysed by means of supposedly simpler predicates (e.g., 'looks red') which we use to describe sense experience. For if a philosopher maintains that 'The apple is red' can be analysed as meaning 'The apple would look red under such and such physical conditions', he is assuming that 'looks red' is logically prior to 'is red', i.e. that it is at least *logically* possible to have the concept 'looks red' *before* we acquire the concept 'is red'. But if the coherence theory of concepts is correct, and we cannot fully understand 'looks red' unless we possess the contrasting concept 'is red', then it would seem that it is *not* logically possible to have the concept 'looks red' before we have the concept 'is red'. This paradox might even lead us to wonder, indeed, whether the conceptual interdependence of 'looks' and 'is' is enough to undermine Lewis's basic assumption that we can make 'expressive judgements' (e.g. 'I seem to see a doorknob', 'It looks as if I am seeing something red') without at the same time asserting something about the nature of 'objective reality'. It is these expressive judgements, according to Lewis, that enable us to escape the coherence theory of justification; and if it should turn out that these judgements all make some covert reference to physical objects, then—depending, of course, on the *kind* of 'covert reference'—it might no longer be possible to make the epistemological distinction that Lewis requires.

There are many subtle facets of this question which cannot be explored here, but for our present purpose it is sufficient to point out that the underlying paradox is easily dissolved if we do not confuse concepts with the words used to express them. It is a genetic fact, but a fact with philosophical implications, that when a child first begins to use the word 'red' with any consistency he applies it to things that *look* red to him whether these things are, as we should say, 'really red', or whether they are merely made to appear red by abnormal conditions of observation. Thus the child calls white things 'red' when he sees them through red glass. In fact at this stage the child says 'red' just in those circumstances in which we, as adults, could truthfully say 'looks red to me now', so that it would not be unreasonable to assert that the child is using 'red' to express a primitive form of the concept 'looks red'. To call this a 'primitive form' of the concept 'looks red' is to acknowledge that in some sense the child cannot *fully* understand adult usage until he is able to distinguish things that merely look red from things that really are red; but we must not suppose that the child somehow *loses* his primitive concept when he acquires a more sophisticated one. As Lewis points out in Chapter III of *Mind and the World Order*,[2] the scientist and the non-scientist are able to share what Lewis calls 'our common world' precisely because the scientist does not necessarily forget how to use words in their non-technical senses; and for the same reason there is no inconsistency in maintaining that even as adults we continue to have *a* concept 'looks red' which is logically prior to our concept 'is red'.

To grant Lewis this crucial point is not to deny that the *vocabulary* of 'looks' and 'seems' expressions that we use to describe sense experience is in some respect derivative from the *vocabulary* that we use to describe the physical world. Thus when Lewis describes his sense experience by saying 'I seem to see a doorknob' his choice of words appears to reflect a linguistic rule to the effect that a sense experience should be 'named after' its normal condition (in this case the condition of actually seeing a real doorknob). But such a rule, like the rule in some societies that sons should be named after their fathers, is merely a *baptismal* rule. The fact that Young Rufus is named after Old Rufus does not prevent us from learning to recognize Young Rufus before we have met Old Rufus. Analogously, the fact that key words in our 'looks' and 'seems' expressions are inherited from our 'is' expressions does not prevent the child from consistently identifying things that look red to him (or situations in which he seems to see a doorknob) before he can consistently identify things that *are* red (or situations in which he really sees an 'objective' doorknob). If we do not confuse baptismal rules with semantical rules (e.g., the semantical rule followed by the child who says 'red' when something looks red to him) the coherence theory of concepts does not seem to be incompatible with Lewis's theories of meaning and knowledge. Let us turn, therefore, to the coherence theory of justification.

II

Philosophers have sometimes construed the problems of justification as though they were problems concerning the knowledge

_____

[2] New York, 1929; hereafter referred to as MWO.

possessed by a social group; and it does of course make perfectly
good sense to ask what statements *we* (e.g. you and I, our 'culture
circle', etc.) are justified in believing, and why we are justified
in believing them. But Lewis seems clearly to be right in maintaining that such a question cannot be answered without first
answering a more fundamental, egocentric, question: Why am *I*, at
the present moment, justified in believing some statements and not
justified in believing other statements? This is to be interpreted as
an epistemological question—not as an ethical question to which
someone might in principle reply: 'Because you will be happier (or
more loyal to your friends) if you believe these statements rather
than those'; and the ambiguous expression 'justified in believing' is
to be interpreted so that we may assert without self-contradiction
that someone is justified in believing a statement he does not in fact
believe. It is helpful, therefore, to reformulate the question as a
question about the 'epistemic warrant' (or, for short, 'warrant')
that statements have 'for me' at a particular time; and in these
terms I think that the heart of the coherence theory of justification,
as Lewis probably construes it, is the thesis that *ultimately* every
statement that has some degree of warrant for me has that particular degree of warrant because, and only because, it is related by
valid principles of inference to (that is to say 'coheres with') certain
other statements.

To explain why I have used and italicized the word 'ultimately' in
formulating this central thesis of the coherence theory, and to
facilitate comparison with alternative theories of justification, it is
helpful to refine the issue still further and construe the coherence
theory as an answer to the question: What properties or characteristics of a statement may serve to increase its warrant? This
question may in turn be formulated in a slightly different way by
employing the term 'warrant-increasing property', interpreted so
that, in saying that a statement S has a warrant-increasing property
P for a particular person at a particular time, we imply that S
would be *less* warranted, and that *not-S* would be *more* warranted,
for that person at that time if, other things remaining the same, S
did not have property P. In this terminology the question becomes:
What properties of statements are warrant-increasing properties?

It is clear that advocates of the coherence theory would want to
reply that, if P is a warrant-increasing property of statement S, P
might consist simply in S's being validly inferable from certain
other statements of a specified kind. In such a case, since the

warrant of S is increased, so to speak, by the *fact that* S is validly inferable from certain other statements, P might appropriately be called an 'inferential' property. Advocates of the coherence theory would surely be willing to grant, however, that there are non-inferential properties (e.g., the property of being believed by scholars with such and such characteristics) which might also increase the warrant of a statement; but to preserve coherence as the ultimate court of appeal they would insist that such a non-inferential property (P') can be a warrant-increasing property of a statement S only if a particular statement *about* S—the statement, namely, 'If S has property P then S is true'—is validly inferable from (coheres with) certain other specified statements.[3] (This requirement might be met, for example, if P' were the property of being believed by certain scholars and if there were evidence that these scholars have usually had correct beliefs about statements similar to S in certain respects.) Thus we may say that the coherence theory of justification maintains that, if P is a warrant-increasing property of S, then either (1) P is an inferential property, or (2) P is a warrant-increasing property only because the statement 'If S has the property P then S is true' has an inferential warrant-increasing property. It is convenient to summarize this by saying that all warrant-increasing properties, according to the central thesis of the coherence theory, must be 'ultimately inferential'.

To convert this central thesis into a fully determinate coherence theory, it would have to be elaborated in two ways. (1) We should have to specify the 'valid' principles of inference, deductive and inductive, that determine whether one statement coheres with, and thus confers warrant on, another. And (2) we should have to specify the nature of the 'certain other statements' with which a warranted statement must cohere—the class of statements that are, we might say, 'warrant-conferring'. Although the problems involved in (1) are very important—especially those which arise when we ask whether there is a set of principles of inference, and only one set, that can be selected and justified by reapplying the same standard of coherence—these problems are neutral with respect to the central issues at stake between Lewis and the coherence theory. The problems involved in (2), however, are more

---

[3] For simplicity I assume that the non-inferential warrant-increasing property P' is only one step removed from the ultimate appeal to coherence; but in principle there might be a long intervening chain of non-inferential warrant-increasing properties.

directly relevant to these central issues, and we shall return to them
after considering Lewis's position.

III

In clear opposition to the coherence theory of justification, Lewis
flatly denies that all warrant-increasing properties are ultimately
inferential. It is a matter of some importance, which we shall
consider later, that Lewis often discusses the problems of epistemic
justification as problems concerning *judgements*, and may thus be
restricting his attention to the epistemic status of statements that
are actually *believed* (judged to be true) by a particular person at a
particular time. But in any case he maintains that those statements
which do reflect my present judgements about my own present
experience—including statements about sense experience, memory
experience, occurrent feelings, etc.—are *certain* (and hence warranted) for me at the present time, and that their certainty is not
derived directly or indirectly from their coherence with other statements. There is room for debate, however, about the meaning of
the word 'certain' in this context, and I think that Lewis's writings
actually suggest several different alternatives to the coherence
theory of justification.

There are a number of passages in *Mind and the World Order*, in
An Analysis of Knowledge and Valuation,[4] and elsewhere, in which
Lewis says that 'expressive judgements' (e.g. 'I seem to see a doorknob') *cannot be mistaken*. 'One cannot be mistaken', he asserts,
'about the content of an immediate awareness' (MWO 131). This is
perhaps the most extreme alternative to a coherence theory of justification, and is often taken to be the only alternative that Lewis
offers us. In another place in *Mind and the World Order*, however,
Lewis says, interestingly enough: 'All those difficulties which the
psychologist encounters in dealing with reports of introspection
may be sources of error in any report of the given. It may require
careful self-questioning, or questioning of another, to elicit the full
and correct account of the given' (p. 62). This of course seems to
imply that, in some important sense of 'can', our expressive judgements *can* be mistaken, and it suggests the need to distinguish what
we might call 'truth-evaluative' senses of 'certain' from 'warrant-
evaluative' senses of 'certain'. To say that a judgement is certain in
a truth-evaluative sense of the word entails that the judgement is

La Salle, Ill., 1964; hereafter referred to as AKV.

true, but to say that a judgement is certain in a warrant-evaluative sense is merely to say that the judgement (whether it be in fact true or false) is completely warranted in some specifiable sense of 'completely'. Although Lewis does sometimes assert that expressive judgements cannot be false, I believe that all the *arguments* he gives for the certainty of expressive judgements are arguments to show that these judgements are certain in a warrant-evaluative sense. Indeed Lewis sometimes uses the words 'indubitable' and 'incorrigible' as synonyms of 'certain', and these two words are more naturally interpreted as warrant-evaluative than as truth-evaluative. There is no logical inconsistency in asserting that someone has a false belief which he cannot rationally *doubt* and which he is not in a position to *correct*; consequently there is no inconsistency in asserting that expressive judgements are indubitable and incorrigible, while at the same time granting that some of them may be false.

In defending the doctrine that expressive judgements are certain in a warrant-evaluative sense, Lewis sometimes tries to prove much more than is necessary to refute the coherence theory of justification. Some of his arguments are apparently intended to show that, if I now judge, for example, that it looks as if I am seeing something red, I shall never, at any time in the future, be justified in revoking this judgement. But problems concerning the future revocation of an expressive judgement, at a time when my decision must depend in part on my memory of my present experience, are not directly relevant to the question: Are my *present* expressive judgements certain (and hence warranted) for me *now*? And, if they are, is their warrant derived entirely from coherence? I believe that Lewis's answers to these two questions are (1) that my present expressive judgements, being certain, are not only warranted for me but warranted to so high a degree that no other judgements are *more* warranted for me, and (2) that their warrant is not derived to the slightest degree from coherence nor defeasible through failure to cohere with other judgements. 'There is no requirement of consistency', Lewis asserts, 'which is *relevant* to protocols.'[5]

Again, however, it is important to observe that there are at least three weaker, and therefore perhaps more plausible, positions that are also incompatible with the coherence theory of justification as we have been construing it. It might be maintained (1) that the warrant of an expressive judgement may be increased by its

---

[5] 'The Given Element in Empirical Knowledge', 173. Italics mine.

coherence with other judgements, and to some extent decreased by failure to cohere, but that failure to cohere can never decrease its warrant to a point at which a contradictory judgement would be more (or even equally) warranted. This would allow us to say that my present expressive judgements, although they may be false, are not now *falsifiable* for me. Or it might be maintained (2) that present expressive judgements, although falsifiable by failure to cohere, always have *some* degree of warrant which is not derived from coherence and which is not defeasible through failure to cohere. Or, even more moderately, it might be maintained (3) that expressive judgements have some degree of 'initial' non-inferential warrant which *is* defeasible through failure to cohere—perhaps even allowing, in principle, for the possibility that the contradictory of an expressive judgement may be as fully warranted as any other empirical judgement.[6] Although Lewis's strong position and each of these weaker positions differ markedly from one another, each of them entails a proposition which we may call 'the central thesis of epistemic priority'—the thesis that some statements have some degree of warrant which is independent of (and in this sense 'prior to') the warrant (if any) that they derive from their coherence with other statements. If we decide that there are statements of this kind, our next task is to determine what warrant-increasing property these statements have in addition to properties that are ultimately inferential.

In considering this problem there is a strong temptation for those who accept the thesis of epistemic priority to say that the statement (for example) 'It looks as if I am seeing something red' is warranted (or given some warrant) for me simply by the fact that it *does* look as if I am seeing something red; but to say this seems to imply that the statement is warranted because it is *true*—because it asserts what is in fact the case. To preserve the important distinction between truth and warrant, so that in principle *any* empirical statement may be true but unwarranted, or false but warranted, it would be preferable to maintain that the statement has a certain degree of warrant for me because it is a statement (whether true or

---

[6] Lewis himself defends a position analogous to (3) with respect to present memory judgements about the *past*—as opposed to present judgements about experiences (including memory judgements) occurring in the *present* (AKV 354ff.). H. H. Price's 'Principle of Confirmability' represents an analogous position with respect to judgements about presently perceived material things; see *Perception* (New York, 1933), 185. But 'initial' warrant is derived by Lewis and Price from an 'assumption' or 'principle', and can thus be construed as 'inferential'.

false) that *purports* to characterize (and only to characterize) the content of my present experience. (This could of course be made more precise by the use of examples and other devices.) But this condition is clearly insufficient, for we should not want to hold that *all* statements, including all possible pairs of contradictory statements, have some degree of warrant if they satisfy this requirement.

The obvious way to meet this difficulty is to add the further condition that a statement about my present experience can have some degree of ultimate non-inferential warrant for me only if I believe it to be true. This condition is suggested, as we have already observed, by Lewis's use of the word 'judgement', and I am inclined to think that Lewis would consider these two conditions, taken together, to constitute a *sufficient* condition of epistemic priority. If he were also to maintain that these two conditions are *necessary*, it would not be inappropriate to say that for Lewis expressive judgements are 'self-warranted' (perhaps even 'self-evident'), implying by this, so to speak, that, for a statement about my present sense experience, its being now judged by me to be true is an ultimate warrant-increasing property. Because of the ambiguity of the word 'judgement', however, it is unclear to me whether Lewis would actually consider this second condition (namely that statements with non-inferential warrant must be believed) to be necessary. There are of course many statements which are warranted for me, which I am justified in believing, but which I do not in fact believe; and a philosopher who accepts the thesis of epistemic priority might maintain that among these statements are some that are ultimately warranted, at least in part, non-inferentially. Presumably, however, these non-inferentially warranted statements would all be statements that I would now believe if I had just *decided* whether they were true or false; and thus it would probably be close to the spirit of Lewis's position to maintain that in the last analysis a statement can now have for me only one warrant-increasing property that is not ultimately inferential—that compound property which consists in (1) purporting to characterize (and only to characterize) the content of my present experience, and (2) being a statement that I either now believe to be true or should now believe to be true if I had just decided whether it were true or false.

This formulation of a possible theory of epistemic priority raises a number of important and puzzling questions. We might wonder, for example, whether (2) should include some restriction on the method by which I arrive at my belief, and whether it is possible to formulate such a restriction without circularity. And we might wonder whether the *strength* of my belief (the *confidence* with which I hold it) does not have some role in determining at least the *degree* to which a statement has a warrant that is ultimately non-inferential. Within the limits of this paper, however, I can make only a few concluding remarks about Lewis's criticism of the coherence theory, in particular about his statement, already quoted, that 'no logical relationship, by itself, can ever be sufficient to establish the truth, or the credibility even, of any synthetic judgement.'

IV

This statement, which I think represents the crux of many familiar arguments against the coherence theory, seems to me to reflect a conception of the coherence theory which is unnecessarily narrow and much too narrow to make the theory at all plausible. It is sometimes said (cf. AKV 340) that the coherence theory provides us with no way of distinguishing the actual world from other 'possible worlds', since statements describing any of these worlds will form equally coherent systems; and this seems also to be Lewis's point when he says that a system of statements that stand only because they 'lean against one another' gives us 'no better assurance of anything in it than that which attaches to the contents of a well-written novel'. As we have observed, however, a philosopher who accepts what we have called the 'central thesis' of the coherence theory is not thereby committed to any particular way of identifying the class of 'warrant-conferring' statements with which any warranted statement must ultimately cohere. If he insists that the power to confer warrant resides only in warranted statements, and that warranted statements constitute a perfectly democratic society in which each member receives its warrant from coherence with all the others, then indeed he will not be able to explain why one system of coherent statements is warranted and another is not. But this difficulty can be avoided if he adopts a less democratic position and recognizes an élite class of 'basic' warrant-conferring statements which, although it may include some statements that are not warranted, excludes a great many statements that *are* warranted. If he can identify this class by reference to something other than mere coherence, he may be able, so to speak, to tie the entire set of warranted statements to the possible world in which we actually live. In fact he would then be in a position to agree with Lewis, without giving up the coherence theory, that no logical (inferential) relationship, *by itself*, 'can ever be sufficient to establish the truth, or even the credibility, of any synthetic judgement'.

There are many interesting ways in which we might delimit such a class of basic warrant-conferring statements for a particular person at a particular time, but perhaps the traditional and most plausible way is to restrict this class to statements, whatever their logical form or subject-matter, that are actually believed by that person at that time.[7] If 'believed' is interpreted liberally enough so that this class includes a large number of very general theoretical statements, there is some ground for holding that the inferential relationships among them—and at some points the lack of any inferential relationship—are sufficient to determine which statements are warranted, which statements are not, and the relative degrees of warrant among them.[8] Within this élite class, so to speak, each statement, whether itself warranted or not, would have a voice in determining the epistemic status of every other statement in the class. And statements outside the class—statements which have not yet been thought about, or which, for some other reason are neither believed nor disbelieved—could be said to be 'derivatively' warranted if in fact—whether anybody knows it or not—they cohere with the warranted statements in this warrant-conferring class. This would mean, in effect, that these derivatively warranted statements are second-class citizens: they receive warrant from members of the class of basic warrant-conferring statements (and are thus tied down to the actual world), but they have no independent authority in determining whether any other statement is warranted.

A position of this kind seems to me to avoid Lewis's logical objection to the coherence theory of justification and thus to demonstrate that the issue between this theory and the thesis of

---

[7] Cf. Brand Blanshard, *The Nature of Thought* (New York, 1940), ii. 272: 'What the ultimate standard means in *practice* is the system of present knowledge as apprehended by a particular mind.'

[8] The rules that would determine these things might be similar to those proposed by R. B. Brandt for the selection of warranted memory beliefs (recollections) in his 'Memory Beliefs', *The Philosophical Review*, 64/1 (Jan. 1955), 88. Brandt's rule, however, 'advises accepting recollections when there is no positive support from the system' and is thus compatible with the thesis of epistemic priority.

epistemic priority must ultimately be decided on purely empirical grounds. It is of course difficult to formulate precise criteria for settling such an issue, but advocates of the coherence theory have commonly tried to defend their position by appealing to the actual practices of scientists and other rational men, and presumably these practices are relevant to the issue even if not absolutely decisive. On this basis I think it would be very difficult to defend Lewis's strong position that some statements are certain in a sense that makes coherence *completely* irrelevant to their warrant. But I think, on the other hand, that rational men often believe statements about their own sense experience with much greater confidence than they could justify by inference from other beliefs; and this suggests that we may accept the thesis of epistemic priority and try to choose among the three weaker positions that entail this thesis. It has been my intention in this paper to formulate an issue and not to defend this particular conclusion. But if the thesis of epistemic priority is, as I think, correct, the methodological consequences are momentous whether or not we accept Lewis's doctrine of certainty. For at least we can say in that case that Lewis has always been right in maintaining that the major task of a theory of empirical knowledge is to show how it is possible—by means of a theory of meaning and suitable principles of inference—for statements that have independent, non-inferential, warrant to serve as the ground of all the rest of our empirical knowledge.

X

MORE ON GIVENNESS AND EXPLANATORY COHERENCE

W. SELLARS

I

1. Historically, there have been two competing strands in the concept of a 'self-presenting' state of affairs, that is, the kind of state of affairs access to which is supposed to provide empirical knowledge with its 'foundation'.

2. According to the first strand, a self-presenting stage of affairs is a *fact* (an *obtaining* state of affairs) which is known to obtain, not by virtue of an act of warranted belief, but by virtue of a unique cognitive act which is more basic than that of any believing however warranted.

3. The main thrust of this position is directed against what it decries as 'representationalism,' the view that whatever other conditions they must satisfy to constitute knowledge, cognitive acts are, in the first instance, representations.

4. Representationalism can take different forms. That which is most prevalent today stresses the quasi-linguistic character of cognitive acts, the idea that they belong to a framework of signs and symbols which, whether innate or acquired, enables organisms which possess it to construct representations of themselves in their environment.

5. A more traditional form stresses a distinction between two 'modes of being' which objects and states of affairs may have: (*a*) actual being—roughly, the being which something has independently of being an object of thought; (*b*) intentional inexistence, the being something has when it is thought of, *qua* thought of—Descartes's 'representative' or 'objective' reality.

Reprinted by permission of the publisher, from G. Pappas (ed.), *Justification and Knowledge* (1979), 169–82. Copyright © 1979 by D. Reidel Publishing Company, Dordrecht, Holland.

6. According to the latter form, our cognitive access to the world consists *exclusively* in the occurrence of mental acts in which objects and events have intentional in-existence. The term 'exclusively' is of the essence, for it is representationalism in the (supposedly) pejorative sense by virtue of denying that we have any other cognitive access to the world than by such acts. Whatever other features these acts may have, in no case do they involve, nor are they accompanied by what the anti-representationalist would characterize as a 'direct' cognitive access to 'the facts themselves' in their character as factual.

7. The representationalist grants, of course, that certain cognitive acts have a *special* character by virtue of which they are capable of yielding knowledge of certain privileged matters of fact. The possession of this special character would either guarantee that a representational act is true, or at least give a high antecedent probability to the proposition that this was the case.

8. Just how this special character is to be conceived, classical representationalists found it difficult to say. As a matter of fact, careful reading of the texts reveals that most, if not all, representationalists covertly introduced a non-representational mode of cognitive access—interestingly enough, to representational acts themselves. Because of this fact, Immanuel Kant might well have been the first thoroughgoing representationalist.

9. They took it for granted that one could 'notice', 'compare' and 'consider' one's mental acts, and to do these things was, in effect, to have non-representational knowledge of these acts as being what they are, e.g., a representation of a tree. Such awareness would simply be a special case of what anti-representationalists refer to as unmediated or direct apprehension of matters of fact.

10. That Descartes, like Locke, covertly introduced a non-representational element into his theory of knowledge along the above lines is, I think, clear. He did, however, also insist that certain representational acts have, in addition to their character as representations, a special property—which he referred to as 'clarity and distinctness'—which plays the role described in paragraph 7 above.

11. Such a property might be called a knowledge-making property, by analogy with what in moral philosophy are called right-making characteristics.[1]

---

[1] Cf. Chisholm, *Perception* (Ithaca, 1957), 30–2.

12. Of course, a coherent representationalist who argues that all cognitive access to the world is a matter of the occurrence of representational acts need not take clarity-cum-distinctness to be *the* knowledge-making property, or even *a* knowledge-making property. In any case it seems more appropriate to a priori knowledge than to knowledge of particular matters of fact.

13. With respect to the latter, the representationalist might propose some mode of causal confrontation of the knowing by the known. The connection would be a knowledge-making property of the representational act, and would give it a cognitive virtue which other kinds of representations do not have.

14. The contemporary representationalist who stresses the linguistic analogy might well argue that the causal relationship between the knowing and the known in introspective, perceptual, and memory judgements is reflected by the presence of demonstrative components in the representational act.

15. To develop this theme, however, would require the formulation of a theory of intentionality which does justice to both the logical and the causal dimensions of discourse about mental acts, and this topic is much too large to be more than adumbrated on the present occasion.[2]

16. Representationalists typically become touchy when asked whether our only access to the fact, when it is a fact, that an act has a knowledge-making property (whatever it might be) is by the occurrence of a further representational act. And, indeed, the question whether representationalism can be so formulated as to alleviate this touchiness is a central theme in disputes pertaining to 'foundationalism'.

17. From this perspective, the alternative to representationalism is the view that we have a direct access to the *factuality* of certain privileged facts unmediated by representational acts, whether quasi-linguistic episodes (e.g., tokens of Mentalese) or conceptual acts in which states of affairs have 'representative being' or intentional in-existence.

18. According to this alternative, our direct or non-representational access to these privileged facts (call it 'direct apprehension') provides a cognitive stratum which 'underlies', 'supports', or 'provides a foundation for' cognitive acts of the representational

---

[2] I have, however, discussed it at length on a number of occasions, thus *Science and Metaphysics* (London, 1968), ch. 3–5; most recently in *Naturalism and Ontology* (Atascadero, 1980), chs. 4–5.

category. If we call the latter 'beliefs', then while some justified true beliefs may merit the term 'knowledge', they rest on a foundation of direct apprehensions which are not special cases of beliefs, but belong to a radically different category.

19. According to this line of thought, then, a self-presenting state of affairs is one which is either directly apprehended, or of such a kind as to be capable of being directly apprehended should the corresponding question arise. Direct apprehension or direct apprehendibility would be a source of epistemic authority.

20. Notice that for a state of affairs to be self-presenting, as thus construed, it must obtain, that is, be a fact rather than a mere possibility.

21. Now one who takes this line might deny that direct apprehensions themselves have intrinsic epistemic value and restrict terms of epistemic appraisal, thus 'evident' or 'warranted', to *beliefs*, and, hence, to propositions whose epistemic status does not require that they be true.[3]

22. One might accordingly argue that the self-presentingness of self-presenting states of affairs is a 'prime mover unmoved' (to borrow Chisholm's useful metaphor)[4] of epistemic authority, that is, that the direct apprehension or apprehendibility of a state-of-affairs is a source of evidentness or warrant, but itself neither warranted nor unwarranted.

23. Or, to put it differently, one might claim that their special relation to self-presenting *facts* is a knowledge-making property of certain *beliefs*.

24. To make this move, however, would be paradoxical, for it involves denying that the direct apprehension of a fact is itself *knowledge*. For direct apprehension, by those who have evolved the concept, is almost invariably taken to be the very paradigm of knowledge 'properly so-called'.

25. On the other hand, to hold that an act of direct apprehension is subject to epistemic appraisal as, for example, *evident* seems to point in the direction of representationalism. How could items so sharply contrasted, as *apprehensions* and *representations* are by the anti-representationalist, both be ascribed epistemic value without equivocation? The anti-representationalist programme is not without its problems.

---

[3] Otherwise put, 'to states of affairs whose epistemic status does not require that they obtain'. Cf. the preceding paragraph.

[4] *Theory of Knowledge*, 2nd edn. (Englewood Cliffs, NJ, 1977), 25.

26. The classical alternative to this conception of a self-presenting state of affairs as a fact which is either directly apprehended or capable of being directly apprehended should the appropriate question arise is, of course, that of the representationalist. According to the latter account a self-presenting state of affairs is one which is such that if the relevant person at the relevant time occurrently believes (judges) it to obtain, the believing would have high epistemic worth and, indeed, would be non-inferentially warranted or self-evident.

27. Notice, as pointed out above, that this alternative is compatible with the idea that self-presenting states of affairs *need not obtain* (be *facts*). It is also compatible with the idea that when a self-presenting state of affairs *does* obtain, it is a factor which contributes (causally) to bringing about the occurrent belief (should such arise) that it does obtain. (See paragraphs 13–15 above.)

28. The distinctive feature of this account is that the *self-presentingness* of a self-presenting state of affairs is to be understood in terms of the idea that the *factual* category to which the state of affairs belongs, for example, that of being one's occurrent mental state of the present moment, is an (epistemic) value-making property of the state of affairs.

29. Whereas 'direct apprehension' can masquerade as a non-value-laden term (see paragraph 24 above).

II

30. Now it seems eminently clear to me that in his excellent paper on 'Coherence, Certainty, and Epistemic Priority',[5] Roderick Firth rejects the radical distinction between *beliefs* and *direct apprehensions* which is central to the first account of self-presenting states.

31. In his reconstruction of the concept of givenness the central theme is the idea that certain judgements have, in his terminology, an ultimately non-inferential warrant-increasing property.

32. He alternates between speaking of 'judgements' (which I have been calling 'occurrent beliefs') and of 'statements'; but it seems clear that he is using the term 'statement' not to refer to verbal performances, but as a surrogate for 'proposition' in that sense in which propositions are *contents* of beliefs (that is, are that which is believed). I think that he is implicitly making an analogical

[5] Essay IX in this collection.

use of Strawson's distinction between sentences and the statements they can be used to make on particular occasions, to emphasize that judgements have the conceptual counterparts of the indexical features of statement-utterances.

33. Firth distinguishes (pp. 168–9) two modes of *inferential* warrant-increasing properties which statements may have. I shall paraphrase his distinction, referring to the two kinds simply as 'the first kind' and 'the second kind'.

(1) A statement, *S*, has an inferential warrant-increasing property, *P*, of the *first* kind, if *P* consists in the fact that *S* is 'validly inferable from certain other statements of a specified kind'.

(2) A statement, *S*, has an inferential warrant-increasing property, *P*, of the *second* kind, if the meta-statement, 'if *S* has the property *P*, then *S* is likely to be true'[6] has an inferential warrant-increasing property, *P′*, of the *first* kind.

34. Firth refers to both 'deductive' and 'inductive' inference. The former is reasonably unproblematic. On the other hand he does not clearly specify the scope of 'inductive'. The example he gives is a case of what is usually called 'simple' or 'instantial' induction. Nevertheless the fact that he parenthetically ties 'inferable from' to 'coheres with'[7] leaves the door open to the possibility of expanding the scope of 'inductive inference' to include other modes of non-deductive explanatory reasoning.

35. Whether or not he is prepared to avail himself of this option— and if so, to what extent—is a matter of crucial importance, for on it hinges the ultimate significance of his distinction between inferential and non-inferential warrant-increasing properties.

36. In any event, Firth illustrates inferential warrant-increasing properties of the *second* kind by 'the property of being believed by certain scholars', for example, I take it, by members of the relevant academy. It belongs to the *second* kind because the meta-statement,

If a statement, *S*, has the property of being believed by certain scholars, then *S* is likely to be true,

has the property of being inductively inferable from a statement to the effect that 'these scholars have usually held correct beliefs

---

[6] Firth writes 'true' where I have put 'likely to be true'—but that is simply a symptom of his lack of concern for inferential warrant-increasing properties of the *second* kind.

[7] p. 169, 1. 12.

about statements similar to *S* in certain respects':[8] and this property is an inferential warrant-increasing property of the *first* kind.

37. What, then, is a *non-inferential* warrant-increasing property? Clearly, as far as the *extension* of the concept is concerned, it is a warrant-increasing property (WP) which belongs to neither of the above two kinds. As for the *intension* of the concept, the contrast between non-inferential WPs and inferential WPs of the *first* kind is unproblematic.

38. Again, if the 'inferential' WP, *P'* of the meta-statement,

Statements which have *P* are likely to be true,

is construed as the property of having inductive support in the instantial sense, the contrast between inferential WPs of the *second* kind and non-inferential WPs is equally unproblematic.

39. As a matter of fact, even if one counts the acquisition of a *theory* by a substantial degree of confirmation as a variety of acquiring inductive support, the distinctions remain reasonably straightforward.

40. But suppose that *P'* is the property of belonging to a theory of persons as representers of themselves-in-the-world, which, although it has good explanatory power and is capable of refinement by inductive procedures, *was not* (and, indeed, could not have been) *arrived at* by inferences guided by inductive canons however broadly construed. Would *P'* be an *inferential* WP or an *explanatory* but not *inferential* WP?

41. It might be thought that the question as to how the theory was 'arrived at' is one which belongs to the 'order of discovery' *rather than* 'the order of justification'. But reflection on the fact that to answer a question of the form 'Is *x* justified in ∅-ing?' requires taking *x*'s historical situation into account should give one pause.

42. I shall return to this theme in a moment. For the time being I note only that in the essay in question, Firth does not touch on these topics, although the issues they raise suggest possibilities which are in keeping with one aspect of his enterprise, which is, as I would put it, to reconcile as far as possible the claims of those who stress warrantedness grounded in explanatory coherence (among whom I count myself) with the claims of those who stress the non-inferential warrantedness[9] of certain empirical statements (among

[8] p. 169.

[9] A warrantedness, however, which may be *inferential* in *something like* Firth's account of inferential WPs of the *second* kind.

whom I also count myself). I shall attempt to push Firth in the direction of Firth-Bosanquet.

III

43. But before arguing the case for the primacy of the concept of explanatory coherence in epistemic evaluation, it will be helpful to take a careful look at Firth's account of the non-inferential warrantedness of certain empirical statements. It will also help in defining our problem to examine the connection he finds between the concept of non-inferential warrant and that of what he calls 'epistemic priority'.[10]

44. He begins by suggesting that 'the statement . . . "it looks to me as if I am seeing something red" . . . has a certain degree of warrant for me because it is a statement (whether true or false) that *purports* to characterize (and only to characterize) the content of my present experience.' To which he adds, finding this to be too permissive, 'a statement about my present experience can have some degree of ultimate non-inferential warrant for me only if I believe it to be true'.

45. Separating out the chaff introduced by the ambiguities of the word 'statement', this amounts to the idea that the property (P_E) of being a judgement about, and exclusively about, my present experience is a non-inferential WP.

46. This requires that the meta-judgement,

MJ_1: Judgements which have P_E are likely to be true,

if itself warranted, has a warrant which, *as Firth is using the term*, is non-inferential.

47. Assuming, for the moment, that MJ_1 *is* warranted, and having in mind the question raised in paragraph 40 above, let me provisionally characterize MJ_1 as a

non-inductively warranted warrant principle

and contrast it with

MJ_2: Judgements which are believed by certain scholars are likely to be true.

which can be characterized as an

inductively warranted warrant principle.

[10] pp. 168 ff.

48. Notice that in the second passage quoted in paragraph 44, Firth refers to 'degree[s] of *ultimate* non-inferential warrant' (italics mine). What he has in mind, of course, is that while the property of being believed by certain scholars (e.g., members of the American Geographical Society) is not an *inferential* property of geographical statements, so that it would be incorrect to classify its character as a WP as its being an *inferential* WP, yet it would be equally incorrect to classify it as a *non-inferential* WP, for it owes its character as a WP to its *own* inferential property of being an inductively established sign of probable truth. Although itself a non-inferential property of geographical statements, it *has* a higher order inferential property which is the ground of its ability to contribute warrant to geographical statements. It is by virtue of this fact that it is an inferential WP of the *second* kind. And it is in this sense that it is not an *ultimately* non-inferential WP.

49. Thus, when Firth tells us that P_E, the property of being exclusively about one's own experience of the present moment, is an *ultimately* non-inferential WP, he means that P_E is not only not an inferential property of the judgements in question, but that, unlike being believed by members of the AGS, it is not a WP by virtue of itself having an inferential property.

50. In other words, Firth is committed to the idea that MJ_1, which characterizes P_E as a WP, either itself has no WP or, if it does, has a WP which is non-inferential.

51. Since, however, Firth does not press the question as to whether MJ_1 does or does not have a WP, the possibility arises that he is emphasizing that it does not belong in the same box as MJ_2, that is, that its WP (if it has one) is not *inductive*. This would leave open the possibility that its WP, if any, is either non-inferential, or inferential but non-inductively so (cf. paragraph 47).

52. These considerations make it clear that the question '*Does* MJ_1 have a WP?' or, to put the matter bluntly, 'Is there any *reason* to accept MJ_1?' can no longer be deferred.

53. A negative answer would, on the face of it, bring to shipwreck the enterprise of making sense of the epistemic evaluation of empirical propositions. On the other hand, an affirmative answer would immediately raise the question '*What* WP does MJ_1 have?' or '*What* reason is there to accept MJ_1?'

54. And to these questions the only available answers, given the Firthian context in which they arise, are: (1) it is self-evident or axiomatic that it is reasonable to accept MJ_1; (2) it is reasonable to

accept MJ_1 *because* if it is false, no empirical statements are warranted.

55. Both these answers would turn us aside with a stone instead of the bread which, in spite of all the dialectical niceties, we intuitively feel must be there. Self-evidence is too atomistic an interpretation of the authority of epistemic principles; while the second answer—which amounts to the old slogan 'This or nothing' —is too weak, in that we do seem to have some insight into *why* something like the epistemic principles so lovingly polished by Firth and Chisholm are true. What has gone wrong?

IV

56. Firth formulates what he calls 'the central thesis of epistemic priority' as 'the thesis that some statements have some degree of warrant which is independent of (and in this sense "prior to") the warrant (if any) which they derive from other statements'.[11] He thinks that this thesis is correct, and concludes that 'Lewis has always been right in maintaining that the major task of a theory of empirical knowledge is to show how it is possible . . . for statements that have independent non-inferential warrant to serve as the ground of all of the rest of empirical knowledge.'[12]

57. Now it is clear that some principles which assert that a certain property of empirical statements is a WP are themselves statements which belong to the content of empirical knowledge thus

MJ_2: Statements which are accepted by the AGS are likely to be true

is not only a *criterion* for assessing geographical knowledge claims; it is itself an empirical statement and, indeed, an inductively confirmed knowledge claim in its own right.

58. But what of MJ_1? And what of such principles[13] as

MJ_3: If a person ostensibly perceives (without ground for doubt) something to be $\emptyset$ (for appropriate values of $\emptyset$) then it is likely to be true that he perceives something to be $\emptyset$.

MJ_4: If a person ostensibly remembers (without ground for doubt) having ostensibly perceived something to be $\emptyset$

---

[11] p. 172.
[12] p. 176.
[13] Adapted from Chisholm's principles B and D, *Theory of Knowledge*, 80–1.

(for appropriate values of $\emptyset$) then it is likely to be true that he remembers ostensibly perceiving something to be $\emptyset$.

Might not these also be *both* principles which provide criteria for adjudicating certain empirical knowledge claims *and* empirical knowledge claims in their own right? [14]

59. Now if an affirmative response took the form of a claim that MJ_1, MJ_3, and MJ_4 are *empirically confirmed* knowledge claims—thus putting them in a box with MJ_2—a sensitive nerve would be touched. Would not such a claim involve a vicious circularity?

60. Since it is obvious that they cannot be empirical generalizations which owe their epistemic authority to confirmation by instances, one might look for a less direct mode of confirmation by experience.

61. Even if indirectly, however, an appeal must ultimately be made to the fruits of introspection, perception, and memory. Sooner or later we would be confronted by such pairs of statements as

> It is reasonable to accept MJ_1, MJ_3, and MJ_4 because they are elements in a theory T which coheres with our introspections, perceptions, and memories. Our ostensible introspections, perceptions, and memories are likely to be true because they fall under MJ_1, MJ_3, and MJ_4.

62. How, we are inclined to expostulate, could it be reasonable (at t) to accept T *because* it is supported by our introspective, perceptual, and memory judgements (IPM judgements), if it is *because* they fall under MJ_1, MJ_3, and MJ_4 that it is reasonable to accept these IPM judgements?

63. Consider

> Jones accepts T for the reason that IPM judgements support T;
>
> Jones accepts IPM judgements for the reason that they fall under T.

This would seem to be no more rational on Jones's part than the situation described by

> Jones saves money in order to maintain his bank account;

---

[14] After all, can it not be argued that lawlike statements are both empirical hypotheses *and* material rules of inference?

Jones maintains his bank account in order to facilitate his saving money.

64. We might say that in these two cases Jones is being unreasonable because his motivation is circular. They can be compared with cases in which a person is unreasonable because acting from a self-contradictory intention. Of course, the circle must not be too small (or the contradiction too blatant) if the concept of such a case is to be coherent.

65. To be distinguished from such 'subjective' unreasonableness is the objective ungroundedness[15] which would obtain if the following *per impossible* were true:

> What makes it reasonable for Jones to accept *T* is *simply* the fact that *T* is supported by the IPM judgements which it is reasonable for Jones to accept.

> What makes it reasonable for Jones to accept these IPM judgements is *simply* the fact that they are likely to be true by virtue of falling under *T*, which it is reasonable for Jones to accept.

66. It should therefore be clear, if it was not already, that what we were groping for in paragraph 58 was a way in which it could be *independently* reasonable to accept MJ_1, MJ_3 and MJ_4 in spite of the fact that *a* ground for accepting them is the fact that they belong to *T*, which we suppose to be an empirically well-confirmed theory.

67. I think that such a way can be found by following a strategy developed in two essays on the reasonableness of accepting inductive hypotheses.[16] As a matter of fact, the following considerations are necessary to round out the argument of those essays.

68. Such an expanded account might well be called 'Epistemic Evaluation as Vindication'. Its central theme would be that achieving

[15] It is important to distinguish between two possible constructions of 'It is reasonable for Jones to do *A because A*-ing would bring about *X*. Thus

> R_1: The fact that *A*-ing would being about *X* makes it reasonable for Jones to do *A*.
> R_2: It is reasonable for Jones to do *A* for the reason that by *A*-ing he (himself) would bring about *X*.

In R_1 what is reasonable is simply the doing of *A*, and the fact that *A* would bring about *X* is the *ground* of this reasonableness. In R_2 what is reasonable is the doing of *A with a certain intention or purpose*, i.e. that of bringing about *X* by doing *A*.

[16] 'Induction as Vindication', in *Philosophy of Science*, 31 (1964), reprinted in *Essays in Philosophy and its History* (Dordecht, 1974); and 'Are There Non-deductive Logics?' in *Essays in Honor of C. G. Hempel*, ed. N. Rescher (Dordrecht, 1970).

a certain end or goal can be (deductively) shown to require a certain integrated system of means. For the purposes of this necessarily schematic essay, the end can be characterized as that of being in a *general* position, so far as in us lies, to *act*, that is, to bring about changes in ourselves and our environment in order to realize *specific* purposes or intentions.

69. In the above-mentioned essays I argued that among the necessary means to this end is the espousal of certain patterns of reasoning, specifically those involved in the establishing of statistical hypotheses, laws, and theories.

70. Although I did have *something* to say about how these various patterns of reasoning are interrelated, I treated each 'mode of probabilification' as though it stood on its own feet and said relatively little about how these dimensions of 'prima-facie' reasonableness combine and interact to generate probabilities 'all things considered'.[17]

71. And, in particular, I had nothing to say about the probability of observation statements—though it is obvious that the probability of an inductive hypothesis is a function of the probability of the observational premises which are mustered to support it.

72. In the language of the present essay, I had nothing to say about the probability which attaches to ostensible introspections, perceptions, and memories (IPM judgements).

73. If challenged, I would have appealed to something like MJ_1, MJ_3, and MJ_4 and argued that they are true. If asked why it is reasonable to accept them, I would have argued that they are elements in a conceptual framework which defines what it is to be a finite knower in a world one never made.

74. In short I would have appealed to a more encompassing version of what I have been calling theory *T*.

75. To be one who makes epistemic appraisals is to be in this framework. And to be in this framework is to appreciate the interplay of the reasonablenesses of inductive hypotheses and of IPM judgements.

76. Now in the case of particular theories, for example, the corpuscular theory of light, one can imagine that one gets into the conceptual framework of the theory by a process of inductive reasoning. One *entertains* the framework and finds it inductively

---

[17] After all, my philosophical purpose was to exhibit inductive reasoning as a form of practical reasoning, and by so doing to throw light on the very concept of probability.

reasonable to espouse it. One espouses it *for the reason that* it is inductively reasonable to do so, and one is *being reasonable* in so doing.

77. But can one espouse theory *T for the reason that* it is inductively reasonable to do so, and be *reasonable* in so doing? We have already seen that the answer is 'No!'.

78. Clearly we must distinguish the question 'How did we get into the framework?' from the question 'Granted that we are in the framework, how can we justify accepting it?' In neither case, however, is the answer 'by inductive reasoning' appropriate.

79. Presumably the question 'How did we get into the framework?' has a causal answer, a special application of evolutionary theory to the emergence of beings capable of conceptually representing the world of which they have come to be a part.

80. As to the second question, the answer, according to the proposed strategy, lies in the necessary connection between being in the framework of epistemic evaluation and being agents. It is this connection which constitutes the objective ground for the reasonableness of accepting *something like* theory *T*.

81. I say 'something like' theory *T*, for we are now at the moment of truth and must get down to specifics. Thus, what does all of the above metaphysical chatter about frameworks have to do with the rationality of accepting MJ_1, MJ_3, and MJ_4?

82. The answer is that since agency, to be effective, involves having reliable cognitive maps of ourselves and our environment, the concept of effective agency involves that of our IPM judgements being likely to be true, that is, to be correct mappings[18] of ourselves and our circumstances.

83. Notice, then, that if the above argument is sound, it is reasonable to accept

MJ_5: IPM judgements are likely to be true,

simply on the ground that unless they *are* likely to be true, the concept of effective agency has no application.

84. Now for the linchpin. We must carefully distinguish between having good reason to accept MJ_5 and having good reason to accept a proposed *explanation* of *why* IPM judgements are likely to be true.

85. To explain why IPM judgements are likely to be true *does* involve finding inductive support for hypotheses concerning the

---

[18] May I call them pictures?

mechanisms involved and how they evolved in response to evolutionary pressures. And *this* obviously presupposes the reasonableness of accepting IPM judgements.

86. To borrow a Firthian locution, MJ_5 is epistemically prior to the reasonableness of particular IPM judgements, whereas particular IPM judgements are epistemically prior to *explanations* of the likely truth of IPM judgements.

87. Some twenty-two years ago I wrote

> If I reject the framework of traditional empiricism, it is not because I want to say that empirical knowledge has *no* foundation. For to put it this way is to accept that it is really 'empirical knowledge so-called,' and to be put in a box with rumors and hoaxes. There is clearly *some* point to the picture of knowledge as resting on a level of propositions—observation reports—which do not rest on other propositions in the same way as other propositions rest on them. On the other hand, I do wish to insist that the metaphor of 'foundation' is misleading in that it keeps us from seeing that if there is a logical dimension in which other empirical propositions rest on observation reports, there is another logical dimension in which the latter rest on the former.[19]

To the extent that this passage was one of my notorious promissory notes, I hope that the present essay provides *some* of the cash.

88. I will conclude by rounding out the considerations advanced in paragraphs 85–6. They explain why I wrote in paragraph 80 that there is an objective ground for accepting 'something like' theory *T*; for, as it exists at any one time, theory *T* is a complex which includes MJ_5 *and* attempts to explain *why* IPM judgements are likely to be true. The latter enterprise is still unfinished business.

89. It is in the former respect that it constitutes the conceptual framework which spells out the 'explanatory coherence' which is the ultimate criterion of truth.[20]

---

[19] 'Empiricism and the Philosophy of Mind', in *Minnesota Studies in the Philosophy of Science*, i, ed. H. Feigl and M. Scriven (Minneapolis, 1956); reprinted with minor alterations in *Science, Perception and Reality* (London, 1963). The passage occurs on p. 170 of *SPR*.

[20] I have, of course, neglected in this essay the equally important and no less difficult topic of deductive reasonableness.

XI

PERCEPTION, VISION, AND CAUSATION

P. SNOWDON

It is believed by some that reflection on many of our psychological notions reveals that they can be instantiated by an object only if some sort of causal condition is fulfilled. Notions to which it has been supposed this applies include those of remembering, knowing, acting for a reason and perception.[1] I wish here to discuss the application of such a view to this last case, an application which is, I think, often believed to be more or less obviously correct, or at least to be as obviously correct as it ever is.[2] Although the present discussion is primarily of causal theories of perception (or more accurately, of one case of perception, namely vision), some elements in it may be relevant to the assessment, or understanding, of causal theories for some other psychological notions. The reason this may be so is that the principal argument used to support a causal theory of perception of this sort exhibits a similar form to arguments used to support some causal theories elsewhere and involved in any consideration of how strongly causal theories of perception are supported is the task of getting clear about the force of arguments with that structure.

Reprinted by courtesy of the Editor of the Aristotelian Society and the author from *Proceedings of the Aristotelian Society*, 81 (1980–1), 175–92, © 1981.

[1] See C. B. Martin and M. Deutscher, 'Remembering', *Philosophical Review* 75 (1966), A. I. Goldman, 'A Causal Theory of Knowing', *Journal of Philosophy* 64 (1967), D. Davidson, 'Actions, Reasons, and Causes', *Journal of Philosophy* 60 (1963) and H. P. Grice, 'The Causal Theory of Perception', Essay III in this collection.

[2] David Wiggins, for example, talks of 'the finality of Grice's argument about perception', 'Freedom, Knowledge, Belief and Causality' in G. N. A. Vesey, ed., *Knowledge and Necessity* (London, 1970), 137. P. F. Strawson describes the view as 'obvious' in his 'Perception and its Objects', Essay V in this collection.

I

I want to begin by characterizing the causalist viewpoint—a viewpoint first propounded by Grice, and endorsed and added to in an impressive tradition, containing Strawson, Pears, and Peacocke (and, of course, many others).[3] In contrast to this assenting tradition, there has also been a dissenting one, but the points raised in it have seemed to most people not strong enough to threaten the causal theory.[4]

The view is defined by three claims. I shall specify them for the visual case, rather than for the more general case of perception itself.

The first claim is this; it is necessarily true that if a subject S sees a public object O then O causally affects S. I shall call this the causal thesis. Different theorists may (and do) disagree about how to explain the required relation of causal dependence and may (and do) differ about quite what sort of objects the claim should be formulated for. I want to ignore these variations.

The causal claim says nothing about what effect O must have on S. The second claim fills that gap and asserts: (2) O must produce in S a state reportable in a sentence beginning 'It looks to S as if . . .', where those words are interpreted both phenomenologically (rather than as ascribing, say, a tentative judgement by S) and, in Quine's terms, notionally rather than relationally. I shall call this the effect thesis, and refer to the alleged effects as looks-states (or L-states).

The third thesis amounts to a comment on the status of the other two. It says (3) theses (1) and (2) represent requirements of our ordinary concept, or notion, of vision. It is thus asserting, notably, that the causal thesis is, in some sense, a conceptual truth. I shall call this the conceptual thesis.[5]

---

[3] See P. F. Strawson, 'Causation in Perception', in *Freedom and Resentment* (London, 1974), D. F. Pears, 'The Causal Conditions of Perception', *Synthese*, 33 (1976), and Christopher Peacocke, *Holistic Explanation* (Oxford, 1979).

[4] The 'dissenting tradition' includes A. R. White, 'The Causal Theory of Perception', *Aristotelian Society*, Suppl. vol. 35 (1961), Jenny Teichman, 'Perception and Causation', *Proceedings of the Aristotelian Society*, 71 (1970–1), Jaegwon Kim, 'Perception and Reference without Causality', *Journal of Philosophy*, 74, (1977), and (perhaps), Michael Dummett 'Common Sense and Physics', 35–6, in G. F. Macdonald, ed., *Perception and Identity* (London, 1979).

[5] Grice describes himself as 'characterizing the ordinary notion of perceiving', p. 71. Strawson talks of 'the general idea' of 'causal dependence' being 'implicit' in 'the concept of perception', in 'Causation in Perception', 83.

It is, of course, very hard to say precisely what the conceptual thesis is claiming, but it seems reasonable to suggest that part of what is involved in a truth's being a conceptual one is that it is supportable (but not necessarily only supportable) in a distinctive way. And at least part of what is distinctive about the way is that there is a restriction on the data to which appeal can be made in the supporting argument. A somewhat rough way of specifying the restriction is that the data must be relatively immediately acknowledgeable by any person, whatever their education, who can count as having the concept in question. The aim of the restriction is to exclude any facts of which we can become aware only in the context of certain activities (for example, carrying out experiments, or becoming acquainted with the results of experiments, or reading psychological textbooks) which need not be indulged in by just anyone who has the concept. It has to be asked, therefore, whether any good argument satisfying this constraint exists for the causal thesis.

Now, that the causal thesis is true is something which most educated people would accept, and it is fair to suppose that its truth is a matter of relatively common knowledge. In this it resembles, say, the claim that the earth goes round the sun, or the claim that there has been evolution. It should, though, be clear that its having this status is no ground for accepting that the conceptual thesis is correct. For it is obvious that, despite there being widespread acquaintance with the conclusion, the fundamental justification of the causal thesis may rely on data outside the restricted class.

Theses 1–3 constitute the theory the support and correctness of which I wish to assess, but, of course, there is another claim, which anyone subscribing to this position would accept. It is that it is not sufficient for a subject to see an item that the item relate to the subject in accordance with the requirements of the first two theses. The problem then is to isolate the further conditions which will rule out deviant ways in which an object can fulfil the earlier two. Contributions to the assenting tradition, as I have called it, are mainly attempts to refute earlier purported solutions, combined with suggestions as to better ones.

The theory which has been specified is a causal theory of vision. There are, of course, structurally parallel theories about the other actual senses, but there is also a parallel thesis about perception itself, which is, probably, the one which is most often explicitly endorsed. There is, though, a reason for concentrating on the more specific visual claim, namely that it is possible thereby to avoid discussing a lacuna in the standard argument for the more general thesis. Thus the usual (although not invariable) procedure is to provide an argument for (say) the visual thesis, but to draw as a further immediate consequence the general thesis about perception. However, the more specific claim does not entail the general conclusion and something needs to be said in support of the move.

II

The main argument for the described position which was originally propounded by H. P. Grice, I shall consider in the next section. But before taking that up, there are some remarks by Professor Strawson, which are, I think, aimed at providing support for the causal and conceptual thesis (at least, I shall interpret them that way) and on which I wish very briefly to comment.

Strawson says this:

The idea of the presence of the thing as accounting for, or being responsible for, our perceptual awareness of it is implicit in the pre-theoretical scheme from the very start. For we think of perception as a way, . . . of informing ourselves about the world of independently existing things: we assume, that is to say, the general reliability of our perceptual experiences; and that assumption is the same as the assumption of a general causal dependence of our perceptual experiences on the independently existing things we take them to be of. The thought of my fleeting perception as a perception of a continuously and independently existing thing implicitly contains the thought that if the thing had not been there, I should not even have seemed to perceive it. It really should be obvious that with the distinction between independently existing objects and perceptual awareness of objects we already have the general notion of causal dependence of the latter on the former, even if this is not a matter to which we give much reflective attention in our pre-theoretical days.[6]

Now this is a very suggestive but also a very concise passage, in which it seems possible to detect three, no doubt intended to be interlocking, considerations. The first is as follows. Perception (of objects) is thought to be a way of acquiring information about the world. This amounts to (or at least involves) the assumption that experiences which are perceptual are, in general, reliable. This assumption is the same as the belief that if an experience is perceptual of object O it is causally dependent on that object.

[6] Strawson, 'Perception and its Objects', 103.

To assess this we need to explain what the assumption of the reliability of perceptual experience is supposed to be. One plausible way to view it is this: we treat experiences which we take to be perceptual as reliable in the sense that how it seems in these experiences to us to be is, by and large (in general), the way our environment actually is. If that, however, is the correct interpretation then it seems wrong to suppose that the reliability assumption is equivalent to the causal claim. In the first place, the mere assumption that if an experience is perceptual then it is causally dependent on the object it is a perception of, does not have as a consequence that appearances in these cases are even more or less accurate. This point, though, is unimportant, since all that is needed by the line of thought is that the reliability assumption requires the causal one, not that there is an equivalence. There is, however, no logical requirement here, since this sort of reliability could be present, if, say, our perceptions and the states of the world were joint effects of some other cause which produced the match. The reply is possible that it is excessively rigid to interpret 'requires' as 'entails', but it needs then to be explained what kind of transition between the assumptions is involved. There is, I think, a reason for doubting that any transition of a sufficiently interesting sort can be made here. Thus, we can re-express the reliability assumption (on the present interpretation, and limiting it to vision for convenience) as follows; if our experience is a case of an object O looking certain ways to us (that is, is visually perceptual of object O) then (by and large) O is how O looks. In so far as a causal assumption is implicit in this claim it would be that how an object looks is causally dependent on (amongst other things) how the object otherwise is. To unearth this causal assumption, though, is not to unearth a commitment to the causal thesis, for what if anything has been revealed is the assumption that when an object is seen, its being seen a certain way (that is, how it looks) causally depends on the nature of the object, which amounts in no way to the view that what it is for the object to be seen (a certain way) is for it to affect the viewer. An analogy is this; it is one thing to admit that whether A is heavier than B is, in part, causally determined by (say) A's previous history, another to hold that A's being heavier than B is a matter of A (or A's previous history) having an effect on B.

   The second consideration in favour of the theory is the claim that to think of someone as perceiving an object implies that if the item perceived had not been there then the subject would not have even seemed to perceive it. To avoid triviality here we must treat 'seem to perceive it' as equivalent to 'seem to perceive something of its character'. Now, taken that way, it does not seem that this claim is unrestrictedly true. There are two sorts of counterexample (which I shall specify for the visual case). The first is where a subject sees an object in an environment which would have appeared the same to him even if that object had not been present in it. For example, a man can see a coin immediately behind which is an identical coin, so that removal of the front coin would not alter the scene. The second is when a subject sees an object in circumstances which would have given him an hallucination of just such an object if the item had not been present. For example, a man can see a clock the noise from which is the only thing preventing a drug he has already taken from giving him the hallucination of a clock. Suppose, however, that the counterfactual is true. The belief that it implies the causal thesis relies on the assumption that the claim 'If S sees O at t then if O had not been present things would have seemed a different way to S' implies 'If S sees O at t then (the presence of) O causally accounts for how it seems to S', an assumption which would be correct if the consequent of the first of these conditionals (itself a conditional) entailed the consequent of the second (a causal claim). It is unobvious that there is any such entailment, for the first consequent merely records a dependence of one fact on another, and there can, surely, be dependencies where the relation is not causal dependence. (An example would be; if I had not parked on those yellow lines I would not have broken the law.) The causal thesis is not, therefore, an immediate implication of the remark under discussion.

Finally, it is true that we draw a distinction between (say) sighting an object and the object sighted, and that means that for there to be a sighting more must obtain than presence of the object, but it is not obvious that this extra is the object's having an effect on the sighter.

The causal thesis remains, therefore, to be supported, and I want next to determine how good the main argument is.

III

The main argument relies on the acceptance of something implied by (but not implying) the looks-thesis, namely, the claim that if S

sees *O* then *S* is in an *L*-state.[7] This is, surely, highly plausible, and not something I wish to question.[8] The argument also assumes that if *S* sees *O* then *O* exists. (Rather than calling that an assumption we might say—the theory just deals with sightings of actual objects.)

The argument itself (sometimes expressed with extreme brevity) has three stages. The first consists in the presentation of certain interesting possible cases of visual experience. The second consists in judging of these that they are cases where certain, what we might call, candidate objects involved are not seen. The third stage is simply an inference to the correctness of the causal thesis.

Now, the following are examples of the sort which are given. (*a*) Lady Macbeth has the hallucination that there is blood on her hands, there in fact being none. Her nurse then smears on some blood. (*b*) A man is facing a pillar of a certain character and it looks to him as if there is in front of him an object of that character. However between him and the pillar is a mirror in which is reflected another pillar. (*c*) A man is facing a clock, it looks to him as if there is a clock, but his experience is the result of a scientist's direct stimulation of his cortex in a way which would have yielded experience of that character even if there had been no clock.

The intention is to specify possible cases fulfilling three conditions. First, the two basic necessary requirements for an object-sighting are met. Second, they are cases where there is no sighting of the 'candidate' object. Third, there is an absence of any sort of causal dependence of the looks-state on that object.

Now, it is dubious that the descriptions of the cases necessitate the fulfilment of the last two features. For example, to consider the second requirement and case (*a*), it may be that smearing blood on Lady Macbeth stops the hallucination and enables her to see the blood. Again, considering the third requirement, and (*b*), it may be that the pillar behind the mirror is depressing a light-switch which controls the illumination of the reflected pillar. However, it seems clear that there are possible cases matching the descriptions and fulfilling these features, and it is very natural to interpret the

[7] For expositions see Grice, pp. 69–70, Strawson, 'Causation in Perception', 83, Wiggins 'Freedom; Knowledge, Belief and Causality', 137.

[8] It should be clear that the claim I am here accepting just means; if *S* sees *O* then it is true to say of *S* that it looks to him to be some way. The talk of *L*-states is merely abbreviatory of that. I am not, as will emerge, granting the ontological picture the causalist has in mind when formulating it this way (i.e. in terms of states).

description of the examples as introducing cases of this sort. When taken this way, I shall call them U-cases ('U' for unseen).

If, then, we allow such cases are possible, we must agree that it is not enough for a subject to see an object that the object be present and it looks as if there is an object of that character present. That much is established, but it is not conclusively established that the causal thesis is correct. All we have is the claim that there are possible cases where (i) S is in an L-state appropriate to seeing O, (ii) O is in his environment, (iii) the L-state is not causally dependent on O; and (iv) O is not seen. That such cases are possible does not entail that there are no cases where S and O are so related as to fulfil (i) to (iii) but in which O is seen by S.

If there is no entailment, how should we think of the move from accepting that in the described cases the object is not seen to accepting the causal thesis? We should, I want to propose, view it as a suggested inference to the best explanation. The issue raised is; why, in U-cases, are the mentioned objects not sighted? The causal theorist is suggesting that they are not sightings because of the lack of causal connection. It is a plausible suggestion because the absence of such a causal connection is a prominent element in the cases, and there is no other obvious explanation.

A question that arises at this point is where this interpretation leaves the conceptual thesis. Plainly, if the argument given is to be, not only a good reason for accepting the causal thesis, but, as well, a reason of a sort which licenses the conceptual thesis as a gloss on the status of its conclusion, then, in line with the elucidation of that gloss proposed earlier, the 'data' it relies on should be acknowledgeable by (more or less) anyone who has mastered the concept (of vision). The data in our case consist of the supposed facts reported in the judgements about the specified examples to the effect that they are not cases of (appropriate) vision. Now, it seems that these facts are of the right sort, for they are ones which are recognized by people who have no specialist information about vision at all. Hence, if the argument is a good one the conceptual thesis is warranted.

Now treating the argument in the way suggested leaves the causal thesis with the status of an attractive explanatory hypothesis. It would seem incautious, though, to be confident of its correctness without giving some consideration to other hypotheses, of which we can, I think envisage two sorts. The first sort of alternative which we might call non-radical, stays fairly close to the causal theory in structure, in that it allows that it makes sense to regard the looks-state as something causally produced by the seen object, but it claims that, none the less, we can best explain why the U-cases are not cases of vision by adding to our theory of vision an extra condition (or set of conditions) which requires less than the full causal connection proposed by the causalist.

There is no argument demonstrating that this strategy is in principle wrong, but it is hard to see how it can work. If different U-cases are explained by different features, then (i) a sense, which it is hard to resist, that there is a unified explanation is not satisfied, and (ii) there will be a suspicion that either the various features do not cover all U-cases or they do but at the cost of turning out to be equivalent to the causalist's explanation. If, in contrast, there is a single, non-causal but non-radical, explanation, what is it? The reason I do not wish to pursue this idea further is really that there is what I call a radical alternative which has the advantage that it can, at least, be specified and developed.

IV

To introduce the radical idea, in the form in which I shall develop it, consider this line of thought which bears some formal resemblance to the main argument. Its aim is to support a theory of what it is for A to be married to B. We agree, surely, that if A is married to B then A is a spouse. But it is clear that A could be a spouse and B also be around when A became a spouse without A being married to B. For example, suppose that when A became a spouse the ceremony at which it happened was one to which B's presence was completely irrelevant. It would have gone ahead exactly as it did whether B had been there or not. However, this case suggests something else that is needed: not only must A be a spouse, with B around when A became a spouse, but B's presence must have been causally relevant to A's becoming a spouse. Of course, this is still not sufficient, since the residing clergyman (or what have you) also fulfils this condition. So we might consider adding that for A to be married to B is for B to be causally relevant to A's being a spouse in the way in which . . . etc.

There is, of course, the analogue of the non-radical reply even here; 'it is rather strong to require causal dependence, let us, instead, rule out certain ways for B to be involved.'

Plainly both the argument and this reply lack plausibility. But why? A shot at explaining why this theory moves in the wrong direction, an explanation having two stages, is as follows; (i) the best theory we could offer of what it is to be a spouse is simply that it is to be married to someone or other; (ii) so, replacing in the original theory the notion of being a spouse by its explanation, we see that the original is trying to add conditions to the requirement that A be married to someone, which guarantee that A is married to B. But this is absurd, in that if we could explain what must apply to someone in order to be married to A, all we need to do to explain what it is for B to be married to A is to say that the someone to whom those conditions apply is B. Now, the more radical non-causalist response to the main argument is to allege that to draw a causal conclusion on its basis is similarly absurd.

We have, so far, then, an analogy and a general suggestion, and what is needed is a specific proposal to carry out the general suggestion. Pursuing the analogy, what is needed is a suggested theory about the supposed effect-end in the causal theory which renders its treatment in the causal theory, as the effect, absurd.

Such a suggestion can be extracted from J. M. Hinton's article (*Mind*, 1967) 'Visual Experiences'. Hinton's idea is that the best theory for the state of affairs reported by 'I seem to see a flash of light' (or 'I seem to see an F') is that it is a case of either my seeing a flash of light or my having the illusion of a flash of light (or my seeing an F or my having the illusion of an F). The claim, then, is that the best theory of seeming to see is disjunctive. For our purposes, the suggestion becomes that a theory of the same structure and content applies to the state of affairs reported by 'It looks to S as if there is . . .'.

But this suggestion as it stands is mistaken, for far from being the best theory, the explaining disjunction is not even coextensive with the state it is offered as explaining. There are at least two sorts of counterexamples. (i) The disjunction is true if S sees an F. But S might see an F which does not look like an F, in which case it might well not look to S as if there is an F. For example, S might be seeing a rabbit which had been shaved and painted to look like a cat. (ii) It seems we can have illusions which are not visual—for example auditory or tactile ones. Consider a kind of thing—say an explosion —which is both sightable and can be felt. Then S might be having the illusion of such a thing in virtue of how it feels to him. It would not follow that it looked to him as if there was an explosion.

Hinton's example—of a flash of light—masks the second difficulty, in that it is only sensible to treat an illusion of it as visual.

We can avoid these objections by offering the following revised disjunction:

> it looks to *S* as if there is an *F*; (there is something which looks to *S* to be *F*) *or* (it is to *S* as if there is something which looks to him (*S*) to be *F*).

Let us assume that it is correct. Now, if we make this assumption it seems that the visual case does resemble the spouse-example. Thus, we replace the supposed effect, by what it is best explained to be. We are given, that is, that there is some way *F* such that either something looks that way to *S* or it is to *S* as if something looked that way. How can we add to this to guarantee that *O* is seen? The answer, surely, is that *O* is seen so long as it is overall a case of something's looking *F* to *S*, rather than its being to *S* as if something looked that way, and *O* is the something that looks that way. But for *O* to be that something is not for *O* to bring about the separate state of affairs of something's looking *F*, it is, evidently, simply for *O* to be the something; that is, for *O* to look that way.

On the assumption that this theory is correct, we can provide an alternative explanation for the status of the *U*-cases. This explanation relies on the claim that an object is seen only if it looks some way to the subject and on noticing that we are given in the description of the *U*-cases information which makes it likely that the cases are not ones where the specified objects look some way. The information is precisely that what *actually* went on *would have gone on* whether the objects were present or not. But if that is true they could not have been cases in which the objects were looking some way to the subject, since that could not have obtained in the absence of the object.[9]

A comment that it would be natural to make at this stage is that if the discussion so far is tenable, the main argument is rejectable if a disjunctive theory is correct, but little has been said as to quite

---

[9] It may be objected, 'you are still left with an unexplained distinction between an object's looking *F* to *S* and it merely being to *S* as if something looks *F* to him, and you have not shown that the best account of this is not a causal theory for the former.' These remarks are true, but that the alternative explanation to the normal one relies on distinctions for which no explanation is provided does not discredit it as an explanation. How could it avoid this feature? Since it remains a possible explanation, its role in the present argument is not affected. So if the best account of the distinction involves a causal theory of the relational disjunct, another argument than the main one is needed.

what a disjunctive theory is claiming, and even less as to precisely what a non-disjunctive account would be. The request in this comment for further elucidation is totally reasonable, but difficult to respond to adequately.

The phrase so far used to explain the disjunctive approach has been that the disjunct gives 'the best theory'. Something like this is needed because even someone who accepts the picture involved in the causal theory could agree that the claim resulting from a bi-conditional between 'it looks to S as if . . .' and the disjunction expresses a truth, hence the contrasting (disjunctive) theory cannot be identified as the requirement that such a bi-conditional be true. Further, I see no help, in an account of the dispute, in saying that for the disjunctive theorist the disjunct *gives the meaning* of 'It looks to S as if . . .' whereas for the causalist it does not, since the fairly superficial factors which might make a remark about meaning appropriate in the case of the phrase 'is a spouse', are not present in our case. Without these factors, such a remark fails to illuminate what is in dispute.

But we are able to add vividness to the contrast by expressing it this way. The non-disjunctive theorist espouses a picture in which there is in all cases a single sort of state of affairs whose obtaining makes 'looks'-ascriptions true. This sort of state of affairs is common to such diverse cases as seeing a cricket ball and having an after-image with one's eyes shut tight. This obtaining of such states is intrinsically independent of the arrayed objects surrounding a subject, but will, so long as it is suitably produced by them, constitute a sighting of them. If it is not suitably caused it is not a sighting.

The disjunctive picture divides what makes looks-ascriptions true into two classes. In cases where there is no sighting they are made true by a state of affairs intrinsically independent of surrounding objects; but in cases of sightings the truth-conferring state of affairs involves the surrounding objects.

It is this picture, rather than the claim that the *actual* formula given to express the disjunctive theory adequately does so, which constitutes the core-idea, on the basis of which radical alternative explanation can be given.

V

If the present suggestion is correct, the next question to settle is whether a disjunctive theory is correct. If it is, then the main argument fails and the theory it is supposed to support is incorrect; if it is not, it is still possible that the non-radical rejection of the argument is the right response, but it cannot be said that the structure of the causalist theory is absurd.

It is, of course, impossible to settle this question now, but what I want to do instead is to propose a sketchy line of thought which relies on claims which seem intuitively plausible and which favours the disjunctive approach. In this line of thought an important role is initially played by demonstrative judgements—that is, those expressible in the words 'that is an F'.

Let us suppose that the visual scene you are scanning contains only what appears or looks to be a single faint light. If you hold, there and then, that you can actually see a real faint light-bulb, you will also hold of the thing which looks to be a faint light that it (that thing) is a light bulb. You will hold a judgement that you could express to yourself in the words 'That is a light bulb'. We can put the same point this way; if you are in doubt as to whether the judgement expressed by 'that is a light bulb' is correct, then, in these circumstances, you will, also, be in doubt as to whether you are seeing a light bulb.

It is tempting to generalize this by saying; if S holds that he can see an F then he must accept that there is a certain item of which he is correct in demonstratively identifying it as an F. This would be a mistake since the direct tie between the self-ascribed perceptual claim and the demonstrative identification present in the first case derives from its extremely simple character. Thus it is consistent and possible for me to hold in a case where there are three distinct objects apparently seen that I can see Boycott's bat even though I am not prepared to make of any of them the identification of it as the bat, simply because I do not know which it is. Still, it is evident in this sort of case that if I do not hold a disjunction of identificatory judgements correct, I will not hold that I see the bat.

So far, the tie between demonstratives and judgements about seeing has been presented in terms of a tie between perceptual judgements about yourself that you would make and demonstrative identifications you would make. But surely the tie is more general and, as a first shot, we might express it this way:

(S) (O) (If S sees O and O is an F then there is some object to which S is so related that if he were to demonstratively identify it as an F the judgement would be correct.)

Now, we can add to this, I suggest, a further principle which we are inclined to hold; let us restrict ourselves to the visual case; consider a scene that you can see and the public objects in it; now we can imagine a list of all the true identificatory demonstrative judgements you could have there and then made of the elements in the public scene. The second principle claims that if you encounter such a scene and are not at that time having after-images, a partial hallucination, or undergoing any experiences of that sort, then the previously specified set of true identificatory demonstrative judgements contains all the true demonstrative judgements you could there and then have made on the basis of your current *visual* experience. The best support for this is contained in the challenge; try to specify an extra demonstrative judgement.

Holding this in mind, we can return to the contrast between the disjunctive and non-disjunctive theories of looks-states. This time I want to concentrate on the non-disjunctive picture (theory) and to link it with the preceding claims.

The picture of perception it involves can be explained as follows; when we have an after-image (say) there is an L-state produced in a certain way, a way which rules out its being a perception of an object. Further what we are talking about when we speak of the image itself is, as it were, an element in the visual impression (or L-state) in this case. When we see (say) a faint light there is also such a state produced, but this time it is produced by the faint light, which is therefore, not in the same way an element in it. However, the sort of element produced in both types of case is the same; that the instance of the sort in the first case is an after-image whereas the instance in the second is not, is due entirely to the difference in how the elements are produced. It seems to be carried by this that the subject is related in the same way in both cases to the elements in the impression (= the effect).

I want now to assume that we can make (true and false) demonstrative-type judgements about what I am calling the elements in the L-state. To recognize that this is plausible (though not, I hope, certain) consider the following case. It looks to you as if there is a faint light before you. You are not, however, sure whether you are seeing a faint light or having an after-image. Now you might pose the question thus; what is that—an after-image or a faint light? In fact you are having an image and you persuade yourself that you are; the question then receives the answer; *that* is an after-image. Prima facie, this is a (true) instance of the kind of demonstrative judgement which I am assuming can be made.

Consider next, a related but different example. S is in fact seeing a faint light. Initially he believes (wrongly) that he is having an after-image. Granting the previous assumption, we can ascribe to him the demonstrative judgement—that is an after-image—supposed true by him of what it is he takes to be the image. However, he subsequently realizes he is not having an after-image but rather seeing a faint light; he comes to hold of that that it is a faint light. The problem to be faced is; what relation obtains between his initial, incorrect, demonstrative judgement and his subsequent one?

Now, on the present picture (and given our assumption) there are two possible erroneous judgements the man might have been making at the beginning. Either he judged of what was the faint light that it was an after-image or he judged of an element in the impression (produced in fact by the faint light) that it was an after-image. The latter demonstrative judgement was also of course erroneous. But the new demonstrative judgement as well, on this picture, has two possible interpretations. Either he is judging (correctly) of what is the faint light that it is a faint light; or (incorrectly) of an element in the L-state that it is a faint light. He should, on this picture, be able, however, to make a new and correct demonstrative judgement about the elements in the L-state; namely, that it (that) is an element of an L-state produced by a faint light in a certain way. So there are two possible truth-accruing changes S could make in his demonstrative judgements. He could move from 'that is an after-image' to 'that is a faint light', where his demonstrative picks out the faint light; or he could move from 'that is an after-image' to 'that is an element in an L-state caused in a certain way by a faint light' given that he was identifying an element in the impression. But it seems plain, now, that this is incompatible with the second principle which most of us accept, for it requires the existence of true identificatory judgements outside the class which the principle claims to be exhaustive. This theory as to what the effect in perception is, allied to our assumption about the permissibility of demonstrative judgements, is committed to the possibility of a 'language-game' which cannot be played.

So, to sustain the picture of the effect as a common visual element whose presence constitutes the truth of a looks-claim, it seems we must either (i) modify the assumption that demonstrative judgements are possible of 'elements' in 'impressions' or (ii) abandon the principle. Two modifications of the first assumption seem possible. The first tries to accommodate the case which made the initial assumption plausible, by claiming (i) where the visual effect is produced in a way that means it is not a case of perception, demonstrative judgements can be made about its elements, but (ii) where it is produced in a perception-making way, demonstrative identifications are not possible in respect of its elements but only in respect of the influencing object. Now, this may be a correct result, but it is impossible, I think, for this picture to explain why it is correct. For, why should ancestry affect identifiability? The second modification is more radical; (i) no elements in the L-state can be demonstratively identified, only objects, so to speak, in the world can be so identified; (ii) a subject who when actually having an after-image thinks he is seeing a faint light and thinks to himself 'that is a faint light' really makes no mistaken judgement with those words at all; his mistake is to suppose that he has made a judgement; (iii) a person seeing a light but believing that he is having an after-image may be allowed to make a demonstrative judgement to the effect that that is an after-image, but, of course, it can only be corrected in one way. I leave undecided whether such a view is acceptable.

However, even if it is, a difficulty still remains. For if we cannot demonstratively identify elements in impressions, there are certain psychological attitudes we can have towards the visual states which we are, in some sense, aware of when we have after-images. We can be interested by, concentrate on, be distracted by, scrutinize and attempt to describe them. Now, on the present interpretation of the causal theory with L-states as visual effects it is committed to there being in cases of vision features of this sort (though distinctly brought about). This seems to amount to supposing that in ordinary cases of vision we can have the cited psychological attitudes to features quite distinct from the object which produces them (i.e. the object seen). But, this is not at all obviously true; certainly it is not a supposition we are commonly inclined to make.[10]

[10] I intend the argument here as a challenge to supporters of the causal theory to explain where it goes wrong, rather than as a serious attempt to show they have gone wrong. There are three lines of reply available; (i) to agree that in ordinary perception we cannot have the cited attitudes to anything but the perceived objects, but to deny the claim that in (for example) after-imaging there are 'elements' we can have the attitudes to; (ii) to agree that we can have such attitudes in cases like after-

VI

There is nothing in the previous discussion which amounts to a disproof of the causalist viewpoint (that is, of the conjunction of theses (1)–(3)). If the disjunctive account of looks-states is correct, then thesis (2) is incorrect, hence the overall position also is. Even if the disjunctive theory is not acceptable, and theses (1) and (2) are admissible, the overall position may still be wrong if the refutation of the disjunctive theory involves considerations external to those permitted by the conceptual thesis. (So an assertion of the disjunctive theory is not needed for a rejection of the present causalist view.) However, what I hope to have made some sort of case for is not so much a rejection of the causalist viewpoint as non-acceptance of it.

The issue of the proper attitude to the overall position should be sharply distinguished from the issue of the proper attitude to the causal thesis (thesis (1)). There are, I think, good empirical reasons for believing that to see an object is for it to have, in a certain sort of way, a certain sort of effect. Thus, (i) it seems physically necessary for S to see O that O have an effect on S, and we can either think of the affecting as a *de facto* necessary condition for another relation's obtaining (namely, seeing) or treat the seeing *as* the affecting. The parsimonious naturalist will incline to the latter. (ii) There are things about us (for example, certain capacities for avoiding, if we want to, or hitting, if we want to, objects) which we hold vision explains; I assume that these capacities can, in fact, also be traced to the ways in which the objects affect us. This seems to support an identity and with it thesis (1). If this is correct, the question that emerges is; given thesis (1) is true, why does it matter that there is no proof of it which licenses its status as a 'conceptual' truth? But that, like much else, I propose to leave hanging in the air.

imagings, but to claim we also have them to 'elements' distinct from the perceived objects in perceptual cases: (iii) to agree that there is a prima-facie puzzle about what we are able to attend to but to allege that our inability in the ordinary perception case does not show that there is no common visual element shared by it and (say) after-imaging. I have said nothing to block any of these options.

XII

CRITERIA, DEFEASIBILITY, AND KNOWLEDGE

J. McDOWELL

One can sometimes tell what someone else feels or thinks by seeing and hearing what he says and does. It is very common for philosophers to interpret this idea so that 'what he says and does' is taken to allude to a basis for knowledge of what the person feels or thinks. Their thought of a basis here has two elements. The first is that the basis is something knowable in its own right: this is, knowledge of the basis could have this status—be *knowledge*—independently of the status of what it is a basis for. The second is that judgements about what the person feels or thinks emerge as knowledgeable in favourable cases because of an inferential relation in which they stand to the basis. (This need not imply that the knower arrives at such judgements by inference: see below.) The notion of a criterion, as used by Wittgenstein in connection with this sort of knowledge, is often interpreted on these lines. In earlier parts of the lecture from which this excerpt is taken, I argue that in view of the defeasibility of the inferential relation —which is necessitated by the first of the two elements mentioned above, and freely acknowledged by proponents of this sort of interpretation—we have no real explanation of how the relation could be knowledge-sustaining; for even in the most favourable cases it remains possible, for all one knows, that the beliefs about what is said and done which are to stand as one's basis (in virtue of their role as criteria) are both true and known to be true, while the conclusions which rest on them are false and hence not known at all. But the idea I began with—and Wittgenstein's notion of a criterion—does not need to be interpreted in such a way as to attract this response. 'From what he says and does' can be an appropriate answer to 'How do you know what he feels?' (say)—so that what he says and

Reprinted with revisions and additions from *Proceedings of the British Academy*, 68 (1982), 455–79, © 1982 the British Academy. Used by permission.

does can be one's criterion for what he feels, in the quite non-technical sense of 'way of telling'—without any implication that 'what he says and does' stands in for something more specific, capable of being established independently of one's judgement as to how the person feels, and warranting the claim of that judgement to be knowledgeable. Knowledge that one is confronted by a criterion for the person's feeling as one judges him to (if we allow ourselves to use the word 'criterion' in this less ordinary way) can be an exercise of the very same (of course fallible) capacity that we speak of when we say that one can tell what someone feels from what he says and does: not an epistemically independent capacity whose deliverances ground the epistemic status of judgements as to how people feel.

The possibility of this second interpretation is liable to be obscured from us by a certain tempting line of argument. On any question about the world independent of oneself to which one can ascertain the answer by, say, looking, the way things look can be deceptive: it can look to one exactly as if things were a certain way when they are not. (This can be so even if, for whatever reason, one is not inclined to believe that things are that way.[1] I shall speak of cases as deceptive when, if one were to believe that things are as they appear, one would be misled, without implying that one is actually misled.) It follows that any capacity to tell by looking how things are in the world independent of oneself can at best be fallible. According to the tempting argument, something else follows as well: the argument is that since there can be deceptive cases experientially indistinguishable from non-deceptive cases, one's experiential intake—what one embraces within the scope of one's consciousness—must be the same in both kinds of case. In a deceptive case, one's experiential intake must *ex hypothesi* fall short of the fact itself, in the sense of being consistent with there being no such fact. So that must be true, according to the argument, in a non-deceptive case too. One's capacity is a capacity to tell by looking: that is, on the basis of experiential intake. And even when this capacity does yield knowledge, we have to conceive the basis as a *highest common factor* of what is available to experience in the deceptive and the non-deceptive cases alike, and hence as something that is at best a defeasible ground for the know-

---

[1] On the 'belief-independence' of the content of perception, see Gareth Evans, *The Varieties of Reference* (Oxford, 1982), 123.

ledge, though available with a certainty independent of whatever might put the knowledge in doubt.

This line of thought is an application of the Argument from Illusion. I want now to describe and comment on a way of resisting it.

We might formulate the temptation that is to be resisted as follows. Let the fallible capacity in question be a capacity to tell by experience whether such-and-such is the case. In a deceptive case, what is embraced within the scope of experience is an appearance that such-and-such is the case, falling short of the fact: a *mere* appearance. So what is experienced in a non-deceptive case is a mere appearance too. The upshot is that even in the non-deceptive cases we have to picture something that falls short of the fact ascertained, at best defeasibly connected with it, as interposing itself between the experiencing subject and the fact itself.[2]

But suppose we say—not at all unnaturally—that an appearance that such-and-such is the case can be *either* a mere appearance *or* the fact that such-and-such is the case making itself perceptually manifest to someone.[3] As before, the object of experience in the deceptive cases is a mere appearance. But we are not to accept that in the non-deceptive cases too the object of experience is a mere appearance, and hence something that falls short of the fact itself. On the contrary, we are to insist that the appearance that is presented to one in those cases is a matter of the fact itself being disclosed to the experiencer. So appearances are no longer conceived as in general intervening between the experiencing subject and the world.[4]

The idea of a fact being disclosed to experience is in itself purely negative: a rejection of the thesis that what is accessible to

2 The argument effects a transition from sheer fallibility (which might be registered in a 'Pyrrhonian' scepticism) to a 'veil of ideas' scepticism: for the distinction, see Richard Rorty, *Philosophy and the Mirror of Nature* (Oxford, 1980), 94 n. 8 and 139 ff.

3 In classical Greek, 'φαίνεται σοφὸς ὤν [word for word: he appears wise being] generally means *he is manifestly wise*, and φαίνεται σοφὸς εἶναι [word for word: he appears wise to be], *he seems to be wise . . .*' William W. Goodwin, *A Greek Grammar* (London, 1894), 342.

4 See the discussion of a 'disjunctive' account of 'looks' statements in Paul Snowdon's 'Perception, Vision, and Causation', Essay XI in this volume; and, more generally, J. M. Hinton's *Experiences* (Oxford, 1973)—a work which I regret that I did not know until this lecture was virtually completed, although I expect that this section grew out of an unconscious recollection of Hinton's articles 'Experiences', *Philosophical Quarterly*, 17 (1967), 1–13, and 'Visual experiences', *Mind*, 76 (1967), 217–27.

experience falls short of the fact in the sense of being consistent
with there being no such fact. In the most straightforward application of the idea, the thought would be that the fact itself is
directly presented to view, so that it is true in a stronger sense that
the object of experience does not fall short of the fact: the object of
experience *is* the fact. But a less straightforward application of the
idea is possible also, and this is what seems appropriate in at least
some cases of knowledge that someone else is in an 'inner' state, on
the basis of experience of what he says and does. Here we might
think of what is directly available to experience in some such terms
as 'his giving expression to his being in that "inner" state': this is
something that, while not itself actually being the 'inner' state of
affairs in question, nevertheless does not fall short of it in the sense
I explained.[5]

In *Philosophical Investigations* 1§354, Wittgenstein writes:

The fluctuation in grammar between criteria and symptoms makes it look
as if there were nothing at all but symptoms. We say, for example:
"Experience teaches that there is rain when the barometer falls, but it also
teaches that there is rain when we have certain sensations of wet and cold,
or such-and-such visual impressions." In defence of this one says that these
sense-impressions can deceive us. But here one fails to reflect that the fact
that the false appearance is precisely one of rain is founded on a definition.

That is, it is not experience that teaches us a connection between
rain and appearances that it is raining; that connection is not
merely symptomatic. If there is a general thesis about criteria
applied here, it will be on these lines: one acquires criterial
knowledge by confrontation with appearances whose content is, or
includes, the content of the knowledge acquired. (This would fit
both the sorts of case I have just distinguished: obviously so in the
straightforward sort, and in the less straightforward sort we can say

[5] In my 'On "The Reality of the Past"' (in C. Hookway and P. Pettit, eds.,
Action and Interpretation (Cambridge, 1978), I proposed a position, about
'knowledge of other minds', which might be accused of assimilating the second sort
of case to the first. The plausibility of the assimilation in a particular case depends
on the extent to which it is plausible to think of the particular mode of expression as,
so to speak, transparent. (This is quite plausible for facial expressions of emotional
states: see Wittgenstein, *Zettel* (Oxford, 1967), §§220–5. But it is not very plausible
for 'avowals', except perhaps in the special case of the verbal expression of
thoughts.) The motivation for my proposal in that paper was the wish to deny that
our experiential intake, when we know one another's 'inner' states by experience,
must fall short of the fact ascertained in the sense I have introduced; it was a mistake
to suppose that this required an appeal, across the board, to a model of direct
observation.

that an appearance that someone is giving expression to an 'inner' state is an appearance that he is in that 'inner' state.)

Now defenders of the conception of criterial knowledge that I questioned in the first section of the lecture resist the accusation that their view makes criteria function in the awareness of knowers as mere proxies for the states of affairs known on the basis of the criteria, by virtue of yielding premises for inferences to those states of affairs; and this thesis about match in content might promise a neat justification for denying that criterial knowledge is the upshot of inherence.

The content of inferential knowledge, one might suggest, is generated by a transformation of the content of some data, whereas here the content of the knowledge is simply presented in the data. But this does not establish the coherence of a position in which criteria are conceived as objects of experience on the 'highest common factor' model, but the accusation that criteria function as proxies can be rejected. If the object of experience is in general a mere appearance, as the 'highest common factor' model makes it, then it is not clear how, by appealing to the idea that it has the content of the knowledge that one acquires by confrontation with it, we could save ourselves from having to picture it as getting in the way between the subject and the world. Indeed, it is arguable that the 'highest common factor' model undermines the very idea of an appearance having as its content that things are thus and so in the world 'beyond' appearances (as we would have to put it).

This has a bearing on a question I raise in the earlier section of the lecture, in which I query whether the idea of a criterion as an independently ascertainable and defeasible basis can make it intelligible how it can be knowledge that such a basis yields. Consider a situation in which someone supposedly has such knowledge, as compared with a situation in which someone experiences the same independently ascertainable circumstance but, since the state of affairs for which it is a 'criterion' does not obtain (the defeasible support is defeated), he lacks the knowledge in question: can the blankly external obtaining of the fact, in the first case, make it intelligible that the subject knows, though he is supposedly indistinguishable, in the reach of his experience, from the subject who does not know? Suppose someone is presented with an appearance that it is raining. It seems unproblematic that if his experience is in a suitable way the upshot of the fact that it is raining, then the fact itself can make it the case that he knows that it is raining. But that

seems unproblematic precisely because the content of the appearance is the content of the knowledge. And it is arguable that we find
that match in content intelligible only because we do not conceive
the objects of such experiences as in general falling short of the
meteorological facts. That is: such experiences can present us with
the appearance that it is raining only because when we have them as
the upshot (in a suitable way) of the fact that it is raining, the fact
itself is their object; so that its obtaining is not, after all, blankly
external.[6] If that is right, the 'highest common factor' conception
of experience is not entitled to the idea that makes the case unproblematic. It would be wrong to suppose that the 'highest common
factor' conception can capture, in its own terms, the intuition that
I express when I say that the fact itself can be manifest to experience:
doing so by saying that that is how it is when, for instance, experiences as of its raining are in a suitable way the upshot of the fact
that it is raining. That captures the intuition all right; but—with
'experiences as of its raining'—not in terms available to someone
who starts by insisting that the object of experience is the highest
common factor, and so falls short of the fact itself.

The 'highest common factor' conception has attractions for us
that cannot be undone just by describing an alternative, even with
the recommendation that the alternative can cause a sea of philosophy to subside. The most obvious attraction is the phenomenological argument: the occurrence of deceptive cases experientially
indistinguishable from non-deceptive cases. But this is easily
accommodated by the essentially disjunctive conception of appearances that constitutes the alternative. The alternative conception
can allow what is given to experience in the two sorts of case to be
the same *in so far as* it is an appearance that things are thus and so;
that leaves it open that whereas in one kind of case what is given to
experience is a mere appearance, in the other it is the fact itself
made manifest. So the phenomenological argument is inconclusive.

A more deep-seated temptation towards the 'highest common
factor' conception might find expression like this: '*Ex hypothesi* a
mere appearance can be indistinguishable from what you describe
as a fact made manifest. So in a given case one cannot tell for
certain whether what confronts one is one or the other of those.
How, then, can there be a difference in what is given to experience,
in any sense that could matter to epistemology?' One could hardly

---

[6] This fits the first of the two sorts of case distinguished above; something
similar, though more complex, could be said about a case of the second sort.

countenance the idea of having a fact made manifest within the reach of one's experience, without supposing that that would make knowledge of the fact available to one.[7] This protest might reflect the conviction that such epistemic entitlement ought to be something one could display for oneself, as it were from within; the idea being that that would require a non-question-begging demonstration from a neutrally available starting-point, such as would be constituted by the highest common factor.[8]

There is something gripping about the 'internalism' that is expressed here. The root idea is that one's epistemic standing on some question cannot intelligibly be constituted, even in part, by matters blankly external to how it is with one subjectively. For how could such matters be other than beyond one's ken? And how could matters beyond one's ken make any difference to one's epistemic standing?[9] (This is obviously a form of the thought that is at work in the argument from earlier in the lecture which I have recently reconsidered.) But the disjunctive conception of appearances shows a way to detach this 'internalist' intuition from the requirement of non-question-begging demonstration. When someone has a fact made manifest to him, the obtaining of the fact contributes to his

[7] This is to be distinguished from actually conferring the knowledge on one. Suppose someone has been misled into thinking his senses are out of order; we might then hesitate to say that he possesses the knowledge that his senses (in fact functioning perfectly) make available to him. But for some purposes the notion of being in a position to know something is more interesting than the notion of actually knowing it. (It is a different matter if one's senses are actually out of order, though their operations are sometimes unaffected: in such a case, an experience subjectively indistinguishable from that of being confronted with a tomato, even if it results from confrontation with a tomato, need not count as experiencing the presence of a tomato. Another case in which it may not count as that is a case in which there are a lot of tomato façades about, indistinguishable from tomatoes when viewed from the front: cf. Alvin Goldman, 'Discrimination and Perceptual Knowledge', Essay II in this volume. One counts as experiencing the fact making itself manifest only in the exercise of a (fallible) capacity to *tell* how things are.)

[8] The hankering for independently ascertainable foundations is familiar in epistemology. Its implications converge with those of a Dummett-inspired thesis in the philosophy of language: namely that the states of affairs at which linguistic competence primarily engages with extra-linguistic reality, so to speak, must be effectively decidable (or fall under some suitable generalization of that concept). See G. Baker, 'Defeasibility and Meaning', in P. M. S. Hacker and J. Raz, eds, *Law, Morality, and Society* (Oxford, 1977), 26–57, at pp. 50–1. For criteria as decidable, see e.g. C. Wright, 'Anti-realist Semantics: The Role of *Criteria*', in G. Vesey, ed., *Idealism: Past and Present* (Cambridge, 1982), 230.

[9] See e.g. Laurence Bonjour, 'Externalist Theories of Empirical Knowledge', *Midwest Studies in Philosophy*, 5 (1980), 53–74.

epistemic standing on the question. But the obtaining of the fact is precisely not blankly external to his subjectivity, as it would be if the truth about that were exhausted by the highest common factor.[10]

However, if that reflection disarms one epistemological foundation for the 'highest common factor' conception, there are other forces that tend to hold it in place.[11]

Suppose we assume that one can come to know that someone else is in some 'inner' state by adverting to what he says and does. Empirical investigation of the cues that impinge on one's sense-organs on such an occasion would yield a specification of the information received by them; the same information could be available in a deceptive case as well. That limited informational intake must be processed, in the nervous system, into the information about the person's 'inner' state that comes to be at one's disposal; and a description of the information-processing would look like a description of an inference from a highest common factor. Now there is a familiar temptation, here and at the analogous point in reflection about perceptual knowledge of the environment in general, to suppose that one's epistemic standing with respect to the upshot of the process is constituted by the availability to one's senses of the highest common factor, together with the cogency of the supposed inference.

When one succumbs to this temptation, one's first thought is typically to ground the cogency of the inference on a theory. But the conception of theory as extending one's cognitive reach beyond the confines of experience requires that the theory in question be attainable on the basis of the experience in question. It is not enough that the experience would confirm the theory: the theory must involve no concept the formation of which could not intelligibly be attributed to a creature whose experential intake was limited in the way envisaged. And when we try to conceive knowledge of the 'inner' states of others on the basis of what they do and say,

[10] The disjunctive conception of appearances makes room for a conception of experiential knowledge that conforms to Robert Nozick's account of 'internalism', at p. 281 of *Philosophical Explanations* (Oxford, 1981); without requiring, as he implies that any 'internalist' position must (pp. 281–2), a reduction of 'external' facts to mental facts.

[11] Nozick must be a case in point. His drawing of the boundary between 'internal' and 'external' (see n. 10 above) must reflect something like the 'highest common factor' conception; and in his case that conception cannot be sustained by the 'internalist' intuition that I have just tried to disarm.

or perceptual knowledge of the environment in general, on this model, that condition seems not to be met.[12]

Keeping the highest common factor in the picture, we might try to register that thought by grounding the cogency of the inferences on 'grammar' rather than theory; this would yield something like the conception of criteria that I have questioned. But that this would be a distortion is suggested by the fact that we have been given no idea of how to arrive at specifications of the content of the supposed 'grammatically' certified warrants, other than by straight-forward empirical investigation of what impinges on someone's senses on occasions when we are independently prepared to believe that he has the knowledge in question. The truth is that, for all their similarity to inferences, those processings of information are not transitions within what Wilfrid Sellars has called 'the logical space of reasons',[13] as they would need to be in order to be capable of being constitutive of one's title to knowledge. Acquiring mastery of the relevant tracts of language is not, as acquiring a theory can be, learning to extend one's cognitive reach beyond some previous limits by traversing pathways in a newly mastered region of the 'space of reasons'. It is better conceived as part of being initiated into the 'space of reasons' itself.[14]

I want to end by mentioning a source for the attraction of the 'highest common factor' conception that lies, I think, as deep as any. If we adopt the disjunctive conception of appearances, we have to take seriously the idea of an unmediated openness of the experiencing subject to 'external' reality, whereas the 'highest com-

[12] To the point here is Wittgenstein's polemic against the idea that 'from one's case' one can so much as form the idea of someone else having, say, feelings. On the case of perception in general, see e.g. P. F. Strawson, 'Perception and its objects', Essay V in this volume.

[13] 'Empiricism and the Philosophy of Mind', in Herbert Feigl and Michael Scriven, eds., *The Foundations of Science and the Concepts of Psychology and Psychoanalysis* (Minnesota Studies in the Philosophy of Science I, Minneapolis, 1956), 253–329, at p. 299.

[14] Two supplementations to these extremely sketchy remarks. First: when we allow theory to extend someone's cognitive reach, we do not need to find him infallible in the region of logical space that the theory opens up to him; so we do not need to commit ourselves to the idea that the theory, together with the content of experience, must *entail* the content of the putative knowledge. Second: the rejection of the inferential model that I am urging does not turn on mere phenomenology (the absence of conscious inferences). Theory can partly ground a claim to knowledge even in cases in which it is not consciously brought to bear; as with a scientist who (as we naturally say) learns to see the movements of imperceptible particles in some apparatus.

mon factor' conception allows us to picture an interface between them. Taking the epistemology of other minds on its own, we can locate the highest common factor at the facing surfaces of other human bodies. But when we come to consider perceptual knowledge about bodies in general, the 'highest common factor' conception drives what is given to experience inward, until it can be aligned with goings-on at our own sensory surfaces. This promises to permit us a satisfying conception of an interface at which the 'inner' and the 'outer' make contact. The idea that there is an interface can seem compulsory; and the disjunctive conception of appearances flouts that intuition—twice over, in its view of knowledge of others' 'inner' states.[15]

No doubt there are many influences that conspire to give this picture of the 'inner' and the 'outer' its hold on us. The one I want to mention is our proneness to try to extend an objectifying mode of conceiving reality to human beings. In an objectifying view of reality, behaviour considered in itself cannot be expressive or significant: not human behaviour any more than, say the behaviour of the planets.[16] If human behaviour is expressive, that fact resides not in the nature of the behaviour, as it were on the surface, but in its being the outwardly observable effect of mental states and goings-on. So the mind retreats behind the surface, and the idea that the mental is 'internal' acquires a quasi-literal construction, as in Descartes, or even a literal one, as in the idea that mental states are 'in the head'.[17]

Modern adherents of this picture do not usually take themselves to be enmeshed in the problems of traditional epistemology. But the objectification of human behaviour leads inexorably to the traditional problem of other minds. And it is hard to see how the pictured interface can fail to be epistemologically problematic in the outward direction too: the inward retreat of the mind under-

[15] Am I suggesting that the disjunctive conception of appearances precludes the idea that experience mediates between subject and world? It depends on what you mean by 'mediate'. If experience is conceived in terms of openness to the world, it will not be appropriate to picture it as an interface. (I am sceptical whether such a conception of experience is available within the dominant contemporary philosophy of mind.)

[16] See Charles Taylor, *Hegel* (Cambridge, 1975), 3–11.

[17] This movement of thought can find support in the idea that the mental is conceptually captured by introspective ostensive definition. (That idea is perhaps naturally understood as a response to the obliteration of the notion of intrinsically expressive behaviour.) But some versions of the position are not notably introspectionist.

mines the idea of a direct openness to the world, and thereby poses the traditional problems of knowledge about 'external' reality in general. Without the 'highest common factor' conception of experience, the interface can be left out of the picture, and the traditional problems lapse. Traditional epistemology is widely felt to be unsatisfying; I think this is a symptom of the error in the 'highest common factor' conception, and, more generally, of the misguidedness of an objectifying conception of the human.

NOTES ON CONTRIBUTORS

ROBERT NOZICK is Professor of Philosophy at Harvard University. He is the author of two major works, *Anarchy, State and Utopia* (1974) and *Philosophical Explanations* (1981).

ALVIN GOLDMAN is now Professor of Philosophy at the University of Arizona. He is the author of *A Theory of Human Action* (1970), many articles on epistemology, and most recently *Epistemology and Cognition* (1986).

H. P. GRICE is Emeritus Professor of Philosophy at the University of California at Berkeley. He is the author of influential articles on the philosophy of language, and has more recently been working on rationality and ethics.

DAVID LEWIS is Professor of Philosophy at Princeton University, and author of *Convention: a Philosophical Study* (1969) and *Counterfactuals* (1973). Some of his many articles have recently been collected in his *Philosophical Papers* i (1983) and ii (1986).

SIR PETER STRAWSON is a Fellow of Magdalen College and Waynflete Professor of Metaphysical Philosophy in the University of Oxford. Among his books are *Individuals* (1959), *The Bounds of Sense* (1966), and *Freedom and Resentment* (1974).

FRANK JACKSON is Professor of Philosophy at the Australian National University; he was formerly at Monash University. He has published many articles in philosophical journals, and is the author of *Perception: A Representative Theory* (1977).

DAVID ARMSTRONG was Professor of Philosophy at the Australian National University. Among his books are *Perception and the Physical World* (1961), *A Materialist Theory of the Mind* (1968), and *Belief, Truth and Knowledge* (1973).

FRED DRETSKE is Professor of Philosophy at the University of Wisconsin. He is the author of *Seeing and Knowing* (1969) as well as of *Knowledge and the Flow of Information* (1981).

RODERICK FIRTH is Professor of Philosophy at Harvard University. He has written extensively on epistemology and the theory of perception.

WILFRED SELLARS is Professor of Philosophy at the University of Pittsburgh. His books include *Science, Perception and Reality* (1963) and *Science and Metaphysics* (1966).

PAUL SNOWDON is a Fellow of Exeter College, Oxford.

JOHN MCDOWELL is Professor of Philosophy at the University of Pittsburgh; he was formerly a fellow of University College, Oxford. He has written influential articles on the philosophy of language and on moral philosophy.

FURTHER READING

This list is intended merely to provide a sufficient background to the papers in this collection.

1. SCEPTICISM

T. Clarke, 'The Legacy of Scepticism', *Journal of Philosophy*, 69 (1972), 754–69.

J. Dancy, *An Introduction to Contemporary Epistemology* (Oxford, 1985), ch. 1.

B. Stroud, *The Significance of Philosophical Scepticism* (Oxford, 1984).

P. Unger, *Ignorance* (Oxford, 1975).

2. THEORIES OF KNOWLEDGE

M. Chisholm, *Theory of Knowledge*, 2nd edn. (Englewood Cliffs, NJ, 1977), ch. 6.

F. Dretske, 'Conclusive Reasons', *Australasian Journal of Philosophy*, 49 (1971), 1–22, reprinted in G. Pappas and M. Swain, eds., *Essays on Knowledge and Justification* (Ithaca, NY, 1978).

A. I. Goldman, 'A Causal Theory of Knowing', *Journal of Philosophy*, 64 (1967), 355–72, reprinted in G. Pappas and M. Swain, eds., *Essays on Knowledge and Justification* (Ithaca, NY, 1978).

A. I. Goldman, *Epistemology and Cognition* (Harvard, 1986), ch. 3.

M. Swain, 'Epistemic Defeasibility', *American Philosophical Quarterly*, 11 (1974), 15–25, reprinted in G. Pappas and M. Swain, eds., *Essays on Knowledge and Justification* (Ithaca, NY, 1978).

3. PERCEPTION (GENERAL)

F. Jackson, *Perception* (Cambridge, 1977).

G. Pitcher, *A Theory of Perception* (Princeton, 1971).

I. Rock, *An Introduction to Perception* (New York, 1975).

4. THE OBJECTS OF PERCEPTION

J. Cornman, *Perception, Science and Common Sense* (New Haven, 1975).

F. Dretske, *Knowledge and the Flow of Information* (Cambridge, Mass., 1981), 153–68.
B. O'Shaughnessy, 'Seeing the Light', *Proceedings of the Aristotelian Society*, 85 (1985), 193–218.
H. Robinson, 'The General Form of the Argument for Berkeleian Idealism', in J. Foster and H. Robinson, eds., *Essays on Berkeley* (Oxford, 1985), esp. pp. 170–7.

5. THE CAUSAL THEORY OF PERCEPTION

M. Davies, 'Function in Perception', *Australasian Journal of Philosophy*, 61 (1983), 409–26.
C. Peacocke, *Holistic Explanation: Action, Space, Interpretation* (Oxford, 1979), ch. 2.
D. Pears, 'The Causal Theory of Perception', *Synthese*, 33 (1976), 41–74.
P. F. Strawson, 'Causation in Perception', ch. 4 of his *Freedom and Resentment and Other Essays* (London, 1974).

6. SENSATION AND COGNITION

C. McGinn, *The Character of Mind* (Oxford, 1982), ch. 1.
B. O'Shaughnessy, *The Will: A Dual Aspect Theory* (Cambridge, 1980), 168–74.
C. Peacocke, *Sense and Content* (Oxford, 1983), ch. 1.

7. FOUNDATIONALISM AND COHERENTISM

R. Chisholm, *Theory of Knowledge*, 2nd edn. (Englewood Cliffs, NJ, 1977).
K. Lehrer, *Knowledge* (Oxford, 1974), chs. 7–9.
C. I. Lewis, 'The Given Element in Empirical Knowledge', *Philosophical Review*, 61 (1952), 168–75; reprinted in R. Chisholm and R. Swartz, eds., *Empirical Knowledge* (Englewood Cliffs, NJ, 1973).

8. INTERNALISM AND EXTERNALISM

W. P. Alston, 'Internalism and Externalism in Epistemology', *Philosophical Topics*, 14 (1986), 179–221.
L. Bonjour, 'Externalist Theories of Empirical Knowledge', in P. French *et al.*, eds., *Midwest Studies in Philosophy*, v, *Studies in Epistemology* (Minneapolis, 1980), 53–73.

A. I. Goldman, 'The Internalist Conception of Justification', in P. French *et al.*, eds., *Midwest Studies in Philosophy*, v, *Studies in Epistemology* (Minneapolis, 1980), 27–51.

9. THE ADVERBIAL THEORY OF SENSATION

R. Chisholm, *Theory of Knowledge* (Englewood Cliffs, NJ, 1977), 26–30.

W. Sellars, 'The Adverbial Theory of the Objects of Sensation', *Metaphilosophy*, 6 (1975), 144–60.

P. Butchvarov, 'Adverbial Theories of Consciousness', in P. French *et al.*, eds., *Midwest Studies in Philosophy, v, Studies in Epistemology* (Minneapolis, 1980), 261–80.

INDEX OF NAMES